Albert Ali Salah   Theo Gevers
Nicu Sebe   Alessandro Vinciare

Human Behavior Understanding

First International Workshop, HBU 2010
Istanbul, Turkey, August 22, 2010
Proceedings

Springer

Volume Editors

Albert Ali Salah
University of Amsterdam
Informatics Institute
1098 XG Amsterdam, The Netherlands
E-mail: a.a.salah@uva.nl

Theo Gevers
University of Amsterdam
Informatics Institute
1098 XG Amsterdam, The Netherlands
E-mail: th.gevers@uva.nl

Nicu Sebe
University of Trento
Dept. of Information Engineering and Computer Science
I-38123 Trento, Italy
E-mail: sebe@disi.unitn.it

Alessandro Vinciarelli
University of Glasgow
Dept. of Computing Science
Glasgow G12 8QQ, UK
E-mail: vincia@dcs.gla.ac.uk

Library of Congress Control Number: 2010931103

CR Subject Classification (1998): I.5, H.5.2, I.4, I.4.8, I.2, I.2.10

LNCS Sublibrary: SL 6 – Image Processing, Computer Vision, Pattern Recognition, and Graphics

ISSN	0302-9743
ISBN-10	3-642-14714-3 Springer Berlin Heidelberg New York
ISBN-13	978-3-642-14714-2 Springer Berlin Heidelberg New York

springer.com

© Springer-Verlag Berlin Heidelberg 2010
Printed in Germany

Typesetting: Camera-ready by author, data conversion by Scientific Publishing Services, Chennai, India
Printed on acid-free paper   06/3180

Lecture Notes in Computer Science 6219

Commenced Publication in 1973
Founding and Former Series Editors:
Gerhard Goos, Juris Hartmanis, and Jan van Leeuwen

Editorial Board

Preface

It was a great pleasure to organize the First International Workshop on Human Behavior Understanding (HBU), which took place as a satellite workshop to International Conference on Pattern Recognition (ICPR) on August 22, 2010, in Istanbul, Turkey. This workshop arose from the natural marriage of pattern recognition with the rapidly advancing area of human behavior analysis. Our aim was to gather researchers dealing with the problem of modeling human behavior under its multiple facets (expression of emotions, display of relational attitudes, performance of individual or joint actions, etc.), with particular attention to pattern recognition approaches that involve multiple modalities and those that model actual dynamics of behavior.

The contiguity with ICPR, one of the most important events in the pattern recognition and machine learning communities, is expected to foster cross-pollination with other areas, for example temporal pattern mining or time series analysis, which share their important methodological aspects with human behavior understanding. Furthermore, the presence of this workshop at ICPR was meant to attract researchers, in particular PhD students and postdoctoral researchers, to work on the questions of human behavior understanding that is likely to play a major role in future technologies (ambient intelligence, human–robot interaction, artificial social intelligence, etc.), as witnessed by a number of research efforts aimed at collecting and annotating large sets of multi sensor data, collected from observing people in natural and often technologically challenging conditions.

This proceedings volume contains 13 papers presented at the workshop, as well as the abstracts of the keynote talks by Ramesh Jain (UCI) and Ivan Laptev (INRIA), and a summarizing paper by the editors. We received 29 submissions in total, and each paper was peer-reviewed by two members of the Technical Program Committee.

We would like to thank our Program Committee members and reviewers for their rigorous feedback, and our keynote speakers for their contributions. We also thank the ICPR organization team, most importantly Aytül Erçil and Osman Rahmi Fıçıcı for their support. The website of the workshop was created by Hamdi Dibeklioğlu and maintained by Osman Rahmi through its countless updates.

August 2010

Albert Ali Salah
Theo Gevers
Nicu Sebe
Alessandro Vinciarelli

Organization

Conference Co-chairs

Albert Ali Salah	University of Amsterdam, The Netherlands
Theo Gevers	University of Amsterdam, The Netherlands
Nicu Sebe	University of Trento, Italy
Alessandro Vinciarelli	University of Glasgow, Ireland

Technical Program Committee

Oya Aran	IDIAP, Switzerland
Manuele Bicego	University of Verona, Italy
Jeffrey Cohn	University of Pittsburgh, USA
Hazim Ekenel	Karlsruhe University, Germany
Jordi Gonzáles	Universidad Autónoma de Barcelona, Spain
Jonathan Gratch	University of Southern California, USA
Dirk Heylen	University of Twente, The Netherlands
Seong-Whan Lee	Korea University, South Korea
Vittorio Murino	University of Verona, Italy
Fabio Pianesi	University of Trento, Italy
Ioannis Pitas	University of Thessaloniki, Greece
Eraldo Ribeiro	Florida Institute of Technology, USA
Michael S. Ryoo	Electronics and Telecommunications Research Institute, South Korea
Albert Ali Salah	University of Amsterdam, The Netherlands
Marc Schroder	DFKI Language Technology Lab, Germany
Bjorn Schuller	Technical University Munich, Germany
Nicu Sebe	University of Trento, Italy
Metin Sezgin	Koç University, Turkey
Jianhua Tao	Institute of Automation Chinese Academy of Sciences, China
Matthew Turk	University of California Santa Barbara, USA
Hezy Yeshurun	Tel Aviv University, Israel

Additional Reviewers

Hamdi Dibeklioğlu	Cem Keskin	Hee-Deok Yang
Mika Fischer	Myung-Cheol Roh	Zeynep Yücel
Hua Gao	Lukas Rybok	

Table of Contents

Social Signals

Challenges of Human Behavior Understanding

Albert Ali Salah[1], Theo Gevers[1], Nicu Sebe[2], and Alessandro Vinciarelli[3]

[1] Institute of Informatics, University of Amsterdam,
Amsterdam, The Netherlands
{a.a.salah,th.gevers}@uva.nl
[2] Dept. of Information Engineering and Computer Science
University of Trento
Trento, Italy
sebe@disi.unitn.it
[3] Department of Computing Science
University of Glasgow
Glasgow, Scotland
vincia@dcs.gla.ac.uk

Abstract. Recent advances in pattern recognition has allowed computer scientists and psychologists to jointly address automatic analysis of of human behavior via computers. The Workshop on Human Behavior Understanding at the International Conference on Pattern Recognition explores a number of different aspects and open questions in this field, and demonstrates the multi-disciplinary nature of this research area. In this brief summary, we give an overview of the Workshop and discuss the main research challenges.

1 Introduction

Domains where human behavior understanding is a crucial need (e.g., human-computer interaction, affective computing and social signal processing) rely on advanced pattern recognition techniques to automatically interpret complex behavioral patterns generated when humans interact with machines or with others. This is a difficult problem where many issues are still open, including the joint modeling of behavioral cues taking place at different time scales, the inherent uncertainty of machine detectable evidences of human behavior, the mutual influence of people involved in interactions, the presence of long term dependencies in observations extracted from human behavior, and the important role of dynamics in human behavior understanding.

The target topics of the Human Behavior Understanding (HBU) Workshop reflect some of the old and new questions in this domain:

- Social behavior analysis & modeling, multimodal behavior patterns
- Temporal patterns
- Facial, gestural and voice-based affect recognition
- Sign-language recognition
- Human motion analysis

A.A. Salah et al. (Eds.): HBU 2010, LNCS 6219, pp. 1–12, 2010.

- Pattern recognition applied to novel sensors
- Pattern discovery in personal sensor networks, reality mining
- Smart environments
- Human-computer interaction
- Benchmarking studies on novel databases
- New feature selection and extraction methods
- Mathematical description and integration of contextual information
- Behavioral biometrics

Some of these topics have been actively researched for a long time, like the analysis of face, voice, and bodily signals, yet these are taken up to new levels of difficulty by relaxing some of the simplifying constraints. Research focuses now on more natural settings with uncontrolled conditions, real-time operation requirements and interaction dynamics. Furthermore, domain-specific semantic information is drawn into the picture as we move from generic techniques to specific applications. This re-focusing is partly done by introducing richer taxonomies and increasing volumes of multi-modal data.

This chapter is meant as a summary of the issues covered in the Workshop, and subsequently, it is neither a balanced treatment of the domain, nor an extensive survey of all open questions. In Section 2 we distinguish between different spatio-temporal scales of human behavior. In its largest scale, patterns are discovered in the collective behavior of masses. Section 3 deals with the most heavily researched area of behavior analysis, pertaining to visual sensors. The visual patterns are usually shorter in their temporal extent, but we see that the temporal aspects are gaining importance in this modality as well. Section 4 focuses on social signal processing, which adds social semantics to signal processing. Finally, we conclude in Section 5 and give pointers to further reading material on some of the key issues.

2   Temporal Levels of Behaviors

It is possible to look at behaviors at different temporal levels. The microscopic behaviors happen in a short time frame, and have to be analyzed as such. A blink of the eye, a rapid hand gesture, a yawn can all be seen as microscopic behaviors. On the other hand, the movement of masses over longer temporal and spatial scales also contains recognizable patterns, and these can be said to exist in a macroscopical scale. The continuous range that stretches between these extremes contains many problems that are approached with a host of pattern recognition methods.

One of the areas in which different temporal scales come together is ambient intelligence. In [1], daily activities of people living in a sensed environment (like eating, using a computer, reading, watching television, etc.) are analyzed. The smaller time frame in which the activity is actually performed and the larger time frame which is composed of longer segments prone to contain the activity are combined in a hierarchical framework. Here, SVM classifiers predict locally ongoing activities, and Conditional Random Fields are used to refine the prediction by estimating time segments of global activities.

While most of the papers submitted to the HBU Workshop dealt with be-havior dynamics on a microscopical scale, we admitted work on both types of patterns. In [2], daily activity patterns of individuals are analyzed using large collections of mobile phone data. These reveal that activity patterns within a given area of work strongly resemble each other. As more data are available from the population, it becomes possible to create *reality mining* applications and discover behavior patterns [3].

The diversity in the behavior-related patterns suggests the possibility of using diverse sensors in their assessment. Modern mobile phones are equipped with a host of sensors, thus allowing unprecedented opportunities of personal data col-lection. In [4], body-worn miniature inertial and magnetic sensors were used the collect data for activity classification. Each sensor unit used in the study com-prises a triaxial gyroscope, a triaxial accelerometer, and a triaxial magnetometer. Using multiple types of sensors potentially increases the cost of a given system, but offers great increase in robustness. Especially in the context of ambient in-telligence, multimodal analysis of behavior opens up new venues of applications such as behavioral biometrics and automated care for the elderly. In [1], infrared and object motion sensors are used in conjunction to classify daily activities in a sensor-equipped home setting.

The human behavior is not restricted to physical actions and behaviors. Many people now have a presence on the Web, and exhibit social networking behavior that is becoming ever more relevant. In the keynote talk of Ramesh Jain [5], the *macroscopic behavior* of masses on the Web is investigated.

3   Visual Action Recognition

Vision is currently the most heavily used sensory modality in the analysis of human behavior. Visual human action recognition concerns the detection and tracking of people, and more generally, the understanding of human behaviors from image sequences involving humans [6,7]. Automated vision-based analysis of human actions finds many applications in surveillance, ambient assisted living, concept-based video retrieval, automatic sports video annotation and summa-rization, customer behavior analysis for marketing and gaming. So far a scalable and widely applicable system for this purpose remains elusive.

3.1   Tracking the Body

Tracking of humans and human behavior inherently involves estimation of body pose, locations and movements of body parts, interaction with objects, and some-times also gaze estimation. While estimating the pose means determining the location and the orientation for an object, humans manifest more complex pose aspects. Pose estimation can be a post processing step in a tracking algorithm, or it can be an active part of the tracking process. Recent approaches to tracking favor particle filtering based methods, as these can maintain multiple proba-bilistic hypotheses with respect to a parametrized body posture at any given time [8].

Pose estimation can be approached with different methods. A model of the human shape can be used in constraining the interpretation of the pose. In model-free pose estimation, the pose can be represented as a set of feature points, as a combination of simple shapes, or with stick-figures, which connect points with lines. [9] introduced the motion history image to represent human body movement. [10] recently extended this paradigm to propose a spatio-temporal silhouette representation, called silhouette energy image to characterize motion and shape properties. The challenges in this problem are dealing with both indoor and outdoor conditions, real-time operation, low level features extraction, motion analysis, and saliency computation, multi-camera fusion, among others.

While some methods aim at tracking and labelling the body parts in 2D, others try to map 2D sequences of image observations into 3D pose representations. In some cases, equipment is available to obtain depth information from the scene. Two papers in this collection describe such systems. In [11], a trinocular camera system is used for this purpose. In [12] input from multiple cameras are fused to determine the gesture trajectories of humans performing signs. In both approaches, hidden Markov model (HMM) is the classifier of choice to effect temporal classification.

The use of an explicit model of a person's kinematics, shape, and appearance in an analysis-by-synthesis framework is a widely investigated approach to human pose estimation from video [13]. In these approaches the model is used to synthesize an appearance from the current parametrization of the model, which is compared to the actual appearance. The discrepancy is minimized by changing the parameters appropriately, to a point where the model is able to synthesize a close match of the appearance. At that point, the converged parameters can be directly used to represent the pose of the person. The direct model pose estimation can de subdivided in multiple view 3D pose estimation [14] and monocular 3D pose estimation. For a detailed overview on methods of pose estimation, see [15].

Once the people are tracked and spatio-temporal features are extracted, action classification can take place. In recent work, static SIFT features were shown to perform well for many detection tasks, while histogram of oriented gradient (HoG) and histogram of optical flow (HoF) features were successful for action recognition [16]. Yet the temporal dimension is taken into account in only a few low-level descriptors: A 3D Harris operator that describes spatio-temporal interest points was described in [17]. In [18] human actions were modelled as three-dimensional shapes induced by the silhouettes in the space-time volume. [19] presented a spatio-temporal interest point detector, and analyzed a number of cuboid descriptors for action recognition. Most approaches opt for temporal integration of spatial descriptors, using different forms of dynamic Bayesian networks [20].

3.2   The Context

Automatic detection of an action may involve complex spatiotemporal and semantic reasoning. To constrain this problem, contextual cues are used. For the integration of contextual information, we need to define the context properly. It can mean several things:

1. Geometrical scene properties, i.e. 3D composition of the scene. The scene can be classified by using visual cues into one of the possible scene classes.
2. Scene type, i.e. the content and context of the scene. This property can be derived via texture analysis, and indicate indoor vs. outdoor, or common locations like street, football field, etc.
3. Objects in the scene: The objects of interaction provide valuable contextual cues.
4. Persons in the scene: The number of persons in the scene, and their visual features can provide contextual cues.
5. Temporal context: Detection of other prior actions will influence the detection of related actions. Interaction semantics would be in this category, and hence this is probably the richest source of contextual information.

The application setting mostly determines what kind of contextual cue will be used in each setting. There are marked differences between content-based retrieval of actions from movies and detection of actions from one or more surveillance cameras. In the latter the cameras are mostly static, providing poorer context, as opposed to constructed narratives of films. There are also lots of self-occlusions, and the scale of action is typically much smaller. In a surveillance setting real-time operation is usually essential. On the other hand, videos can be processed in an offline fashion, have often higher resolution and scale for people performing the actions, engineered camera perspectives, moving and zooming camera angles. Furthermore, multimedia solutions often come to rescue where vision-based processing fails; subtitles (text), speech (transcript), social tags and file name associations are used to label videos. In one of the keynotes of the HBU Workshop, Ivan Laptev discusses several supervised and weakly-supervised approaches for action recognition in movies [21].

3.3 Benchmarking

Increased interest in human action/activity recognition in recent years resulted in several benchmarking and database annotation efforts. In this domain, we observe that the application focus shifts from the recognition of simple, generic human actions to the analysis of activities in a context and/or interactions between humans. The CAVIAR[1] Dataset for instance contains video recordings of settings like city center surveillance and analysis of customer behavior in a shopping mall. Activities include people walking alone, meeting with others, window shopping, entering and exiting shops, and leaving a package in a public place. The latest editions of Performance Evaluation of Tracking and Surveillance (PETS)[2] propose similar challenges such as crowd analysis and tracking of individuals in a crowd.

---

[1] http://homepages.inf.ed.ac.uk/rbf/CAVIAR/
[2] http://www.cvg.rdg.ac.uk/PETS2009/

Recognition of unusual or dangerous actions is important for public infrastructure surveillance, and the existence of CCTV cameras and surveillance by security staff makes automated activity recognition a natural extension in these settings. The automated action recognition technology can support the existing personnel, and reduce the burden of inspection by making potentially interesting actions salient, as well as blocking obviously irrelevant information. The TRECVID[3] challenge for 2010 states that "Detecting human behaviors efficiently in vast amounts surveillance video, both retrospectively and in realtime, is fundamental technology for a variety of higher-level applications of critical importance to public safety and security." For this purpose, a large dataset collected from Gatwick airport is made available in the 2010 challenge.

The recent SDHA (Semantic Descriptions of Human Actions) Challenge[4], organized as a satellite event to ICPR'2010, provides three public databases for various action recognition settings [22]. Some of the labelled actions have complicated semantic associations (e.g., stalking, flirting), which makes the dataset challenging. Further datasets for this type of research are detailed in [23]. In the present collection, [24] provides a detailed survey of evaluation protocols on the KTH action database, which is one of the most studied among these [25].

Apart from individual efforts, a number of previous projects tackled human action recognition from different perspectives. To give a few illustrative examples, the ADVISOR EC-IST project (Annotated Digital Video for Intelligent Surveillance and Optimised Retrieval) aimed at using computer vision algorithms to detect unusual human behavior and to use the developed technologies to improve the effectiveness of existing security operators[5]. The tackled behaviors were blocking, fighting, jumping over barriers, vandalism and overcrowding, all in a public transport scenario. The CAVIAR EC-IST project (Context Aware Vision using Image-based Active Recognition) targeted local image descriptors combined with task, scene, function and object contextual knowledge to improve image-based recognition processes.

3.4   Challenges

The primary challenge in this area is the great range of actions and gestures produced by humans even in relatively restricted domains. Humans use contextual cues extensively to recognize small but discriminative differences. Consider for instance the gestures of an orchestra conductor, which simultaneously specify the rhythm, the style and conductor's interpretation of the piece. A subtle facial expression or posture can convey that the players should play more legato, or the energy in the overall composure of the conductor may suggest forte. The expression of the rhythm can temporarily shift from one hand to the other, as the conductor overlaps the expression of several cues. The gestures will be highly idiosyncratic, yet the orchestra generally knows how to adapt to the conductor.

---

[3] http://trecvid.nist.gov/

[4] http://cvrc.ece.utexas.edu/SDHA2010/index.html

[5] http://www-sop.inria.fr/orion/ADVISOR/default.html

It is the representation of assumed knowledge (i.e. priors) in combination with real-time, adaptive and multi-modal information processing on both sides that makes the problem really difficult for a computer. This problem is investigated under the rubric of social signals.

4   Social Signals

A great class of human behaviors pertain to expressing and recognizing social signals, which have communicative and interactive aspects. Even in the absence of other people, socially formed habits manifest themselves in different ways like facial expressions and idiosyncratic gestures. Studying social interactions and developing automated ways of classifying human social behavior from all kinds of sensors is becoming important not only for natural human-computer interaction, but also for all kinds of applications we have mentioned in the previous section.

4.1   Taxonomies

In [26], a taxonomy is introduced for the analysis of social signals. The verbal signals that are usually direct manifestations of communicative intent are accompanied by *behavioral cues* that serve to convey information about the emotion, personality, status, dominance, regulation and rapport in a given social context. These cues reside in different modalities, like the physical appearance, gesture, posture, facial expression, focus of attention, vocal behavior (e.g., prosody and silences), and even the spatial arrangement of participants during an interaction.

In one of the major efforts directed for social signal processing, the SSPNet[6] project focuses on the analysis of political debates as a rich source of behavioral signals. The project defines the core questions of social signal processing as follows:

1. Is it possible to detect automatically nonverbal behavioral cues in data captured with sensors like microphones and cameras?
2. Is it possible to automatically infer attitudes from nonverbal behavioral cues detected through sensors like microphones and cameras?
3. Is it possible to synthesize nonverbal behavioral cues conveying desired relational attitudes for embodiment of social behaviors in artificial agents, robots or other manufacts?

These questions are generic, in the sense that they apply to many domains of behaviors equally. However, the computational aspects (for both analysis and synthesis) depend largely on the application domain, making the problem difficult or very difficult in each case.

---

[6] http://sspnet.eu/

4.2 Domains for Analysis

The automatic analysis of behavioral cues in a particular domain requires and fosters a decomposition of all activities in that domain. Each such domain has its own challenges and rewards. In the present collection, a number of such domains are investigated. Poggi and D'Errico present a scheme for the annotation of signals of dominance in political debates [27], which are behaviorally rich and interactive settings. In [28] a taxonomy of communicative and non-communicative behaviors of teachers towards their pupils is proposed, which can be used for guiding the development of an automatic analysis tool for a classroom. Such a tool would be a very valuable teaching aid.

In [29], Lepri et al. investigate prediction of personality traits from behavioral cues. A well-known taxonomy proposes five traits as constitutive of people's personality: Extraversion, Emotional Stability, Agreeableness, Conscientiousness, Openness to Experience [30]. In [29], the extraversion-introversion dimension is analyzed using four acoustic features (Conversational Activity, Emphasis, Influence and Mimicry) and one visual feature. In [31], the emotion content of the speech is analyzed and the resulting system is usable as a virtual speech coach for improving public speaking skills. The authors use a discriminative approach, and train SVM classifiers for each type of emotion.

The idiosyncratic variations constitute a major challenge of social signals. In successful dyadic interactions, human subjects exhibit a remarkable adaptivity to these variations. In the study of Özkan and Morency, backchannel feedback in dyadic interactions is analyzed [32]. A feature selection approach is proposed to automatically discover the subset of features relevant to this specific application.

4.3 Face Analysis

Affect-related signals constitute a large portion of nonverbal behavioral cues, and facial expressions are among the most extensively studied signals in this category. These result from movements of the facial muscles as the face changes in response to a person's internal emotional states, intentions, or social communications. Psychological studies suggest that facial expressions, as the main mode for nonverbal communication, play a vital role in human face-to-face communication [33,34]. Computer recognition of facial expressions has many important applications in intelligent human-computer interaction, computer animation, surveillance and security, medical diagnosis, law enforcement, and awareness systems. Therefore, automatic facial expression analysis (from video or images) has received much attention in last two decades [35,36]. Face analysis in conjunction with body and head pose orientation can reveal the attention focus of a person, which can also be a very useful cue in putting a behavior in its proper context [37].

The challenges of face analysis in the present context are finding the correct level of description, feature extraction and representation, spontaneous and posed expression classification, head pose and gaze direction estimation. The Workshop has received a number of submissions on these areas. In [38] spatiotemporal DCT features are used in a boosted classification framework for the classification of face and head gestures. Face detection, tracking and analysis are much more difficult in real-life settings, as the resolution of the face area and the pose show great variations. In [39], a probabilistic approach is proposed for a multi-camera setup to track and recognize faces across difficult conditions.

5   Concluding Remarks

Understanding affective and social behavior of humans with computational tools is receiving increased interest. The present volume demonstrates that pattern recognition is an essential component of research in this area. Researchers seek to analyze patterns emanating from interactions between humans, as well as between humans and computers or smart systems, with the goal of designing more responsive and natural interfaces and applications.

Automatic classification of human behavior involves understanding of bodily motion [7,15,23], gestures and signs [40], analysis of facial expressions [36], and interpretation of affective signals [35]. On a higher level, these signals are integrated with the contextual properties of an application domain. Social signal processing deals with interactions between humans [26]. It integrates verbal cues with rich sets of non-verbal behavioral cues to deeply analyze social interactions. Ambient intelligence deals with smarter environments [41]. In ambient environments, the living space is equipped with many sensors that observe the behavior of humans and with many actuators to make the space responsive to changes in these behaviors. As a more focused application, perceptual user interfaces are concerned with more responsive human-computer interfaces [42,43]. In this domain the computer is given the capacity to detect behavioral changes of its user. The analysis of spatio-temporal dynamics of human actions, observed through different sensory modalities, allows inference and customization on many levels [44,45].

The submissions for the HBU Workshop demonstrate that the range of behaviors in the proposed applications is rapidly expanding. The set of behaviors under study includes concepts that are hard to describe precisely and mathematically. However, recent pattern recognition approaches developed for multimedia retrieval have shown us that a precise description is sometimes not necessary for the recognition of a concept. If an informative feature extraction step is combined with a powerful pattern classifier and a training set with sufficiently rich variation, it may be possible to learn appropriate descriptors for even the most challenging concepts. Subsequently, it is obvious that human behavior understanding will continue to be a very active research area in the near future, and will be instrumental in providing the tools for building more interactive systems.

References

1. Nicolini, C., Lepri, B., Teso, S., Passerini, A.: From on-going to complete activity recognition exploiting related activities. In: Salah, A.A., Gevers, T., Sebe, N., Vinciarelli, A. (eds.) HBU 2010. LNCS, vol. 6219, pp. 26–37. Springer, Heidelberg (2010)

2. Phithakkitnukoon, S., Horanont, T., Di Lorenzo, G., Shibasaki, R., Ratti, C.: Activity-aware map: Identifying human daily activity pattern using mobile phone data. In: Salah, A.A., Gevers, T., Sebe, N., Vinciarelli, A. (eds.) HBU 2010. LNCS, vol. 6219, pp. 14–25. Springer, Heidelberg (2010)
3. Eagle, N., Pentland, A.: Reality mining: sensing complex social systems. Personal and Ubiquitous Computing 10(4), 255–268 (2006)
4. Altun, K., Barshan, B.: Human activity recognition using inertial/magnetic sensor units. In: Salah, A.A., Gevers, T., Sebe, N., Vinciarelli, A. (eds.) HBU 2010. LNCS, vol. 6219, pp. 38–51. Springer, Heidelberg (2010)
5. Jain, R.: Understanding macroscopic human behavior. In: Salah, A.A., Gevers, T., Sebe, N., Vinciarelli, A. (eds.) HBU 2010. LNCS, vol. 6219, p. 13. Springer, Heidelberg (2010)
6. Gavrila, D.: The Visual Analysis of Human Movement: A Survey. Computer Vision and Image Understanding 73(1), 82–98 (1999)
7. Wang, L., Hu, W., Tan, T.: Recent developments in human motion analysis. Pattern Recognition 36(3), 585–601 (2003)
8. Isard, M., Blake, A.: Condensation-conditional density propagation for visual tracking. International Journal of Computer Vision 29(1), 5–28 (1998)
9. Bobick, A., Davis, J.: The recognition of human movement using temporal templates. IEEE Transactions on Pattern Analysis and Machine Intelligence 23(3), 257–267 (2001)
10. Ahmad, M., Lee, S.W.: Variable silhouette energy image representations for recognizing human actions. Image and Vision Computing 28(5), 814–824 (2010)
11. Hahn, M., Quronfuleh, F., Woehler, C., Kummert, F.: 3d mean-shift tracking and recognition of working actions. In: Salah, A.A., Gevers, T., Sebe, N., Vinciarelli, A. (eds.) HBU 2010. LNCS, vol. 6219, pp. 101–112. Springer, Heidelberg (2010)
12. Richarz, J., Fink, G.A.: Feature representations for the recognition of 3D emblematic gestures. In: Salah, A.A., Gevers, T., Sebe, N., Vinciarelli, A. (eds.) HBU 2010. LNCS, vol. 6219, pp. 113–124. Springer, Heidelberg (2010)
13. Ali, S., Shah, M.: Human action recognition in videos using kinematic features and multiple instance learning. IEEE Transactions on Pattern Analysis and Machine Intelligence 32(2), 288–303 (2010)
14. Kehl, R., Gool, L.: Markerless tracking of complex human motions from multiple views. Computer Vision and Image Understanding 104(2-3), 190–209 (2006)
15. Moeslund, T., Hilton, A., Krüger, V.: A survey of advances in vision-based human motion capture and analysis. Computer Vision and Image Understanding 104(2-3), 90–126 (2006)
16. Laptev, I., Marszalek, M., Schmid, C., Rozenfeld, B.: Learning realistic human actions from movies. In: IEEE Conference on Computer Vision and Pattern Recognition, pp. 1–8 (2008)
17. Laptev, I.: On space-time interest points. International Journal of Computer Vision 64(2), 107–123 (2005)
18. Gorelick, L., Blank, M., Shechtman, E., Irani, M., Basri, R.: Actions as space-time shapes. IEEE Transactions on Pattern Analysis and Machine Intelligence 29(12), 2247–2253 (2007)
19. Dollar, P., Rabaud, V., Cottrell, G., Belongie, S.: Behavior recognition via sparse spatio-temporal features. In: 2nd Joint IEEE Int. Workshop on Visual Surveillance and Performance Evaluation of Tracking and Surveillance, pp. 65–72 (2005)
20. Rius, I., GonzÃ les, J., Varona, J., Roca, X.: Action-specific motion prior for efficient Bayesian 3D human body tracking. Pattern Recognition 42(11), 2907–2921 (2009)

21. Laptev, I.: Recognizing human action in the wild. In: Salah, A.A., Gevers, T., Sebe, N., Vinciarelli, A. (eds.) HBU 2010. LNCS, vol. 6219, p. 87. Springer, Heidelberg (2010)
22. Ryoo, M., Aggarwal, J.: Hierarchical recognition of human activities interacting with objects. In: IEEE Conference on Computer Vision and Pattern Recognition, pp. 1–8 (2007)
23. Poppe, R.: A survey on vision-based human action recognition. Image and Vision Computing 28(6), 976–990 (2010)
24. Gao, Z., Chen, M.Y., Hauptmann, A., Cai, A.: Comparing evaluation protocols on the KTH dataset. In: Salah, A.A., Gevers, T., Sebe, N., Vinciarelli, A. (eds.) HBU 2010. LNCS, vol. 6219, pp. 88–100. Springer, Heidelberg (2010)
25. Schuldt, C., Laptev, I., Caputo, B.: Recognizing human actions: A local SVM approach. In: International Conference on Pattern Recognition, vol. 3, pp. 32–36. IEEE Computer Society, Los Alamitos (2004)
26. Vinciarelli, A., Pantic, M., Bourlard, H.: Social signal processing: Survey of an emerging domain. Image and Vision Computing 27(12), 1743–1759 (2009)
27. Poggi, I., D'Errico, F.: Dominance signals in debates. In: Salah, A.A., Gevers, T., Sebe, N., Vinciarelli, A. (eds.) HBU 2010. LNCS, vol. 6219, pp. 163–174. Springer, Heidelberg (2010)
28. D'Errico, F., Leone, G., Poggi, I.: Types of help in the teacher's multimodal behavior. In: Salah, A.A., Gevers, T., Sebe, N., Vinciarelli, A. (eds.) HBU 2010. LNCS, vol. 6219, pp. 125–139. Springer, Heidelberg (2010)
29. Lepri, B., Kalimeri, K., Pianesi, F.: Honest signals and their contribution to the automatic analysis of personality traits - a comparative study. In: Salah, A.A., Gevers, T., Sebe, N., Vinciarelli, A. (eds.) HBU 2010. LNCS, vol. 6219, pp. 140–150. Springer, Heidelberg (2010)
30. John, O., Srivastava, S.: The Big Five Trait Taxonomy: History, Measurement, and Theoretical Perspectives. In: Pervian, L., John, O. (eds.) Handbook of personality: theory and research. The Guilford Press, New York (1999)
31. Pfister, T., Robinson, P.: Speech emotion classification and public speaking skill assessment. In: Salah, A.A., Gevers, T., Sebe, N., Vinciarelli, A. (eds.) HBU 2010. LNCS, vol. 6219, pp. 151–162. Springer, Heidelberg (2010)
32. Ozkan, D., Morency, L.P.: Concensus of self-features for nonverbal behavior analysis. In: Salah, A.A., Gevers, T., Sebe, N., Vinciarelli, A. (eds.) HBU 2010. LNCS, vol. 6219, pp. 75–86. Springer, Heidelberg (2010)
33. Ekman, P., Rosenberg, E.: What the face reveals: Basic and applied studies of spontaneous expression using the Facial Action Coding System (FACS). Oxford University Press, USA (2005)
34. Mehrabian, A.: Nonverbal communication. Aldine (2007)
35. Zeng, Z., Pantic, M., Roisman, G., Huang, T.: A survey of affect recognition methods: Audio, visual, and spontaneous expressions. IEEE Transactions on Pattern Analysis and Machine Intelligence 31(1), 39–58 (2009)
36. Salah, A., Sebe, N., Gevers, T.: Communication and automatic interpretation of affect from facial expressions. In: Affective Computing and Interaction: Psychological, Cognitive and Neuroscientific Perspectives. IGI Global (to appear)
37. Yücel, Z., Salah, A.: Head pose and neural network based gaze direction estimation for joint attention modeling in embodied agents. In: Proc. 31st Annual Conference of Cognitive Science Society (2009)
38. Cinar Akakin, H., Sankur, B.: Spatiotemporal-Boosted DCT Features for Head and Face Gesture Analysis. In: Salah, A.A., Gevers, T., Sebe, N., Vinciarelli, A. (eds.) HBU 2010. LNCS, vol. 6219, pp. 64–74. Springer, Heidelberg (2010)

39. Utsumi, Y., Iwai, Y., Ishiguro, H.: Face tracking and recognition considering the camera's field of view. In: Salah, A.A., Gevers, T., Sebe, N., Vinciarelli, A. (eds.) HBU 2010. LNCS, vol. 6219, pp. 52–63. Springer, Heidelberg (2010)
40. Ong, S., Ranganath, S.: Automatic sign language analysis: A survey and the future beyond lexical meaning. IEEE Transactions on Pattern Analysis and Machine Intelligence 27(6), 873–891 (2005)
41. Aarts, E., Encarnação, J.: True visions: The emergence of ambient intelligence. Springer, Heidelberg (2006)
42. Crowley, J., Coutaz, J., Bérard, F.: Perceptual user interfaces: things that see. Communications of the ACM 43(3), 54–64 (2000)
43. Crowley, J.: Context driven observation of human activity. In: Aarts, E., Collier, R.W., van Loenen, E., de Ruyter, B. (eds.) EUSAI 2003. LNCS, vol. 2875, pp. 101–118. Springer, Heidelberg (2003)
44. Guesgen, H., Marsland, S.: Spatio-temporal reasoning and context awareness. In: Handbook of Ambient Intelligence and Smart Environments, pp. 609–634 (2010)
45. Pentland, A.: Looking at people: Sensing for ubiquitous and wearable computing. IEEE Transactions on Pattern Analysis and Machine Intelligence 22(1), 107–119 (2000)

Understanding Macroscopic Human Behavior

Ramesh Jain

Department of Computer Science
University of California, Irvine
Irvine, CA 92697
jain@ics.uci.edu

Abstract. The Web has changed the way we live, work, and socialize. Web-thinking has been influencing how we understand, design, and solve important societal problems and build complex systems. For centuries, emergence has been considered an essential property underlying the way complex systems and patterns emerge out of relatively simple interactions among different components. The Web has compellingly demonstrated results of emergence in understanding human behavior not at an individual level but at different macro levels ranging from social networks to global levels. Recent rapid advances in sensor technology, Web 2.0, Mobile devices, and Web technologies have opened further opportunities to understand macroscopic human behavior. In this talk, we will discuss our approach to build a framework for studying macroscopic human behavior based on micro-events including Tweets and other participatory sensing approaches.

A.A. Salah et al. (Eds.): HBU 2010, LNCS 6219, p. 13, 2010.

Activity-Aware Map: Identifying Human Daily Activity Pattern Using Mobile Phone Data

Santi Phithakkitnukoon[1], Teerayut Horanont[1,2], Giusy Di Lorenzo[1],
Ryosuke Shibasaki[2], and Carlo Ratti[1]

[1] SENSE*able* City Laboratory, School of Architecture and Planning,
Massachusetts Institute of Technology, Cambridge, MA, USA
[2] Department of Civil Engineering, School of Engineering,
The University of Tokyo, Tokyo, Japan
{santi,giusy,ratti}@mit.edu, teerayut@iis.u-tokyo.ac.jp,
shiba@csis.u-tokyo.ac.jp

Abstract. Being able to understand dynamics of human mobility is essential for urban planning and transportation management. Besides geographic space, in this paper, we characterize mobility in a profile-based space (*activity-aware map*) that describes most probable activity associated with a specific area of space. This, in turn, allows us to capture the individual daily activity pattern and analyze the correlations among different people's work area's profile. Based on a large mobile phone data of nearly one million records of the users in the central Metro-Boston area, we find a strong correlation in daily activity patterns within the group of people who share a common work area's profile. In addition, within the group itself, the similarity in activity patterns decreases as their work places become apart.

1 Introduction

For better understanding of the effects of human movement, characterizing human mobility patterns is crucial. For example, without such characterization, the impact of inhabit dynamics in the city cannot be understood. As spatio-temporal and geo-referenced datasets are growing rapidly because of the daily collection of transaction data through database systems, network traffic controllers, sensor networks, and telecommunication data from mobile phones and other location-aware devices, the large availability of these forms of data allows researchers to better characterize human mobility. The additional information of activities associated with human mobility further provides a unique opportunity to better understand the context of human movement, and hence better urban planning and management. In this paper, we develop the *activity-aware map*, which provides information about the most probable activity associated with a specific area in the map. With the activity-aware map and an analysis of a large mobile phone data of nearly one million records of location traces, we are able to construct the individual daily activity patterns. This allows us to carry out a correlation analysis of work area's profile and similarity in daily activity patterns.

A.A. Salah et al. (Eds.): HBU 2010, LNCS 6219, pp. 14–25, 2010.

2   Related Work

A rapidly increasing number of mobile phone users has motivated researchers from various fields to study its social [1][2][3] and economic [4][5][6] impact. With the extensive records of mobile phone data such as calling pattern and location of the mobile phone user, analyses have been performed on numerous aspects including behavioral routine [7][8][9], social proximity [10][11], call prediction [12][13], social closeness [14][15], and human mobility [16][17][18][19][20].

Understanding dynamics of social networks is beneficial to urban planning, public transport design, traffic engineering, disease outbreaks control, and emergency response management. To study dynamics in human mobility, GPS receiver has been handy for researchers in collecting a large real-life traces. Azevedo et al. [16] study pedestrian mobility behavior using GPS traces captured at Quinta da Boa Vista's Park in Rio de Janeiro (Brazil). Movement elements are analyzed from data collected from 120 pedestrians. They find that the velocity and acceleration elements follow a normal distribution while the direction angle change and the pause time measure fit better to lognormal distribution. Based on 226 daily GPS traces of 101 subjects, Lee et al. [17] develop a mobility model that captures the effect of human mobility patterns characterized by some fundamental statistical functions. With analytical and empirical evidence, they show that human movement can be expressed using gaps among *fractal waypoints* [21] (people are more attracted to more popular places).

With a large set of mobile phone data, Candia et al. [18] study spatiotemporal human dynamics as well as social interactions. They investigate the patterns in anomalous events, which can be useful in real-time detection of emergency situation. At the individual level, they find that the interevent time of consecutive calls can be described by *heavy-tailed* distribution, which is consistent with the previous reports on other human related activities. Gonzalez et al. [19] examine six-month trajectory of 100,000 mobile phone users and find a high regularity degree in human trajectories contrasting with estimation by *Levy flight* and *random walk* models. People tend to return a few frequent locations and follow simple repeated patterns despite the diversity of the their travel history. The most recent study in human mobility based on a large mobile phone data by Song et al. [20], whose result is consistent with Gonzalez et al.'s [19] that human mobility is highly predictable. Based on data from 50,000 mobile phone users, they find that predictability in human mobility is independent of distance that each individual regularly travel and show that the predictability is stabled at 93% for all regular traveled distances of more than 10km.

In contrast with other work in human mobility, our work is focusing on human mobility concerning the spatial profile (i.e. type of space or surrounding area such as dinning, shopping, and entertainment) rather than geographical location.

3   Methodology

A number of literature have described geographical human mobility pattern concerning movement of people between multiple locations. Here we are interested in characterizing the mobility not by geographic location but its associated *spatial profile*. This spatial profile-based mobility pattern, in turn, becomes a *human activity pattern*. In addition, our interest expands to investigation of relationship between this activity pattern and demographic of people. Therefore, in this section, we will describe our methodology used in characterizing space, capturing daily activity pattern, as well as preprocessing our dataset.

3.1   Data Preparation

In this research, we use anonymous mobile phone data collected during the period from July 30th, 2009 to September 12th, 2009 by Airsage[22] of about one million users in the state of Massachusetts, which account for approximately 20% of population, equally spread over space. This includes 130 million anonymous location estimations in (latitude,longitude)-coordinates, which are recorded when the users are engaged in communication via the cellular network. Specifically, the locations are estimated at the beginning and the end of each voice call placed or received, when a short message is sent or received, and while internet is connected. Note that these location estimations have an average uncertainty of 320 meters and median of 220 meters as reported by Airsage[22] based on internal and independent tests. For our analysis, we consider the mobile phone data within an area of $33\times42km^2$, which includes 52 cities (Boston, Cambridge, and others) in the county of Essex, Middlesex, Suffolk, and Norfolk as shown in Fig. 1. The list of the counties and their corresponding area covered (in km^2) by this study are shown in Table 1.

Within this area in the map, we need to extract mobility traces of each user from the mobile phone data. As the estimation of the user's location is aggregated

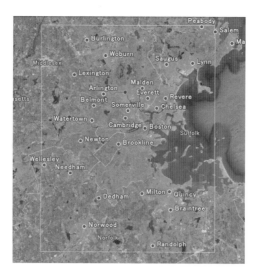

Fig. 1. Area of study in this research, cropped by yellow line

Table 1. List of the counties and their area covered by this study

County	Area covered (km^2)
Essex	110.30
Middlesex	452.52
Suffolk	154.39
Norfolk	26.12

only when network connection is established, mobility thus can be derived as a temporal sequence of locations. To segment these traces into trajectories so that daily mobility pattern of each individual can be identified, we describe here some basic algorithms to extract *trajectory* and *stop* [23].

Let X_k denote a set of sequential traces of user k such that $X_k = \{x_k(1), x_k(2), x_k(3), ...\}$ where $x_k(i)$ is a position i of user k. A trajectory can then be obtained by segmenting X_k with the spatial threshold $\triangle S$. If a distance between adjacent positions is greater than the threshold $(distance(x_k(i), x_k(i + 1)) > \triangle S)$, then the early position $x_k(i)$ becomes the end position of the last trajectory while the later position $x_k(i+1)$ becomes the starting position of the next trajectory. Once the trajectories are detected, a stop can be identified as an event during which the user stays in a specific location for a sufficiently long period of time. As each position i contains location and timestamp, i.e. $x_k(i) = (lat(i), long(i), t(i))$, extraction of a stop depends on time and space. A stop is thus regarded as a sequence of positions $\{x(j), x(j + 1), x(j + 3), ..., x(j + m)\}$ where the distance between any adjacent positions is less than a spatial threshold S_{th} i.e., $distance(x(j), x(j + 1)) < S_{th}$, and time spent within the location is greater than a time threshold T_{th} i.e., $t(m) - t(j) > T_{th}$.

After stops have been identified, *work* location of each user is then estimated as a most frequent stop during the day hours. The information about work location allows us to derive the mobility choices of the users, and detect activity patterns throughout the day.

3.2   Spatial Profiling

To model the space, we construct a virtual grid reference by dividing the map into square cells of size 500 by 500 meters (to compensate location estimation uncertainty). Since our interest is in the activities associated with the space, we thus characterize space based on the type of activities expected to be performed within given space. For example, if restaurants were clustered within a particular area, then this area would be associated with eating activity.

In this study, we consider four different human activities in which people typically spend time engaging on daily basis. These activities are concerning eating, shopping, entertainment, and recreational. Profiling the map according to these activities requires information about the types of places within each cell. To acquire the information regarding these activities, we search for Points of Interest

Table 2. Considered activities and keywords used for POIs search

Activity	Keywords used
Eating	Restaurant, Bakery, Coffee shop
Shopping	Mall, Store, Market
Entertainment	Theater, Bowling, Night club
Recreational	Park, Gym, Fitness

(POIs) for each cell location. We use *pYsearch* (Python APIs for Y! search services) version 3.1 [24] for POI search service, and Reverse Geocoding with *Geopy* (A Geocoding Toolbox for Python) [25] for translating *(latitude, longitude)*-coordinate into a physical address. For each activity category of each cell, we make three search attempts using different keywords. The keywords used for each activity category are listed in Table 2. With the limit of 5,000 queries per day restricted by Yahoo, an extensive amount of search time is required inevitably.

Once POI searches are completed, the number of POIs associated with each activity category is recorded for each cell. The raw *activity distribution map* is then composed of 500x500m^2 cells where each cell contains distribution of each activity. Each cell C_i contains normalized portion of each activity:

$$C_i = [\alpha_i(1), \alpha_i(2), \alpha_i(3), \alpha_i(4)], \tag{1}$$

where $i = 1, 2, 3, ..., N$, N is the total number of cells, and normalized portion of each activity $\alpha_i(a)$ in cell i is computed as

$$\alpha_i(a) = \frac{n_{\alpha_i(a)}}{\sum_{i=1}^{N} n_{\alpha_i(a)}}, \tag{2}$$

where $n_{\alpha_i(a)}$ denotes the number of POIs associated with activity a within the cell i and $a = 1, 2, 3, 4$ corresponds to eating, shopping, entertainment, and recreational activity, respectively.

Based on our POI search, Fig. 2 shows a map with the visual grids and POIs found by 12 different keywords (described in Table 2) in different colors.

To further classify these cells into a more crisp distribution map, we apply k-means algorithm with $k=4$. The resulting *crisp activity distribution map* is depicted in Fig. 3 where each cell is classified to one of the four activities according to Bayes theorem:

$$P(a|n_{\alpha_i(a)}) = \frac{P(n_{\alpha_i(a)}|a)P(a)}{n_{\alpha_i(a)}}. \tag{3}$$

The interest here is to find the most probable activity category a for each of the k clusters. Therefore, for each cluster, we find a that maximizes *a posteriori* (MAP method). So we use Bayes theorem above to compute the posterior probability of each activity category as follows:

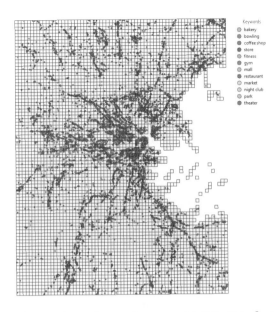

Fig. 2. POI search results on the map with 500x500m^2 visual grids

$$a_{MAP} \equiv \arg\max_a P(a|n_{\alpha_i(a)})$$
$$= \arg\max_a \frac{P(n_{\alpha_i(a)}|a)P(a)}{n_{\alpha_i(a)}}$$
$$= \arg\max_a P(n_{\alpha_i(a)}|a)P(a). \tag{4}$$

3.3   Daily Activity Patterns

Generally, people perform different activities throughout the day. A lot of these activities are repeated on daily basis, e.g. eating around 12pm (noon), jogging in the evening, and hence producing recognizable patterns. With our mobile phone data, each user is more likely to engage in an activity during "stop" rather than on the move. Therefore, for each stop, activity is identified according to the crisp activity distribution map.

To infer a daily activity pattern for each user, we divide 24-hour time scale into eight 3-hour segments starting at 5AM as shown in Fig. 4. So daily activity pattern is simply a sequence of activities performed by the user during each stop throughout the day. For each user, daily activity patterns are collected over the course of the data collection period. Note that, in this study, we consider only weekdays (Monday, Tuesday, Wednesday, Thursday, Friday) as our speculation is that weekday pattern is different from weekend pattern due to typical work schedule and hence different daily activity sequences – this will be addressed and further discussed in our future work.

Fig. 3. Crisp activity distribution map

Fig. 4. The eight 3-hour temporal windows are used to frame the daily activity pattern

To derive the representative daily activity pattern of each user, we simply assign each segment with the most frequent activity during that time interval over the period of data collection. Precisely, if $\lambda_a^d(t)$ represents the count of activity a on d-th day during time segment t (where $t = 1, 2, 3.., 8$), then

$$z(t) = \arg\max_a \sum_{d=1}^{M} \lambda_a^d(t) \tag{5}$$

where $z(t)$ is the assigned activity for time segment t and M is the total number of days.

4   Work Area's Profile and Similarity in Daily Activity Patterns

The activity map and individual daily activity patterns developed in the previous section allows us to conduct a number of studies that can be useful for better understanding of human behavior in the city. In this present research, we are particularly interested in relationship between people's daily activity patterns and the characteristic of their work area. Do people who work in the same area's category (e.g. eating, shopping, etc.) also have similar daily activity patterns? With the same type of work area, how does distance impact the similarity in their daily activity patterns (e.g. do people who work in an urban shopping area have similar activity pattern with people who work in a distant shopping area)? In this current study, we are attempting to answer these two questions.

As a first step, we classify the users into four groups based on their work cell's profiles. Each group then consists of a number of different individual daily activity patterns who have a common work cell's profile. To represent each group's activity pattern, we need to find a group signature for further correlation analyses. The representative daily activity pattern or signature of each group can be obtained in a similar fashion with the individual patterns described in the previous section (using Eq. (5)). The derived signatures are shown in Table 3.

It can be noticed that there is no Eating element appears in any of other group signatures beside its own group (showing in form of a working activity, W). Our speculation is that it could be caused by first, people normally eat at home (breakfasts) and at work or somewhere nearby workplace (lunches), and second, people are not frequently involved in a phone communication while at eating area. Note also that the patterns are derived from weekdays activities so if weekends-only activities are considered, Eating elements could emerge in the group patterns.

To answer the first question, we need to measure similarity in daily activity patterns among individuals within the same group as well as among other groups. To measure distance (dissimilarity) between two daily activity patterns, we use *Hamming distance*, which is normally used to measure distance between two strings of equal length. The distance is essentially the number of positions at which the corresponding symbols are different, which is quite suitable for our case as a series of activities can be considered as symbols. The result of the average Hamming distance within the group is shown in Table 4.

Using group signatures obtained earlier, we then measure dissimilarity between each group signature and other group's individual patterns. The result of this between-group distance is shown in Table 5 in forms of average Hamming distance.

As the result of our first investigation, Fig. 5 illustrates a bar plot intended to make a comparison between within-group and between-group distances where

Table 3. Signature of each group based on work cell's profile. Note: Eat. = Eating, Sho. = Shopping, Ent. = Entertainment, Rec. = Recreational, W = Work cell.

Group	Group's daily activity pattern
Eating	W–W–W–W–Sho.–Rec.–Rec.–Sho.
Shopping	W–W–W–W–Rec.–Rec.–W–W
Entertainment	Sho.–W–W–W–W–Rec.–Sho.–Sho.
Recreational	W–W–W–W–W–Sho.–Sho.–Sho.

Table 4. Average within-group distance

Work cell's profile	Average distance
Eating	4.78
Shopping	2.58
Entertainment	4.67
Recreational	3.61

Table 5. Average between-group distance

	Eating	Shopping	Entertainment	Recreational
Eating	–	6.53	6.60	6.96
Shopping	4.90	–	4.92	5.05
Entertainment	6.43	6.88	–	7.00
Recreational	5.04	4.81	5.13	–

red bars represent within-group distance while blue bars represent between-group distance. Clearly, it shows that within-group distances are less than between-group distances. This implies that people who have a common work cell's profile tend to exhibit more similar daily activity patterns than people who have different work cell's profile.

For the second investigation about the impact of physical distance on the similarity in activity patterns, we decide to proceed by placing a growing spatial window (a circle of an arbitrary radius) onto the map then measure similarity between between the users' activity pattern whose work cell located at the center of the window and other users whose work cells are within the vicinity of the spatial window. The similarity is being measured while the radius of the window grows from a small to larger value. The process is repeated for each activity category. This way, we can see the change(if any) in similarity for each work profile as we move away from the center area. Precisely, we choose to grow the spatial window from the center of Boston area with the radius varying

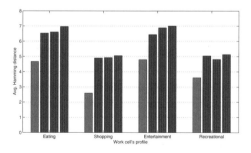

Fig. 5. When users are grouped together based on their work cell's profiles, within-group and between-group distances are illustrated with red and blue bars respectively. This shows higher degree in similarity within the group than between groups.

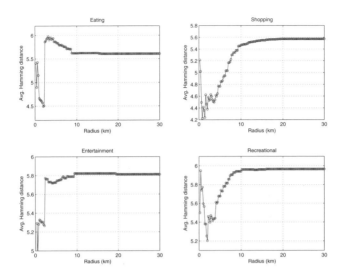

Fig. 6. Dissimilarity in daily activity patterns is measured by average Hamming distance as the radius varies from 0.5km to 30km for each work cell's profile. The center of the growing radius is near the center of city of Boston. Dissimilarity is between the users whose work cells are within the 0.5km radius and other users covered by growing radius.

from 0.5km to 30km. The result for each work category is shown in Fig. 6. We can observe that, overall, the similarity in activity patterns decreases as radius increases, which implies that physical distance has an impact on similarity in daily activity patterns. People whose work area's profile are although the same, their activity patterns tend to deviate more as they work areas become further apart.

In summary, we have observed a strong correlation in daily activity patterns within the group of people who share a common work area's profile. Addition, within the group itself, the similarity in activity patterns decreases as the distance between them increases.

5 Limitations of the Study

There are a number of limitations of this study. First and foremost, the lack of continuity of mobility traces due to the fact that the location is estimated from mobile phone data only when connection with a cellular network is made through either voice, text, or data communication, which constricts us to a smaller number of users that can be analyzed. Secondly, our POI search is constrained by Yahoo's search limit and capability. Lastly, home and work locations are estimated intuitively according to the data provided. Although ground-truth validation is desired, it would be very difficult to perform due to the privacy issue.

6   Conclusions

In this paper, we have developed an activity-aware map that contains most probable activity associated with a specific area in the map based on POIs information. With activity-aware map, we are able to extract individual daily activity patterns from analyzing a large mobile phone data of nearly one million records. Results from our correlation analysis show a strong correlation in daily activity patterns within the group of people who share a common work area's profile. In addition, within the group itself, the similarity in activity patterns decreases as the distance between them increases. This study is the first report of many more to come in using activity-aware map to study inhabitant behavior. So as our future direction, we will continue to investigate on daily activity pattern and its dynamics for better understanding of human dynamics, which in turn benefits urban planning and management.

Acknowledgments. This research has been supported by VWoA Electronic Research Lab, AT&T Foundation, National Science Foundation, MIT Portugal, and all the Senseable City Laboratory Consortium members. We would like to also express our gratitude to Aisage for valuable data.

References

1. Turner, M., Love, S., Howell, M.: Understanding emotions experienced when using a mobile phone in public: The social usability of mobile (cellular) telephones. Telemat. Inf. 25(3), 201–215 (2008)
2. Nickerson, R.C., Isaac, H., Mak, B.: A multi-national study of attitudes about mobile phone use in social settings. Int. J. Mob. Commun. 6(5), 541–563 (2008)
3. Liu, C.C.: Measuring and prioritising value of mobile phone usage. Int. J. Mob. Commun. 8(1), 41–52 (2010)
4. Kauffman, R.J., Techatassanasoontorn, A.A.: International diffusion of digital mobile technology: A coupled-hazard state-based approach. Inf. Technol. and Management 6(2-3), 253–292 (2005)
5. Giray, F., Gercek, A., Oguzlar, A., Tuzunturk, S.: The effects of taxation on mobile phones: a panel data approach. Int. J. Mob. Commun. 7(5), 594–613 (2009)
6. Li, W., McQueen, R.J.: Barriers to mobile commerce adoption: an analysis framework for a country level perspective. Int. J. Mob. Commun. 6(2), 231–257 (2008)
7. Eagle, N., Pentland, A.: Reality mining: sensing complex social systems. Personal and Ubiquitous Computing 10(4), 255–268 (2006)
8. Eagle, N., Pentland, A.: Eigenbehaviors: Identifying structure in routine. Proc. Roy. Soc. A (2006) (in submission)
9. Eagle, N.: Machine perception and learning of complex social systems. Ph.D. Thesis, Program in Media Arts and Sciences, Massachusetts Institute of Technology (2005)
10. Clauset, A., Eagle, N.: Ersistence and periodicity in a dynamic proximity network. In: Proceedings of Discrete Mathematics and Theoretical Computer Science Workshop on Computational Methods for Dynamic Interaction Networks (2007)
11. Eagle, N., Pentland, A., Lazer, D.: Inferring social network structure using mobile phone data. PNAS (2007)

12. Phithakkitnukoon, S., Dantu, R.: Predicting calls — new service for an intelligent phone. In: Krishnaswamy, D., Pfeifer, T., Raz, D. (eds.) MMNS 2007. LNCS, vol. 4787, pp. 26–37. Springer, Heidelberg (2007)
13. Phithakkitnukoon, S., Dantu, R.: Cpl: Enhancing mobile phone functionality by call predicted list. In: Meersman, R., Tari, Z. (eds.) OTM 2008, Part II. LNCS, vol. 5332, pp. 571–581. Springer, Heidelberg (2008)
14. Phithakkitnukoon, S., Dantu, R.: Mobile social group sizes and scaling ratio. AI & Society, Springer (2009)
15. Phithakkitnukoon, S., Dantu, R.: Mobile social closeness and similarity in calling patterns. In: IEEE Conference on Consumer Communications & Networking Conference (CCNC 2010), Special Session on Social Networking, SocNets (2010)
16. Azevedo, T.S., Bezerra, R.L., Campos, C.A.V., de Moraes, L.F.M.: An analysis of human mobility using real traces. In: WCNC 2009: Proceedings of the 2009 IEEE conference on Wireless Communications & Networking Conference, Piscataway, NJ, USA, pp. 2390–2395. IEEE Press, Los Alamitos (2009)
17. Lee, K., Hong, S., Kim, S.J., Rhee, I., Chong, S.: Slaw: A mobility model for human walks. In: Proceedings of the 28th Annual Joint Conference of the IEEE Computer and Communications Societies (INFOCOM), Rio de Janeiro, Brazil. IEEE, Los Alamitos (April 2009)
18. Candia, J., Gonzalez, M.C., Wang, P., Schoenharl, T., Madey, G., Barabasi, A.: Uncovering individual and collective human dynamics from mobile phone records. Journal of Physics A: Mathematical and Theoretical 41(22), 1–16 (2008)
19. Gonzalez, M.C., Hidalgo, C.A., Barabasi, A.L.: Understanding individual human mobility patterns. Nature 453(7196), 779–782 (2008)
20. Song, C., Qu, Z., Blumm, N., Barabasi, A.L.: Limits of predictability in human mobility. Science 327(5968), 1018–1021 (2010)
21. Rhee, I., Lee, K., Hong, S., Kim, S.J., Chong, S.: Demystifying the levy-walk nature of human walks. Technical report, NCSU (2008)
22. Airsage: Airsage wise technology, http://www.airsage.com
23. Calabrese, F., Pereira, F.C., Lorenzo, G.D., Liu, L.: The geography of taste: analyzing cell-phone mobility and social events. In: Proceedings of IEEE Inter. Conf. on Pervasive Computing, PerComp. (2010)
24. pYsearch: Python APIs for Y! search services, http://pysearch.sourceforge.net/
25. Geopy: A Geocoding Toolbox for Python, http://code.google.com/p/geopy/wiki/ReverseGeocoding

From On-Going to Complete Activity Recognition Exploiting Related Activities

Carlo Nicolini[1], Bruno Lepri[2], Stefano Teso[1], and Andrea Passerini[1]

[1] Dipartimento di Ingegneria e Scienza dell'Informazione
Università degli Studi di Trento, Italy
[2] FBK-irst, via Sommarive 18, Povo, Trento, Italy

Abstract. Activity recognition can be seen as a local task aimed at identifying an *on-going* activity performed at a certain time, or a global one identifying time segments in which a certain activity is being performed. We combine these tasks by a hierarchical approach which locally predicts on-going activities by a Support Vector Machine and globally refines them by a Conditional Random Field focused on time segments involving related activities. By varying temporal scales in order to account for widely different activity durations, we achieve substantial improvements in on-going activity recognition on a realistic dataset from the PlaceLab sensing environment. When focusing on periods within which related activities are known to be performed, the refinement stage manages to exploit these relationships in order to correct inaccurate local predictions.

1 Introduction

Automatic monitoring of Activities of Daily Living (ADLs, such as eating, drinking, cleaning, and so on) is an important component for the implementation of advanced services in the fields of Ambient Assisted Living and Assisted Cognition. In assessing the level of self-sufficiency of patients, clinicians consider the capabilities of performing basic ADLs such as cooking and eating [1]. The automatic recognition and tracking of these activities may allow for a more reliable and cheaper automatic reporting to clinicians or relatives. At the same time, it allows for the provision of advanced services that can contribute to older people's independent life: services like reminders, help in activity execution, etc.

As defined in [2], the activity classification task can take at least two guises which differ according to the kind of perspective taken on the activities. The first type is the "complete activity" (CA) recognition task and considers finished activities and asks about their type. This task involves an external perspective on the activity and humans talk about these activities using the perfective tenses as in the following example: A-"What did Mark do yesterday afternoon?", B-"He played basketball". For automatic systems, the task is to assign the right activity label to the unknown segmented and complete one. Different works in activity recognition field dealt with CA task; in particular it has been often used by researchers adopting the object-use approach whereby activities are modeled

A.A. Salah et al. (Eds.): HBU 2010, LNCS 6219, pp. 26–37, 2010.

as sequences of used objects [3,4]. The second kind of classification task, called "on-going activity" recognition task (OGA) takes an internal perspective on activities. The human subject or the automatic system are temporally located inside the activity. In this case, humans would use imperfective tenses or progressive forms: A-"What is Mark doing now?", B-"Mark is playing basketball". So, the task is anchored to a given time and the goal of the human or of the machine is finding signs of the on-going activity and define their type. We can cite some previous works adopting the OGA paradigm; for example, [5,6]. In this paper we are going to deal with both of these tasks (OGA and CA): more precisely, we deal with OGA task using Support Vector Machines (SVM) in order to predict what is happening inside a given small time interval. These local predictions are fed as input to a sequential model, namely a Conditional Random Field (CRF), aimed at performing CA recognition on larger segments of the day. In the real world, people often perform multiple activities concurrently in their daily living; e.g. a person might have the habit of watching TV while ironing. Furthermore, related activities can have quite different recognition complexity. We build on this observation by focusing on time segments involving highly related activities, and exploiting a well-predicted activity to improve recognition of a difficult one. Finally, our evaluation highlights the importance of calibrating the temporal scale at which an activity should be searched for depending on its average duration.

This paper is organized as follows. In Section 2 we discuss some related works on activity recognition. Section 3 describes the sensing environment and the learning algorithms we employed. Experimental results are reported in Section 4, and conclusions are drawn in Section 5.

2   Previous Works

The problem of human activity recognition has received increasing interest in recent years in the pattern recognition and machine learning communities. In particular, good results were achieved both on low-level activities (e.g. ADLs such as sitting, standing, walking, and lying [7,8]), and high-level activities (e.g. eating, watching TV, dishwashing, and cooking [9,10], and office activities [11]). Different sensors were used for activity recognition tasks: several works have explored the use of switches and motion detectors (similar to those used in common alarm systems) to collect data regarding the performance of ADLs [12]. Recently, Logan et al. [5] compared different modalities on data approaching real-world conditions: they collected 104 hours of annotated data of a person living in a house, instrumented with over 900 sensors, including power and water flow inputs, objects and person motion detectors, and RFID tags. They found that 10 infra-red motion detectors outperformed the other sensors on many of the studied activities, especially those that were usually performed in the same location. From a machine learning point of view, most of the work in the activity recognition area is based on supervised algorithms such as Naive Bayes [9], Decision Trees [7,5], Hidden Markov Models [13,8,3,14], Support Vector Machines [13,2], and Conditional Random Fields [14]. In particular, Conditional

Random Fields were found to offer higher overall accuracy than Hidden Markov Models (HMM) for multi-label activity classification, even if HMMs can better discriminate between multiple activities when the training dataset contains unbalanced class labels [14]. A limited number of works used relational learning techniques to deal with activity recognition tasks: [15] used Relational Markov Networks (RMNs) for recognizing activities from location data. Landwher et al [16] introduced a relational transformation based tagging system in order to integrate various principles of inductive logic programming (e.g., search, operators, representations, and background knowledge) with transformation-based tagging (e.g., error-driven search, branch and bound idea).

3   Activity Classification

3.1   The Sensing Environment

PlaceLab is an instrumented home environment operated as a shared research facility. The complete description of the sensing environment can be found in [5]. Logan et al. [5] collected and analyzed data from a couple who lived at the home for a period of 10 weeks. The home is a custom built condominium instrumented with several hundred sensors, including an audiovisual recording system that captures ground truth of the participants activities. The environment contains several classes of sensors, including wired reed switches, power and water flow inputs, objects and person motion detectors, and RFID tags. We focused on infrared (IR) and object motion (OM) sensors, those found in Logan et al. [5] to be the most discriminant.

3.2   Data Preparation

Following Logan et al. [5], we divided each day into $30s$ intervals overlapped by $15s$. We formulated the activity recognition problem as nine binary classification tasks at the interval level, one for each of the nine possible activities. Each interval was labeled positively for a certain activity if it had occurred at any time within it. Note that many activities are not mutually exclusive (i.e. they

Table 1. Activity duration statistics

Activity	Instances	Avg. duration (min)
ActivelyWatchingTV	15	53
DishWashing	21	1
Grooming	28	2
GroupedEating	101	4
Hygiene	20	3
MealPrep	40	2
Reading	29	17
UsingComputer	50	37
UsingPhone	68	3

can both be performed within the $30s$ timeframe) and the problem should be addressed as multi-label rather than multi-class prediction.

We represented an interval as a vector of sensor features, indicating the number of times each sensor was activated during the interval.

Most activities have average durations on the order of a minute, with some like ActivelyWatchingTV or UsingComputer having a far longer duration as showed in Table 1.

In order to account for such temporal correlations we applied a sliding window approach computing average feature vectors on intervals surrounding the one of interest, either separately for past and future (asymmetric) or combining both together (symmetric).

3.3   Local Classification by Support Vector Machines

We addressed each binary classification task at the interval level with an SVM classifier [17]. SVM are state-of-the-art discriminative classifiers capable of efficiently handling thousands of features and learning complex non-linear functions thanks to the kernel trick. Experimental results show substantial improvements over the decision tree classifiers employed in [5], as will be detailed in the experimental section.

3.4   Global Refinement by Conditional Random Fields

CRFs [18] are undirected graphical models conditioned on observation sequences. Linear-chain CRF allow to efficiently model sequential observations and have been successfully applied to a variety of recognition tasks in text classification, bioinformatics and activity recognition, to name a few application domain. Here

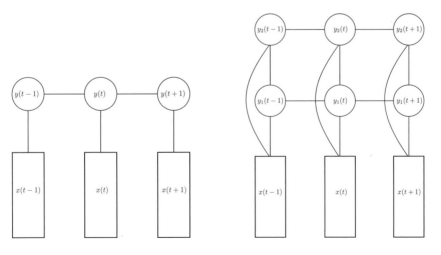

Fig. 1. Graphical model representation of a linear-chain CRF, on the left, and a factorial CRF with two chains, on the right, unrolled for three time intervals. The $x(t)$ nodes represent the predicted OGAs over time, while the $y_i(t)$ variables are the detected CAs.

we employ them as a *refinement* stage, in order to combine sequences of local OGA predictions from multiple related activities into a global CA prediction. Figure 1 shows a graphical representation of the models we employed. The inputs $x(t)$ represent local OGA predictions for all or some of the activities at time interval t. The outputs $y(t)$ represent CA predictions for the activity being globally refined. The model to the left is a plain linear-chain CRF, where a single activity is predicted in output. Connections are provided between outputs at consecutive time instants, with the effect of propagating predictions along the time range. The model to the right is a more complex factorial CRF [19], where multiple activities (two in this example) are jointly predicted. Linear-chain models for each activity are combined by adding co-temporal connections between activities. Note that the higher complexity of the factorial model implies more parameters to be estimated and approximate inference. In conjunction with the scarcity of positive examples for most activities, this often resulted in a performance worsening with respect to the simpler linear-chain case, as will be detailed in the experimental section.

4   Experimental Results

We conducted a leave-one-day-out cross validation procedure as in [5]. The aims of the experimental evaluation are: 1) identifying the most discriminative sensors and time frames (i.e. sizes of the sliding windows) for the different activities; 2) comparing to previous activity recognition approaches on this dataset; 3) verifying the usefulness of sequential models to refine local predictions. In the following we will report experimental results for each of these points. For comparability to [5], we employed area under the ROC curve (AUC) as a figure of merit in all experiments.

For each of the binary classification tasks, we conducted an extensive model selection phase to identify 1) the best set of sensors, IR, OM or IR+OM; 2) the best sliding window size; 3) the best SVM parameters, namely regularization parameter C and kernel type among linear, polynomial or Gaussian with varying width size.

Model selection was conducted by an inner leave-one-day-out cross validation on the training set of the first fold (i.e. the first 8 days), and obtained parameters and feature sets were kept fixed for the outer cross validation.

4.1   Model Selection Results

The best kernel was a second degree polynomial for all activities. Concerning sensor classes, IR sensors performed much better than OM ones. Furthermore, we did not experience significant advantages in combining OM and IR sensors, especially when increasing the size of the sliding window. These results are consistent with those reported in [5] where IR sensors where found to be the most discriminant.

Figure 2 reports AUC values for varying window sizes for the different activities. Both IR and IR+OM results are shown. Two aspects are worth mentioning.

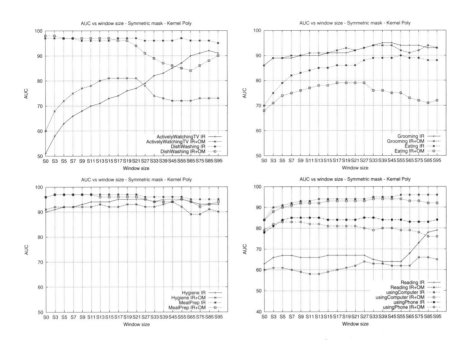

Fig. 2. AUC dependence on window size, comparison between IR and IR+OM for the different activities

First, large differences can be observed in the optimal window size of different activities. This size is actually highly correlated with the average duration of the activity (see Table 1), with the three longest activities, namely ActivelyWatchingTV, Reading (for which the maximum is outsize of the range shown) and UsingComputer, having by far the largest optimal window sizes. Second, IR and IR+OM behave quite differently with respect to optimal window size, with the latter early starting to show performance worsening. This seems to indicate the need to separately optimize window sizes for the two classes of sensors. We plan to investigate this issue in future experiments.

4.2 SVM Results

Table 2 reports experimental comparisons between our local SVM classifiers and the decision trees (DT) used by Logan et al. [5].

SVM substantially outperforms DT in all experiments. The largest improvements can be observed for the three hardest recognition tasks, GroupedEating, Reading and UsingPhone. Note that an appropriate window size is also crucial in achieving these results, especially for the first two activities which perform drastically worse if only the activations in the target interval are considered (see Figure 2). UsingComputer is by far the best predicted activity, as the other activities with AUC > 0.95 have much less positive examples, and AUC is very sensitive to the unbalancing in the data.

Table 2. Leave-one-day-out cross validated AUC (%) for DT and SVM. Optimal window size refers to SVM and was obtained by an inner cross-validation on the training set of the first fold.

Activity	Best win.	SVM$_{AUC}$	DT$_{AUC}$
ActivelyWatchingTV	$s85$	**90**	80
DishWashing	$s3$	**97**	89
Grooming	$s45$	**95**	87
GroupedEating	$s55$	**91**	56
Hygiene	$a19$	**96**	86
MealPreparation	$s11$	**97**	87
Reading	$s135$	**81**	54
UsingComputer	$s95$	**96**	85
UsingPhone	$s9$	**85**	64

4.3   CRF Results

We investigated the usefulness of relying on well-predicted activities in order to improve recognition of more difficult ones. Figure 3 shows the cross-correlation between UsingComputer and Reading, the two activities with highest cross-correlation. Note that activities are frequently co-occurrent (Lag=0), but also frequently follow one after the other within a short time frame.

We employed either the true labels or the local SVM predictions in order to focus on time segments likely to contain one of these activities. We selected segments of consecutive intervals where at least one of the two activities was actually performed or locally predicted to be performed, allowing for a small gap of inactivity (10 intervals) between consecutive positive intervals. We then retained those segments in which each activity was performed for at least 3 intervals. During test, we applied the same selection mechanism to identify candidate time segments.

We experimented with two different models: a linear-chain CRF predicting a single activity, and a factorial CRF jointly predicting Reading and UsingComputer. Each model was input either the margins of the activity being predicted, the margins of both activities, or the margins of all the nine activities.

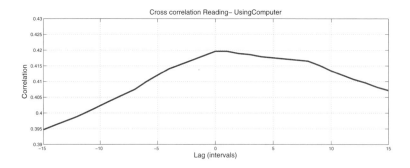

Fig. 3. Cross correlation between Reading and UsingComputer labels

Table 3. Results of CRF experiments. Both training and test data is segmented according to the true labels. A '-' indicates that there are no positive instances of the given activity. L-CRF stands for linear-chain CRF, F-CRF for factorial CRF.

Predictions for Reading									
Prediction	1	2	3	4	5	6	7	8	9
SVM	0.31	–	0.25	0.48	**0.85**	–	0.12	0.55	0.56
L-CRF, Reading	0.38	–	0.5	0.85	0	–	0.66	0.32	0.56
L-CRF, Reading+UsingComputer	0.38	–	0.5	**0.94**	0	–	**0.86**	0.5	0.54
L-CRF, All Activities	**0.45**	–	0.5	0.71	0	–	0.67	**0.68**	0.65
F-CRF, Reading+UsingComputer	0.36	–	0.04	0.61	0.24	–	0.33	0.49	0.48
F-CRF, All Activities	0.42	–	**0.93**	0.55	0	–	0.69	0.5	**0.72**
Predictions for Using Computer									
Prediction	1	2	3	4	5	6	7	8	9
SVM	0.48	–	0.95	0.68	0.8	–	0.79	0.83	0.77
L-CRF, UsingComputer	0.99	–	0.98	0.94	0.9	–	**0.91**	0.76	**0.89**
L-CRF, Reading+UsingComputer	0.98	–	0.98	0.94	0.9	–	0.87	0.78	**0.89**
L-CRF, All Activities	**1**	–	**1**	0.85	**0.97**	–	**0.91**	**0.87**	0.87
F-CRF, Reading+UsingComputer	0.71	–	0.95	0.86	0.78	–	0.79	0.86	0.79
F-CRF, All Activities	0.72	–	0.67	**0.96**	0.14	–	0.87	**0.87**	0.78

Table 3 summarizes the results for the prediction of Reading and UsingComputer with the different CRF models. Each row contains the AUC of the predictions for the given combination of CRF type and inputs, for each day of the test data. The AUCs of the SVM predictor are included for reference. Numbers in

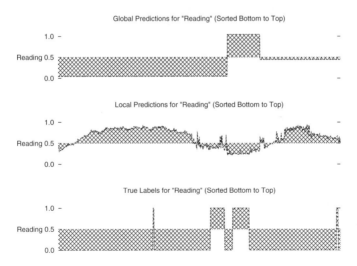

Fig. 4. Plot showing the predictions of the linear-chain CRF for Reading on cross-validation day 7. On the bottom row we report the true labels for Reading. The middle row represents the SVM predictions. The top represents the CRF predictions.

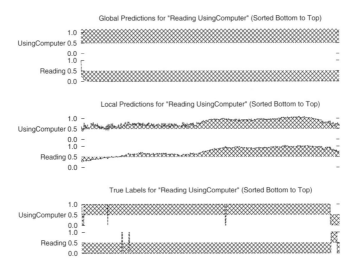

Fig. 5. Plot showing the predictions of the factorial CRF for both Reading and Using-Computer, with all 9 activities as inputs. The predictions refer to day 4. For simplicity, only the labels and local predictions for Reading and UsingComputer are shown.

bold highlight the best result for each test day. Using the true labels to segment both train and test data is clearly infeasible in realistic conditions, where the true labels are not available during the testing stage. However, these experiments allow us to highlight the potential advantages of a sequential refinement stage for CA recognition, abstracting away the problem of identifying candidate periods of the day to focus on.

The first observation is that the linear-chain CRF typically outperforms the SVM, on all days and for both activities, with the sole exception of Reading during day 5. In general the CRF manages to overcome the local predictions. These can be very bad especially in the case of Reading, which is particularly difficult to predict on a local basis. Interestingly, this behavior occurs even if only one input is given. A particular instance of this behavior can be seen in Figure 4, referring to day 7 of the one input case. Here the local predictions are quite bad, but the CRF is able to approximately detect the second large segment of activity.

The factorial CRF does not show this consistent behavior, performing rather worse on some of the test instances. This may be due to the higher complexity of the model, requiring more parameters and approximate inference, and the sparseness of the train data available for Reading. One exception is shown in Figure 5, which refers to the predictions from all activities as inputs on day 4.

We also note that usually increasing the number of inputs improves the prediction for both the linear-chain and factorial models. This fact hints at the positive effect that combining multiple local predictions has on the accuracy of the CRF. As an example, Figure 6 shows how the CRF combines the wrong

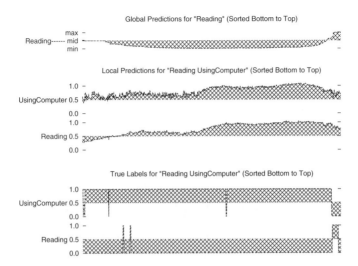

Fig. 6. Plot showing the predictions of Reading with both Reading and UsingComputer as inputs, performed with the linear-chain CRF. The predictions refer to day 4.

Table 4. Results of CRF experiments. Both training and test data is segmented according to the local predictions. A '-' indicates that there are no positive instances of the given activity.

Predictions for Reading									
Prediction	1	2	3	4	5	6	7	8	9
SVM	–	–	–	**0.62**	**0.95**	**0.76**	0.33	0.91	0.74
L-CRF, Reading	–	–	–	0.49	0.42	0.35	0.78	0.1	0.49
L-CRF, Reading+UsingComputer	–	–	–	0.51	0.39	0.23	**0.79**	0.05	0.39
L-CRF, All Activities	–	–	–	0.43	0.36	0.47	0.71	0.63	**0.86**
F-CRF, Reading+UsingComputer	–	–	–	0.46	0.08	0.33	0.71	0.05	0.36
F-CRF, All Activities	–	–	–	0.14	0.02	0.45	0.4	**0.94**	0.8
Predictions for Using Computer									
Prediction	1	2	3	4	5	6	7	8	9
SVM	**0.88**	0.79	–	0.83	**0.96**	0.39	0.88	0.79	0.55
L-CRF, UsingComputer	0.6	**0.97**	–	0.92	0.88	0.48	0.86	**0.9**	0.21
L-CRF, Reading+UsingComputer	0.6	0.88	–	0.85	0.76	0.55	0.83	**0.9**	0.14
L-CRF, All Activities	0	0	–	0.4	0.4	0.47	0.65	0.65	**0.86**
F-CRF, Reading+UsingComputer	0.38	0.85	–	0.67	0.81	**0.67**	0.21	0.48	0.43
F-CRF, All Activities	0.69	0.53	–	**0.99**	0.93	0.48	**0.94**	0.88	0.64

local prediction of Reading with the prediction of UsingComputer to accurately locate both positives and negatives of Reading, even though its SVM prediction is almost completely wrong.

Table 4 summarizes the results of the CRFs when the test and train data are segmented according to the local predictions. In this case, the contributions of the CRF are not as clear cut. For both activities, the best CRF model seems the most complex one, namely a factorial CRF with all 9 activities in input. However, the comparison with the local SVM predictions does not allow to draw clear conclusions, with three wins vs three losses for3.4 Reading, and five wins vs three losses for UsingComputer. Experiments in which training data were segmented according to the true labels did not produce substantially different results. This indicates that further work is needed in order to make CRF predictions more robust to a noisy identification of candidate periods.

5 Conclusion

We addressed the problem of activity recognition from the two perspectives of on-going and complete identification. We showed that by varying the temporal scale at which sensor readings are aggregated, we can account for the different average duration of activities, achieving substantial improvements on the on-going recognition task. The combination of local predictions by CRF sequential models allowed us to refine them into a complete activity recognition prediction. Preliminary results indicate that when focusing on periods containing related activities, this relationship helps to correct inaccurate local predictions, especially in exploiting information on easier activities to improve predictions of a harder one. In order to successfully apply this strategy in a real setting, however, we need to improve its robustness to a noisy identification of these periods, for instance by focusing on reliable predictions only and searching for the more difficult activities in the surroundings of the simpler ones.

Acknowledgments

This research was funded by the Autonomous Province of Trento, Call for proposal Major Projects 2006 (project ACube).

References

1. Katz, S.: Assessing self-maintenance: Activities of daily living, mobility, and instrumental activities of daily living. Journal of American Geriatrics Society 31(12), 712–726 (1983)
2. Lepri, B., Mana, N., Cappelletti, A., Pianesi, F., Zancanaro, M.: What is happening now? detection of activities of daily living from simple visual features. Personal and Ubiquitous Computing (2010)
3. Philipose, M.P.K., Perkowitz, M., Patterson, D.J., Fox, D., Kautz, H., Hähnel, D.: Inferring activities from interactions with objects. IEEE Pervasive Computing 3, 50–57 (2004)
4. Pentney, W., Philipose, M., Bilmes, J.A., Kautz, H.A.: Learning large scale common sense models of everyday life. In: AAAI, pp. 465–470 (2007)
5. Logan, B., Healey, J., Philipose, M., Tapia, E.M., Intille, S.: A long-term evaluation of sensing modalities for activity recognition. In: Krumm, J., Abowd, G.D., Seneviratne, A., Strang, T. (eds.) UbiComp 2007. LNCS, vol. 4717, pp. 483–500. Springer, Heidelberg (2007)

6. Stikic, M., Huynh, T., Van Laerhoven, K., Schiele, B.: Adl recognition based on the combination of rfid and accelerometer sensing. In: 2nd International Conference on Pervasive Computing Technologies for Healthcare 2008 (2008)

7. Bao, L., Intille, S.S.: Activity recognition from user-annotated acceleration data. In: Ferscha, A., Mattern, F. (eds.) PERVASIVE 2004. LNCS, vol. 3001, pp. 1–17. Springer, Heidelberg (2004)

8. Lester, J., Choudhury, T., Borriello, G.: A practical approach to recognizing physical activities. In: Fishkin, K.P., Schiele, B., Nixon, P., Quigley, A. (eds.) PERVASIVE 2006. LNCS, vol. 3968, pp. 1–16. Springer, Heidelberg (2006)

9. Tapia, E.M., Intille, S.S., Larson, K.: Activity recognition in the home using simple and ubiquitous sensors. In: Ferscha, A., Mattern, F. (eds.) PERVASIVE 2004. LNCS, vol. 3001, pp. 158–175. Springer, Heidelberg (2004)

10. Wyatt, D., Philipose, M., Choudhury, T.: Unsupervised activity recognition using automatically mined common sense. In: AAAI, pp. 21–27 (2005)

11. Oliver, N., Horvitz, E., Garg, A.: Layered representations for human activity recognition. In: Fourth IEEE Int. Conf. on Multimodal Interfaces, pp. 3–8 (2002)

12. Ogawa, M., Ochiai, S., Shoji, K., Nishihara, M., Togawa, T.: An attempt of monitoring daily activities at home. In: 22nd Annual International Conference of the IEEE Engineering in Medicine and Biology Society, vol. 1, pp. 786–788 (2000)

13. Blanke, U., Schiele, B.: Scalable recognition of daily activities with wearable sensors. In: Hightower, J., Schiele, B., Strang, T. (eds.) LoCA 2007. LNCS, vol. 4718, pp. 50–67. Springer, Heidelberg (2007)

14. van Kasteren, T., Noulas, A., Englebienne, G., Kröse, B.: Accurate activity recognition in a home setting. In: UbiComp 2008, pp. 1–9. ACM, New York (2008)

15. Liao, L., Fox, D., Kautz, H.: Location-based activity recognition using relational markov networks. In: IJCAI 2005 (2005)

16. Landwher, N., Gutmann, B., Thon, I., Philipose, M., De Raedt, L.: Relational transformation-based tagging for human activity recognition. In: Proceedings of the 6th Workshop on Multi-Relational Data Mining (MRDM), Warsaw, Poland (September 2007)

17. Cristianini, N., Shawe-Taylor, J.: An Introduction to Support Vector Machines. Cambridge University Press, Cambridge (2000)

18. Sutton, C., Mccallum, A.: Introduction to conditional random fields for relational learning. In: Getoor, L., Taskar, B. (eds.) Introduction to Statistical Relational Learning. MIT Press, Cambridge (2006)

19. yu Wu, T., chun Lian, C., jen Hsu, J.Y.: Joint recognition of multiple concurrent activities using factorial conditional random fields. In: 2007 AAAI Workshop on Plan, Activity, and Intent Recognition (2007)

Human Activity Recognition Using Inertial/Magnetic Sensor Units

Kerem Altun and Billur Barshan

Department of Electrical and Electronics Engineering
Bilkent University, Ankara, Turkey
{kaltun,billur}@ee.bilkent.edu.tr

Abstract. This paper provides a comparative study on the different techniques of classifying human activities that are performed using body-worn miniature inertial and magnetic sensors. The classification techniques implemented and compared in this study are: Bayesian decision making (BDM), the least-squares method (LSM), the k-nearest neighbor algorithm (k-NN), dynamic time warping (DTW), support vector machines (SVM), and artificial neural networks (ANN). Daily and sports activities are classified using five sensor units worn by eight subjects on the chest, the arms, and the legs. Each sensor unit comprises a triaxial gyroscope, a triaxial accelerometer, and a triaxial magnetometer. Principal component analysis (PCA) and sequential forward feature selection (SFFS) methods are employed for feature reduction. For a small number of features, SFFS demonstrates better performance and should be preferable especially in real-time applications. The classifiers are validated using different cross-validation techniques. Among the different classifiers we have considered, BDM results in the highest correct classification rate with relatively small computational cost.

Keywords: inertial sensors, magnetometers, human activity recognition and classification, feature selection and reduction.

1 Introduction

Computers have been in peoples' lives for many decades. With rapidly accelerating technology, hand-held computers have already made their way to our daily lives. Human-computer interaction has been an active research area since the introduction of computers; however, it is now becoming essential to design context-aware systems that recognize and interpret human behavior correctly. One aspect of human behavior understanding is the recognition and monitoring of daily activities. A wearable activity recognition system can improve the quality of life in many critical areas, such as ambulatory monitoring, home-based rehabilitation, and fall detection.

Earlier activity recognition systems mostly used vision as the sensing modality [1,2] and that track of research is still going on today [3]. However, vision-based systems can only be used in a confined space, e.g., a house, an office, or

A.A. Salah et al. (Eds.): HBU 2010, LNCS 6219, pp. 38–51, 2010.

a laboratory, with carefully adjusted environmental parameters such as proper illumination. Using cameras can also interfere with the privacy of the individual in question and this may even cause him/her to act differently than normal. Furthermore, when a single camera is used, the 3-D scene is projected onto a 2-D one, with significant information loss. Occlusion or shadowing of points of interest (by human body parts or objects in the surroundings) is circumvented by positioning multiple camera systems in the environment and using several 2-D projections to reconstruct the 3-D scene. This requires each camera to be separately calibrated.

It is said in [4] that "Activity can be best measured where it occurs." Miniature inertial sensors can be flexibly used inside or behind objects without occlusion effects. This is a major advantage over visual motion-capture systems, that require a free line of sight. Because of such restrictions, alternative activity recognition systems, mostly using wearable miniature inertial sensors are being developed. References [5,6,7] provide comprehensive surveys on the use of inertial sensors in motion recognition and analysis.

Inertial sensor based activity recognition systems are used in monitoring and observation of the elderly remotely by personal alarm systems [8], detection and classification of falls [9,10], medical diagnosis and treatment [11], monitoring children remotely at home or in school, rehabilitation and physical therapy [12], biomechanics research [7], ergonomics [13], sports science [14], ballet and dance [15], animation, film making, TV, live entertainment, virtual reality, and computer games [16].

Vision-based systems and inertial sensor based systems are by no means exclusive; in a number of studies, video cameras are used as a reference for comparison with inertial sensor data [17,18,19], whereas in some studies the vision data is integrated or fused with inertial sensor data [20]. Fusion of inertial sensors with magnetometers is also reported in the literature [18,21].

In inertial sensor based systems, there has not been a universal agreement on the number and types of sensors to use, positioning of the sensors, and the methods to use for recognition. Some studies distinguish between postures, i.e., sitting, standing, and lying using the static component of acceleration [8,17,22], whereas some distinguish between as many as 20 activities [22]. Some studies also recognize transitions between postures [8,19,23,24]. The number of sensors used vary between one [8,23] to twelve [4]. To the best of our knowledge, techniques that optimally determine the number, types, and positions of sensors do not exist [22].

This paper presents the results of a comparative study on human activity recognition, using accelerometers, gyroscopes, and magnetometers. We use five sensor modules, each of which includes a triaxial accelerometer, a triaxial gyroscope, and a triaxial magnetometer. We compare the successful differentiation rates, reliability and repeatability of the results, and computational requirements of various classification techniques using two different feature reduction methods.

Fig. 1. Xsens sensor modules and their positioning on the body

2   Classified Activities and Experimental Methodology

The 19 activities that are classified using body-worn miniature sensor units are: sitting (A1), standing (A2), lying down on back and on right side (A3 and A4), ascending and descending stairs (A5 and A6), standing in an elevator still (A7) and moving around in an elevator (A8), walking in a parking lot (A9), walking on a treadmill with a speed of 4 km/hr (in flat and 15° inclined positions) (A10 and A11), running on a treadmill with a speed of 8 km/hr (A12), exercising on a stepper (A13), exercising on a cross trainer (A14), cycling on an exercise bike in horizontal and vertical positions (A15 and A16), rowing (A17), jumping (A18), and playing basketball (A19).

Five MTx 3-DOF orientation trackers are used, manufactured by Xsens Technologies [25]. Each MTx has a triaxial accelerometer, a triaxial gyroscope, and a triaxial magnetometer so that the sensor units acquire acceleration, rate of turn, and Earth-magnetic field data, all in 3-D.

Accelerometers of two of the MTx trackers can sense up to $\pm 5g$ and the other three can sense in the range of $\pm 18g$, where $g = 9.80665$ m/s^2 is the gravitational constant. All gyroscopes in the MTx unit can sense in the range of $\pm 1200°$/sec angular velocities; magnetometers can sense in the range of $\pm 75\mu$T. We use all three types of sensor data in all three dimensions.

The sensors are placed on five different places on the subjects' body, as depicted in Fig.1. Since leg motions in general may produce larger accelerations, two of the $\pm 18g$ sensor units are placed on the sides of the knees (right side of the right knee and left side of the left knee), the remaining $\pm 18g$ unit is placed on the subjects' chest, and the two $\pm 5g$ units on the wrists.

Table 1. Subjects that performed the experiments and their profiles

subject no.	profile			
1	female	age: 25	height: 170 cm	weight: 63 kg
2	female	age: 20	height: 162 cm	weight: 54 kg
3	male	age: 30	height: 185 cm	weight: 78 kg
4	male	age: 25	height: 182 cm	weight: 78 kg
5	male	age: 26	height: 183 cm	weight: 77 kg
6	female	age: 23	height: 165 cm	weight: 50 kg
7	female	age: 21	height: 167 cm	weight: 57 kg
8	male	age: 24	height: 175 cm	weight: 75 kg

Each activity listed above is performed by eight different healthy subjects for 5 min. The profiles of the subjects are given in Table 1. The subjects are asked to perform the activities in their own style and were not restricted on how the activities should be performed. For this reason, there are inter-subject variations in the speeds and amplitudes of some activities. The activities are performed at the Bilkent University Sports Hall, in the Electrical and Electronics Engineering Building, and in a flat outdoor area on campus. Sensor units are calibrated to acquire data at 25 Hz sampling frequency. The 5-min signals are divided into 5-sec segments, from which certain features are extracted.

3   Feature Extraction and Reduction

Each of the five sensor units has nine sensors; thus, 45 signals are available for each 5-sec time window. We calculate the following 26 features for each signal: the minimum and maximum values, the mean value, variance, skewness, kurtosis, 10 equally spaced samples from the autocorrelation sequence, first five peaks of the discrete Fourier transform of the signal and the corresponding frequencies. As a result, $1,170 \, (= 45 \times 26)$ features are available for each 5-sec window for each activity. All features are normalized to the interval $[0, 1]$ to be used for classification.

Because this set of features is quite large and not all features are equally useful in discriminating between the activities, we have investigated different feature reduction methods. Primarily, we reduce the number of features from 1,170 to 30 through principal component analysis (PCA) [26], which is a transformation that finds the optimal linear combinations of the features, in the sense that they represent the data with the highest variance in a feature subspace, without taking the intra-class and inter-class variances into consideration separately. As an alternative to PCA, we considered using sequential forward feature selection (SFFS) and sequential backward feature selection (SBFS) algorithms [26] that use the extracted features themselves instead of linear combinations of features. Since SFFS performed better than SBFS in general, here we report the results of SFFS that adds features one at a time to the selected feature set such that the classification performance is maximized.

4   Classification Techniques

The classification techniques used in this study are: Bayesian decision making (BDM), least-squares method (LSM), k-nearest neighbor algorithm (k-NN), dynamic time warping (DTW), support vector machines (SVM), and artificial neural networks (ANN).

In BDM, we assume that the feature vectors are samples from a multi-variate Gaussian distribution. The mean vector and the covariance matrix of the distribution are estimated using maximum likelihood estimators on the training vectors and the maximum *a posteriori* decision rule is used for classification. LSM is also known as the nearest-mean classifier. The training vectors belonging to each class are averaged. Then, for a test vector, the Euclidean distance to each average vector is calculated. The vector is assigned the class that has the minimum distance. The k-NN and SVM are widely used classifiers (see [26]). DTW is a technique used mostly in speech recognition and aims to find the similarity between two sequences by "warping" them nonlinearly in the time dimension [27,28]. In ANN, we use a three-layer perceptron trained with the back-propagation algorithm [26]. Detailed explanations of these algorithms within the context of human activity recognition can be found in [27,29].

5   Experimental Results

5.1   Results with Features Reduced by PCA

The classification techniques mentioned in Section 4 are employed to classify the 19 different activities using the 30 features selected by PCA. A total of $9,120$ ($= 60$ segments $\times$ 19 activities $\times$ 8 subjects) feature vectors are available, each containing the reduced features of the sensor signals. In the training and testing phases of the classification methods, we use the repeated random sub-sampling (RRSS), P-fold, and subject-based leave-one-out (L1O) cross-validation techniques. In RRSS, we divide the 480 ($= 60$ segments $\times$ 8 subjects) feature vectors from each activity type randomly into two sets so that the first set contains 320 feature vectors (40 from each subject) and the second set contains 160 (20 from each subject). Therefore, two-thirds (6,080) of the 9,120 feature vectors are used for training and one-third (3,040) for testing. This is repeated 10 times and the resulting correct differentiation percentages are averaged.

In P-fold cross validation, the 9,120 feature vectors are divided into $P = 10$ partitions, where the 912 feature vectors in each partition are selected completely randomly, regardless of the subject or the class they belong to. One of the P partitions is retained as the validation set for testing, and the remaining $P - 1$ partitions are used for training. The cross-validation process is then repeated P times (the folds), where each of the P partitions is used exactly once for validation. The P results from the folds are then averaged to produce a single estimation. The random partitioning is repeated 10 times and the average correct differentiation percentage is reported.

Table 2. Correct differentiation rates for all classification methods and three cross-validation techniques. The results of the RRSS and P-fold cross-validation techniques are calculated over 10 runs, whereas those of L1O are over a single run.

method	correct differentiation rate (%) ± one standard deviation		
	RRSS	P-fold	L1O
BDM	99.1 ±0.12	99.2 ±0.02	75.8
LSM	89.4 ±0.75	89.6 ±0.10	85.3
k-NN $(k = 7)$	98.2 ±0.12	98.7 ±0.07	86.9
DTW$_1$	82.6 ±1.36	83.2 ±0.26	80.4
DTW$_2$	98.5 ±0.18	98.5 ±0.08	85.2
SVM	98.6 ±0.12	98.8 ±0.03	87.6
ANN	86.9 ±3.31	96.2 ±0.19	74.3

Finally, we also used subject-based L1O cross validation, where the $7,980$ ($= 60$ vectors $\times$ 19 activities $\times$ 7 subjects) feature vectors of seven of the subjects are used for training and the 1,140 feature vectors of the remaining subject are used in turn for validation. This is repeated eight times such that the feature vector set of each subject is used once as the validation data. The eight correct classification rates are averaged to produce a single estimate. This is similar to P-fold cross validation with P being equal to the number of subjects ($P = 8$), and where all the feature vectors in the same partition are associated with the same subject.

Correct differentiation rates of the classification techniques and their standard deviations are tabulated in Table 2 for the three cross-validation techniques we considered. All of the correct differentiation rates are above 80% with standard deviations usually lower than 0.5% with a few exceptions. From the table, it can be observed that there is not a significant difference between the results of RRSS and P-fold cross-validation techniques. The results of subject-based L1O are always lower than the two. In terms of reliability and repeatability, the P-fold cross-validation technique results in smaller standard deviations than RRSS.

We have implemented the DTW algorithm in two different ways: In the first (DTW$_1$), the average reference feature vector of each activity is used for comparison. As a second approach (DTW$_2$), DTW distances are calculated between the test vector and each of the reference vectors from different classes. The class of the nearest reference vector is assigned as the class of the test vector.

In SVM, following the one-versus-the-rest method, each type of activity is assumed as the first class and the remaining 18 activity types are grouped into the second class. We use a radial basis function kernel $K(\mathbf{x}, \mathbf{x}_i) = e^{-\gamma |\mathbf{x} - \mathbf{x}_i|^2}$ with $\gamma = 4$. In the implementation, LIBSVM toolbox [30] is used in MATLAB environment.

In ANN, we use a network with 30 input neurons (the features), 12 hidden neurons and 19 output neurons. The target output is one for the neuron number that the training vector belongs to, and zero for other neurons. We use the sigmoid function as the activation function. Correct classification for a test vector is achieved when the norm of the difference between actual output and the target output is below a certain threshold.

The confusion matrices for these methods can be found in [28]. We observed that A7 and A8 are the activities most confused with each other. This is because both of these activities are performed in the elevator and the signals recorded from these activities have similar segments. Therefore, confusion at the classification stage becomes inevitable. A2 and A7, A13 and A14, as well as A9, A10, A11, are also confused from time to time for similar reasons. Two activities that are almost never confused are A12 and A17.

Among the classification techniques we considered and implemented, when RRSS and P-fold cross validation techniques are used, BDM gives the highest classification rate, followed by SVM and k-NN. SVM and k-NN methods give the highest classification rates also with subject-based L1O cross validation, but the performance of BDM is not as good. To further compare these three methods, we calculated the correct classification rates using data from subsets of the subjects. All possible subject combinations are considered exhaustively, and those that result in the highest correct classification rates are reported in Tables 3 and 4, using P-fold and subject-based L1O cross validation, respectively. Note that for L1O cross validation (Table 4), the results of a single subject cannot be provided. This is because partitioning in this method is subject-based and requires the availability of data from at least two subjects.

When P-fold cross validation is used, the performances of all three methods are comparable (Table 3). Using data from more than two subjects causes a slight decrease in performance which is expected. When L1O cross validation is used (Table 4), the classification rates are lower than those in Table 3 and it can be also observed that k-NN and SVM are superior to BDM, regardless of the number of subjects used. This means that although data from multiple subjects can be well-approximated by a multi-variate Gaussian distribution, the parameters of the distribution, when calculated by excluding one of the subjects, cannot represent the data of the excluded subject sufficiently well. The performance of BDM and SVM tend to increase with increasing number of subjects (Table 4), indicating that these classifiers generalize better as data from more subjects are included. In the case of BDM, the data may be slowly converging to a multi-variate Gaussian distribution as the number of subjects is increased. In k-NN, there is a slight decrease in performance after the addition of the fourth subject.

5.2   Computational Cost of the Classification Techniques

We also compared the classification techniques based on their computational costs. Pre-processing and classification times are calculated with MATLAB version 7.0.4, on a desktop computer with AMD Athlon 64 X2 dual core processor at 2.2 GHz and 2.00 GB of RAM, running Microsoft Windows XP Professional operating system. Pre-processing/training times and storage requirements of the different techniques are tabulated in Table 5. The pre-processing time of BDM is used for estimating the mean vector and the covariance matrix that need to be

Table 3. Best combinations of the subjects and correct classification rates using P-fold cross validation

BDM		k-NN		SVM	
subject no.	%	subject no.	%	subject no.	%
5	99.0	1	98.9	5	98.5
2,5	99.6	1,2	99.4	1,2	99.4
2,5,6	99.5	1,2,5	99.3	1,2,5	99.4
1,2,4,6	99.5	1,2,5,6	99.1	1,2,5,6	99.3
2,4,5,6,7	99.4	1,2,3,5,6	99.0	1,2,5,6,7	99.1
1,2,3,5,6,7	99.4	1,2,3,4,5,6	98.9	1,2,3,4,5,6	99.0
1,2,3,4,5,6,7	99.2	1,2,3,4,5,6,8	98.8	1,2,3,4,5,6,7	98.9

Table 4. Best combinations of the subjects and correct classification rates using subject-based L1O

BDM		k-NN		SVM	
subject no.	%	subject no.	%	subject no.	%
1,7	64.5	2,6	87.0	2,6	65.7
1,2,7	73.2	2,4,6	90.2	2,6,7	76.6
1,2,6,7	75.9	2,4,6,7	89.8	1,2,6,7	80.0
1,2,3,6,7	75.6	1,2,4,6,7	89.3	1,2,5,6,7	82.0
1,2,3,5,6,7	76.4	1,2,4,6,7,8	88.6	1,2,4,5,6,7	85.0
2,3,4,5,6,7,8	76.8	1,2,4,5,6,7,8	88.1	1,2,4,5,6,7,8	86.9

stored for the test stage. In LSM and DTW_1, the averages of the training vectors for each class need to be stored for the test phase. For k-NN and DTW_2, all training vectors need to be stored. For the SVM, the SVM models constructed in the training phase need to be stored for the test phase. For ANN, the structure of the trained network and the connection weights need to be saved for testing. ANN and SVM require the longest training time.

The resulting processing times of the different techniques for classifying a single feature vector are also given in Table 5. The classification time for ANN is the smallest, followed by LSM, BDM, SVM, and DTW_1 methods. k-NN and DTW_2 take the longest time for classification, but no training time is needed.

5.3   Feature Reduction by SFFS

As another approach to feature reduction, we employ the sequential forward feature selection (SFFS) method. This method is a greedy algorithm for finding the most discriminative features, and is computationally costly. For this reason, we employ this method only for BDM, LSM, and k-NN classifiers. The selected features and the corresponding correct classification rates are presented in order in Table 6. The algorithm is run several times and the run with the most frequently selected features is shown in the table. As an example, the scatter

Table 5. Pre-processing and training times, storage requirements, and processing times of the classification methods. The processing times are given for classifying a single feature vector.

method	pre-processing/training time (ms)			storage requirements	processing time (ms)		
	RRSS	P-fold	L1O		RRSS	P-fold	L1O
BDM	28.98	28.62	24.70	mean, covariance, CCPDF	4.56	5.70	5.33
LSM	6.77	9.92	5.42	av. train. vector for each class	0.25	0.24	0.21
k-NN	–	–	–	all training vectors	101.32	351.22	187.32
DTW$_1$	6.77	9.92	5.42	av. train. vector for each class	86.26	86.22	85.57
DTW$_2$	–	–	–	all training vectors	116.57	155.81	153.25
SVM	7,368.17	13,287.85	10,098.61	SVM models	19.49	7.24	8.02
ANN	290,815	228,278	214,267	connection weights	0.06	0.06	0.06

Table 6. First five features selected by SFFS using BDM, LSM, and k-NN (RL: right leg, LL: left leg, RA: right arm, LA: left arm, T: torso)

BDM			LSM			k-NN		
feature	loc. sensor	%	feature	loc. sensor	%	feature	loc. sensor	%
mean	LL x-acc	33.1	min	RL x-acc	40.0	max	LL x-mag	47.2
DFT pk 5	RL y-mag	57.5	DFT pk 3	T x-gyro	59.0	mean	RL z-mag	84.9
max	LL y-mag	74.8	min	RA x-acc	70.4	mean	RL y-mag	92.4
max	T x-acc	86.0	max	RL x-acc	76.0	max	T x-mag	94.7
mean	RL y-acc	92.0	max	LL z-acc	79.6	min	RL x-mag	96.0

Table 7. Correct classification percentages using the first five features obtained by PCA using BDM, LSM, and k-NN

no. of features	BDM	LSM	k-NN
1	38.4	36.2	34.9
2	52.7	47.1	56.8
3	75.8	67.0	84.3
4	84.1	73.9	90.5
5	90.0	78.0	94.9

plots of the first three selected features are shown pairwise in Fig.2 for the BDM method.

Based on Table 6, it can be concluded that features of magnetometer and accelerometer signals recorded on the legs are more discriminative in general, verifying our previous results on sensor selection and combination [28]. Furthermore, time-domain features are selected more often than frequency-domain features, as also confirmed in a previous study [31]. For the first five features, the classification rates of the k-NN method are higher than BDM and LSM. However, when about 10 features are selected, both the BDM and k-NN methods achieve above 95% correct classification rate. In fact, in most runs, the correct classification rate is around 99%. We note that since feature selection is performed sequentially in SFFS, these features may not be the optimal subsets of

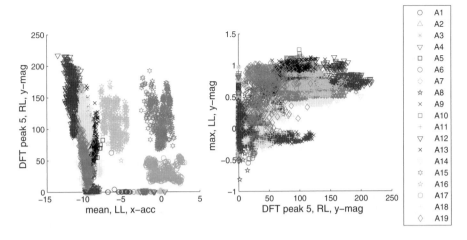

Fig. 2. (color online) Scatter plots of the first three features selected using BDM and SFFS

all features considered together. One should consider all subsets of the total number of features to determine the optimal subsets with a certain number of features. Obviously, this is a very time-consuming process.

Table 7 gives the results of BDM, LSM, and k-NN classifiers when up to first five features selected by PCA are used. Comparing with Table 6, it can be observed that SFFS gives better results, especially for the first few selected features. While the SFFS algorithm tries to maximize the correct classification rate, PCA captures the features with highest variances in the data by making a transformation into principal directions. The difference in performance of the two feature reduction techniques becomes smaller as more features are added to the set.

5.4   Rejection Performances

In this study, the classification performances of the methods are evaluated based on a bounded set of daily activities. The number of possible activities in daily life is much larger than the limited set of 19 activities considered here. Thus, a robust classifier should be able to reject the data from activities that do not belong to any activity class in the set. As an example, we test the rejection performances of LSM and ANN methods using a three-fold activity-based cross-validation scheme. We divide the activities randomly into three sets. At each fold, we train the classifiers using activities from two of the sets and use the remaining one for testing. We train a threshold-based classifier for each activity and each classifier is expected to reject every vector in the test set. A suitable threshold value is estimated and used based on the receiver operating characteristic (ROC) curves [26]. (The ROC curves for BDM, LSM, k-NN, and ANN methods using the data set in this study can be found in [28].)

Following this procedure, the ANN method performed perfectly and 100% of the test vectors are rejected. For the LSM method, the rejection rate is 79%. In accordance with the confusion matrices and ROC curves in [28], incorrectly classified activities are mostly A7, A8, A9, A10, and A11.

5.5   Discussion

Given its very high correct classification rate and relatively small pre-processing and classification times and storage requirements, it can be concluded that BDM is superior to the other classification techniques we considered for the given classification problem. This result supports the idea that the distribution of the activities in the feature space can be well approximated by multi-variate Gaussian distributions. However, its correct classification rate is lower when subject-based L1O cross validation is used. In any case, the low processing and storage requirements of the BDM method make it a strong candidate for similar classification problems.

The k-NN method is also very accurate but it requires considerable amount of time for classification, even though no training time is needed. SVM, although accurate, requires a considerable amount of pre-processing/training time to construct the SVM models. For real-time applications, LSM could also be a suitable choice because it is faster than most methods only at the expense of a slightly lower correct classification rate.

When a small number of features is used in the classification, the SFFS method gives better results than PCA in general (Tables 6 and 7). The correct classification rates obtained by using SFFS and PCA features become similar as more features are included. When about 10 features are used, correct classification rates above 95% are achieved, regardless of whether SFFS or PCA is used in feature reduction. In a real-time application, calculating all the features of the test data and performing PCA would be time consuming. For such a problem, selecting the most discriminative features beforehand by SFFS and calculating only the selected features for the test data would be a suitable approach. Therefore, if only a few features need to be calculated and used, SFFS should be employed because of its better performance with a small number of features and its speed.

6   Conclusions and Future Work

We have presented the results of a comparative study where features extracted from miniature inertial sensor and magnetometer signals are used for classifying human activities. We compared a number of classifiers based on the same data set in terms of their correct differentiation rates and computational requirements. We employed different feature reduction and cross-validation techniques for this purpose.

This work can serve as a guideline in designing context-aware wearable systems that involve recognition of daily activities of an individual. Many context-aware wearable systems are designed to be used by a single person. This work shows that for such applications, a simple quadratic classifier such as BDM is sufficient with almost perfect performance. If such a system is to be used by more than one person, providing training data from all the users is expected to result in above 95% performance. However, it is evident that if, for some reason, such training data is not available, then one must resort to more complex classifiers such as k-NN and SVM that require more computational resources.

There are several possible future research directions that can be explored:

An aspect of activity recognition and classification that has not been much investigated is the normalization between the way different individuals do the same activities. Each person performs a particular activity differently due to differences in body size, style, and timing. Although some approaches may be more prone to highlighting personal differences, new techniques need to be developed that involve time-warping and projections of signals and comparing their differentials. We plan to explore these issues by increasing the number and the variety of subjects used in this study.

To the best of our knowledge, optimizing the positioning, number, and type of sensors has not been much studied. Typically, some configuration, number, and modality of sensors is chosen and used without strong justification.

Detecting and classifying falls using inertial sensors is another important problem that has not been sufficiently well investigated [10], due to the difficulty of designing and performing fair and realistic experiments in this area [6]. Therefore, standard and systematic techniques for detecting and classifying falls still do not exist.

Fusing information from inertial sensors and cameras can be further explored to provide robust solutions in human activity monitoring, recognition, and classification. Joint use of these two sensing modalities increases the capabilities of intelligent systems and enlarges the application potential of inertial and vision systems.

Acknowledgments. This work is supported by the Scientific and Technological Research Council of Turkey (TÜBİTAK) under grant number EEEAG-109E059. The authors would like to thank the anonymous reviewers for their valuable comments and ideas for extending this paper.

References

1. Aggarwal, J.K., Cai, Q.: Human motion analysis: a review. Comput. Vis. Image Und. 73(3), 428–440 (1999)
2. Moeslund, T.B., Granum, E.: A survey of computer vision-based human motion capture. Comput. Vis. Image Und. 81(3), 231–268 (2001)
3. Moeslund, T.B., Hilton, A., Krüger, V.: A survey of advances in vision-based human motion capture and analysis. Comput. Vis. Image Und. 104(2-3), 90–126 (2006)
4. Kern, N., Schiele, B., Schmidt, A.: Multi-sensor activity context detection for wearable computing. In: Aarts, E., Collier, R.W., van Loenen, E., de Ruyter, B. (eds.) EUSAI 2003. LNCS, vol. 2875, pp. 220–232. Springer, Heidelberg (2003)

5. Zijlstra, W., Aminian, K.: Mobility assessment in older people: new possibilities and challenges. Eur. J. Ageing 4(1), 3–12 (2007)
6. Mathie, M.J., Coster, A.C.F., Lovell, N.H., Celler, B.G.: Accelerometry: providing an integrated, practical method for long-term, ambulatory monitoring of human movement. Physiol. Meas. 25(2), R1–R20 (2004)
7. Sabatini, A.M.: Inertial sensing in biomechanics: a survey of computational techniques bridging motion analysis and personal navigation. In: Computational Intelligence for Movement Sciences: Neural Networks and Other Emerging Techniques, pp. 70–100. Idea Group Publishing, USA (2006)
8. Mathie, M.J., Celler, B.G., Lovell, N.H., Coster, A.C.F.: Classification of basic daily movements using a triaxial accelerometer. Med. Biol. Eng. Comput. 42(5), 679–687 (2004)
9. Lindemann, U., Hock, A., Stuber, M., Keck, W., Becker, C.: Evaluation of a fall detector based on accelerometers: a pilot study. Med. Biol. Eng. Comput. 43(5), 548–551 (2005)
10. Kangas, M., Konttila, A., Lindgren, P., Winblad, I., Jämsä, T.: Comparison of low-complexity fall detection algorithms for body attached accelerometers. Gait Posture 28(2), 285–291 (2008)
11. Wu, W.H., Bui, A.A.T., Batalin, M.A., Liu, D., Kaiser, W.J.: Incremental diagnosis method for intelligent wearable sensor system. IEEE T. Inf. Technol. B. 11(5), 553–562 (2007)
12. Jovanov, E., Milenkovic, A., Otto, C., de Groen, P.: A wireless body area network of intelligent motion sensors for computer assisted physical rehabilitation. J. Neuroeng. Rehabil. 2(6) (2005)
13. Pärkkä, J., Ermes, M., Korpipää, P., Mäntyjärvi, J., Peltola, J., Korhonen, I.: Activity classification using realistic data from wearable sensors. IEEE T. Inf. Technol. B. 10(1), 119–128 (2006)
14. Ermes, M., Pärkkä, J., Mäntyjärvi, J., Korhonen, I.: Detection of daily activities and sports with wearable sensors in controlled and uncontrolled conditions. IEEE T. Inf. Technol. B. 12(1), 20–26 (2008)
15. Aylward, R., Paradiso, J.A.: Sensemble: A wireless, compact, multi-user sensor system for interactive dance. In: Proc. Conf. New Interfaces Musical Expression, Paris, France, June 4-8, pp. 134–139 (2006)
16. Shiratori, T., Hodgins, J.K.: Accelerometer-based user interfaces for the control of a physically simulated character. ACM T. Graphic. 27(5) (2008)
17. Aminian, K., Robert, P., Buchser, E.E., Rutschmann, B., Hayoz, D., Depairon, M.: Physical activity monitoring based on accelerometry: validation and comparison with video observation. Med. Biol. Eng. Comput. 37(1), 304–308 (1999)
18. Roetenberg, D., Slycke, P.J., Veltink, P.H.: Ambulatory position and orientation tracking fusing magnetic and inertial sensing. IEEE T. Bio-med. Eng. 54(5), 883–890 (2007)
19. Najafi, B., Aminian, K., Paraschiv-Ionescu, A., Loew, F., Büla, C.J., Robert, P.: Ambulatory system for human motion analysis using a kinematic sensor: monitoring of daily physical activity in the elderly. IEEE T. Bio-med. Eng. 50(6), 711–723 (2003)
20. Tao, Y., Hu, H., Zhou, H.: Integration of vision and inertial sensors for 3D arm motion tracking in home-based rehabilitation. Int. J. Robot. Res. 26(6), 607–624 (2007)
21. Zhu, R., Zhou, Z.: A real-time articulated human motion tracking using tri-axis inertial/magnetic sensors package. IEEE T. Neur. Sys. Reh. 12(2), 295–302 (2004)

22. Bao, L., Intille, S.S.: Activity recognition from user-annotated acceleration data. In: Ferscha, A., Mattern, F. (eds.) PERVASIVE 2004. LNCS, vol. 3001, pp. 1–17. Springer, Heidelberg (2004)
23. Karantonis, D.M., Narayanan, M.R., Mathie, M., Lovell, N.H., Celler, B.G.: Implementation of a real-time human movement classifier using a triaxial accelerometer for ambulatory monitoring. IEEE T. Inf. Technol. B. 10(1), 156–167 (2006)
24. Allen, F.R., Ambikairajah, E., Lovell, N.H., Celler, B.G.: Classification of a known sequence of motions and postures from accelerometry data using adapted Gaussian mixture models. Physiol. Meas. 27(10), 935–951 (2006)
25. Xsens Technologies B.V. Enschede, Holland: MTi and MTx User Manual and Technical Documentation (2009), http://www.xsens.com
26. Webb, A.: Statistical Pattern Recognition. John Wiley & Sons, New York (2002)
27. Tunçel, O., Altun, K., Barshan, B.: Classifying human leg motions with uniaxial piezoelectric gyroscopes. Sensors 9(11), 8508–8546 (2009)
28. Altun, K., Barshan, B., Tunçel, O.: Comparative study on classifying human activities with miniature inertial and magnetic sensors. Pattern Recogn. 43(10), 3605–3620 (2010), doi:10.1016/j.patcog.2010.04.019
29. Preece, S.J., Goulermas, J.Y., Kenney, L.P.J., Howard, D., Meijer, K., Crompton, R.: Activity identification using body-mounted sensors—a review of classification techniques. Physiol. Meas. 30(4), R1–R33 (2009)
30. Chang, C.C., Lin, C.J.: LIBSVM: a library for support vector machines (2001), Software available at http://www.csie.ntu.edu.tw/~cjlin/libsvm
31. Preece, S.J., Goulermas, J.Y., Kenney, L.P.J., Howard, D.: A comparison of feature extraction methods for the classification of dynamic activities from accelerometer data. IEEE T. Bio-med. Eng. 56(3), 871–879 (2009)

Face Tracking and Recognition Considering the Camera's Field of View

Yuzuko Utsumi*, Yoshio Iwai, and Hiroshi Ishiguro

Graduate School of Engineering Science, Osaka University
1–3, Machikaneyama, Toyonaka, Osaka 560–8531, Japan
utsumi.yuzuko@is.sys.es.osaka-u.ac.jp,
{iwai,ishiguro}@sys.es.osaka-u.ac.jp

Abstract. We propose a method that tracks and recognizes faces simultaneously. In previous methods, features needed to be extracted twice for tracking and recognizing faces in image sequences because the features used for face recognition are different from those used for face tracking. To reduce the computational cost, we propose a probabilistic model for face tracking and recognition and a system that performs face tracking and recognition simultaneously using the same features. The probabilistic model handles any overlap in the camera's field of view, something that is ignored in previous methods. The model thus deals with face tracking and recognition using multiple overlapping image sequences. Experimental results show that the proposed method can track and recognize multiple faces simultaneously.

Keywords: Face tracking, Face recognition 3D positional hypotheses, Bayesian framework.

1 Introduction

Recently, security camera systems have been installed in public facilities to crack down on and prevent crimes. Videos from security camera systems are used to find crimes such as violence, theft, and so on. In current security systems, a security guard checks the recorded video, witch typically contains footage of a great number of people, including possible missing persons, stray children, and criminals. If these individuals could be identified and tracked on the video footage, security camera systems would be useful for finding missing persons and stray children and arresting criminals. However, as the security guard checking the video has limited capabilities of finding people, it is impossible for the system to find specific individuals on the security footage. Thus the goal of this research is to track and recognize specific individuals in security camera footage automatically. To achieve this goal, we propose a new method for face tracking in multiple image sequences. Face recognition is the best method for distinguishing people since we normally identify individuals by their faces.

---

* This work was supported by Grant-in-Aid for JSPS Fellows No. 21558.

A.A. Salah et al. (Eds.): HBU 2010, LNCS 6219, pp. 52–63, 2010.

Solving a multi video-based face tracking problem requires three tasks: simultaneously implementing face tracking and recognition, adapting to any changes in facial appearance, and integrating the results of face tracking and recognition in multiple image sequences.

Several video-based face tracking and recognition methods have been proposed in previous studies. Merging of face tracking and recognition has specifically attracted the attention of researchers in the vision community. Fan et al.[1] presented a method using the AdaBoost classifier for tracking and a Modified Probabilistic Neural network (MPNN) for recognition. Other combinations of face tracking and recognition methods such as skin color detection for tracking and PCA for face recognition[2] and SVM for tracking and HMM for recognition[3] have also been proposed. However, using a method that employs different frameworks for face tracking and recognition requires too much time when tracking specific faces in video sequences as features need to be extracted twice. A probabilistic model has been proposed to track and recognize faces in the same framework[4]. Methods based on this model implement effective face tracking and recognition because common features are used for face tracking and recognition.

To handle changes in facial appearance caused by changes in facial orientation, fitting 3D facial models[5] and learning the facial appearance for each orientation[6] have been proposed. Dynamic models such as the Kalman filter[7] and particle filter[8] are used to track faces. Dynamic models track faces robustly even if the tracked face is temporarily occluded. The particle filter is a particularly flexible system because it can represent non-linear motion.

When face tracking and recognition are performed in multiple videos, it is necessary to integrate face tracking information. In pedestrian tracking, stereo matching[2] and homography[9] are applied to integrate the tracking information. Stereo matching and homography are separate from the face tracking and recognition frameworks and additional computational cost is required for the integration. If the pedestrian is occluded, these methods may fail to integrate the tracking information.

As the main contribution of this work, we propose a probabilistic face tracking and recognition model that considers overlap in image sequences. The proposed method tracks and recognizes faces using common features. Since the model considers the camera view, integration of tracking information is performed by calculating probabilities. To cope with changes in facial appearance, we present a facial rotation and translation model. Facial texture information is modeled by Haar-like features. Features are learned by the AdaBoost M1 algorithm for each facial orientation. Experimental results show that the proposed method can track and recognize three individuals in 5 image sequences.

2   Probabilistic Model for Face Tracking and Recognition

The positional hypothesis of face ω_i of person i at time t is represented as $H_{i,t} = (\boldsymbol{x}_{i,t}, \phi_{i,t}, \boldsymbol{x}_{i,t-1}, \phi_{i,t-1}, \cdots, \boldsymbol{x}_{i,t-k}, \phi_{i,t-k})$, where $\boldsymbol{x}_{i,t}$ is the 3D position of face ω_i, and $\phi_{i,t}$ is the rotation angle thereof. We assume that observation

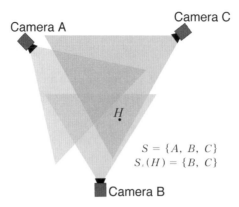

Fig. 1. Fields of views of multiple cameras

$Y_{i,t}^v$ is acquired from camera $s \in S$, where S is a set of cameras in the camera network system. We denote $S_s(H)$ as the set of cameras that can observe person i in the position hypothesis H as shown in Fig. 1. The set of observations $\boldsymbol{Y}_{i,t}$ is defined as follows:

$$\boldsymbol{Y}_{i,t} = \bigcup_{s \in S_s(H)} \boldsymbol{Y}_{i,t}^s. \tag{1}$$

Face recognition is performed by maximizing the joint probability density $p(\omega_i, \boldsymbol{Y}_{i,0}, \boldsymbol{Y}_{i,1}, \cdots, \boldsymbol{Y}_{i,T})$ as follows:

$$\omega_k = \operatorname*{argmax}_{\omega_i} p(\omega_i, \boldsymbol{Y}_{i,0}, \boldsymbol{Y}_{i,1}, \cdots, \boldsymbol{Y}_{i,T}). \tag{2}$$

Due to the computational cost, it is difficult to calculate this joint probability density accurately, and therefore, we assume that each observation arises independently. The joint probability density is represented simply as

$$p(\omega_i, \boldsymbol{Y}_{i,0}, \boldsymbol{Y}_{i,1}, \cdots, \boldsymbol{Y}_{i,T}) = \prod_{t=0}^{T} p(\omega_i, \boldsymbol{Y}_{i,t}). \tag{3}$$

Hence, we can recognize a face to maximize $p(\omega_i, \boldsymbol{Y}_{i,t})$ for each t. We can also track a face by maximizing the probability. $p(\omega_i, \boldsymbol{Y}_{i,t})$ is given by the following equation:

$$
\begin{aligned}
p(\omega_i, \boldsymbol{Y}_{i,t}) &= \int_H p(\omega_i, \boldsymbol{Y}_{i,t}, H_{i,t}) dH. \\
&= \int_H p(\omega_i, \cup_{s \in S_s(H)} \boldsymbol{Y}_{i,t}^s, H_{i,t}) dH.
\end{aligned} \tag{4}
$$

Here we assume that the $\boldsymbol{Y}_{i,t}^s$ are mutually disjoint and independent, and that $p(\omega_i, \boldsymbol{Y}_{i,t})$ can be written as

$$p(\omega_i, \boldsymbol{Y}_{i,t}) = \int_H \prod_{s \in S_s(H)} p(\omega_i, \boldsymbol{Y}_{i,t}^s, H_{i,t}) dH. \tag{5}$$

We also assume that the joint probability density $p(\omega_i, \mathbf{Y}^s_{i,t}, H_{i,t})$ has the probabilistic structure shown in Fig. 2, and that $p(\omega_i, \mathbf{Y}^s_{i,t}, H_{i,t})$ is given as follows:

$$p(\omega_i, \mathbf{Y}^s_{i,t}, H_{i,t}) = p(\mathbf{Y}^s_{i,t}|H_{i,t})p(H_{i,t}|\omega_i)P(\omega_i). \tag{6}$$

Finally, Eq. (2) can be rewritten as follows:

$$\omega_k = \operatorname*{argmax}_{\omega_i} \prod_{t=0}^{T} \int_H \prod_{s \in S_s(H)} p(\mathbf{Y}^s_{i,t}|H_{i,t})p(H_{i,t}|\omega_i)P(\omega_i)dH$$

$$\approx \operatorname*{argmax}_{\omega_i} \prod_{t=0}^{T} \sum_H \prod_{s \in S_s(H)} p(\mathbf{Y}^s_{i,t}|H_{i,t})p(H_{i,t}|\omega_i)P(\omega_i). \tag{7}$$

It is difficult to calculate Eq. (7) because integration over all hypotheses H is impossible. Eq. (7) is, therefore, approximated by using the Monte Carlo method. We describe in detail how the probabilities are calculated in the next section.

2.1 Individual Observed Probability

Probability $P(\omega_i)$ represents the existence of person i in the observable area of the face tracking system. $P(\omega_i)$ can be a function of t or a form thereof that is changed by the system environment. Nevertheless, for simplicity we adopt the discrete uniform distribution given below as the individual observed probability in this paper:

$$P(\omega_i) = \frac{1}{N}, \tag{8}$$

where N is the number of individuals in the facial database.

2.2 Occurrence Probability of the Hypothesis

The probability density $p(H_{i,t}|\omega_i)$ indicates the occurrence probability of hypothesis $H_{i,t}$ corresponding to face ω_i of person i. When the Monte Carlo approximation is adapted to calculate the integration of Eq. (7), it is desirable to generate hypothesis H with the probability $p(H_{i,t}|\omega_i)$. From the above hypothesis generation, Eq. (7) can be calculated as follows:

$$\omega_k \approx \operatorname*{argmax}_{\omega_i} \prod_{t=0}^{T} \sum_H \prod_{s \in S_s(H)} p(\mathbf{Y}^s_{i,t}|H_{i,t})P(\omega_i). \tag{9}$$

The range of the hypothesis can be configured with probability $p(H_{i,t}|\omega_i)$. If the hypothesis that probabilities $p(H_{i,t}|\omega_i)$ and $p(\mathbf{Y}^s_{i,t}|H_{i,t})$ are both low is sampled, and the posterior probability is then calculated, the sampled hypothesis does not affect the posterior probability. Therefore, the hypothesis that probabilities $p(H_{i,t}|\omega_i)$ and $p(\mathbf{Y}^s_{i,t}|H_{i,t})$ are low can be ignored in the calculation of the posterior probability. For efficient calculation, it is also desirable to predict accurate positions of the faces. A complicated probabilistic model may predict a

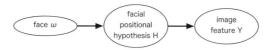

Fig. 2. Probabilistic structure of observations

facial position accurately, but it takes a great deal of time to calculate the predicted position, and this increases the sampling time. To decrease the sampling time, it is possible to track a face using a simple probabilistic model. Therefore, the occurrence probability of hypothesis $p(H_{i,t}|\omega_i)$ is defined in this paper as follows:

$$
\begin{aligned}
p(H_{i,t}|\omega_i) &= \int_H p(H_{i,t}|H_{i,t-1})p(\hat{H}_{i,t-1}|\omega_i) \\
&\approx \sum_H p(H_{i,t}|H_{i,t-1})p(\hat{H}_{i,t-1}|\omega_i),
\end{aligned}
\tag{10}
$$

where $p(H_{i,t}|H_{i,t-1})$ is the transition probability of the hypothesis at the next time interval, and $p(\hat{H}_{i,t-1}|\omega_i)$ is the occurrence probability of the hypothesis updated by the observations. In this paper, we use a random walk model for the transition probability of the hypothesis defined as follows:

$$
p(H_{i,t}|H_{i,t-1}) \sim \mathcal{N}(\boldsymbol{x}_{i,t-1}(H_{i,t-1}), \Sigma),
\tag{11}
$$

where $\boldsymbol{x}_{i,t-1}(H_{i,t-1})$ is the 3D position of face ω_i indicated by hypothesis $H_{i,t}$. $\mathcal{N}(\boldsymbol{\mu}, \Sigma)$ denotes the normal distribution, where μ is the average and Σ is the covariance matrix. The transition probability is described in detail in Section 3.2.

2.3   Likelihood

The likelihood $p(\boldsymbol{Y}_{i,t}^s|H_{i,t})$ represents the possibility of the existence of a face located by the 3D positional hypothesis $H_{i,t}$. A face appearance model is required to calculate this possibility. In this paper, we regard image feature $\boldsymbol{Y}_{i,t}^s$, which expresses a face, as a feature vector extracted around feature points selected by the AdaBoost M1 algorithm[10]. We describe the face appearance model in detail in the next section. It is impossible to compare hypothesis H and image feature $\boldsymbol{Y}$ directly, since both the scale and dimensions are different. Therefore, a mapping $F : H \to \boldsymbol{Y}$ from hypothesis $H_{i,t}$ to image feature $\boldsymbol{Y}$ is needed for the comparison. It is possible that this mapping may distort the shape of the probability distribution, and thus affect the computational results. While it would be better to use a mapping function that does not affect the computational results, such a mapping function remains unknown. Therefore, we use the mapping $F : H \to \boldsymbol{Y}$ implemented by the AdaBoost classifier. The details of the likelihood function are described in Section 3.3.

(a) Feature points (b) Face coordinates

Fig. 3. Face shape model

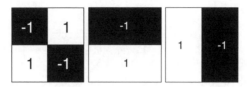

Fig. 4. Haar-like features

3 Implementation

In this section, we explain how the proposed method is implemented. We describe three face models: shape, movement, and texture. We also explain the integration of the joint probability density calculated for each camera.

3.1 Shape Model

Feature points of a face are a representation of the facial shape. In the facial shape model, feature points are selected as shown in Fig. 3(a). These feature points are represented in a face coordinate system as shown in Fig. 3(b). The 3D positional hypothesis denotes the origin of the coordinate system. By using 3D positional hypotheses and face rotation, feature points are projected onto images and facial regions are cropped.

3.2 Movement Model

Facial rotation and translation are modeled in a facial movement model. The proposed system only deals with rotation around the z-axis in the face coordinate system as shown in Fig. 3. We have chosen five facial images, varying from a full frontal image (0 degrees) to facial profiles (-90, -30, 30, and 90 degrees), to represent an individual face. Facial translation is modeled by the random walk model. The position x_t at time t is represented using the position x_{t-1} at time $t-1$ by the following equation:

$$\boldsymbol{x}_t = \boldsymbol{x}_{t-1} + \epsilon_t, \tag{12}$$

where ϵ_t is the random displacement with a normal distribution.

3.3   Texture Model

The texture model consists of image features extracted from face images. We use Haar-like rectangular filters to extract text features as shown in Fig. 4. Haar-like features are effective for face tracking [11] and recognition [12]. To perform face tracking and recognition efficiently, we use the same Haar-like features for both.

The AdaBoost M1 learning algorithm[10] is used for feature selection. Features are selected in descending order of the training error ratios until the classifier of the selected features achieves a desirable false acceptance rate. Five classifiers are built for the five rotation angles ($\pm 90, \pm 30, 0$ degrees) as texture models of an individual face. The likelihood is calculated according to the output of the classifiers as follows:

$$p(\mathbf{Y}_{i,t}^{s}|H_{i,t}) \propto \frac{1}{1 + \exp\left(-\frac{g(\mathbf{Y}_{i,t}^{s})-a}{b}\right)}, \tag{13}$$

where $g(\mathbf{Y}_{i,t}^{s})$ is the output of the classifier and a, b are the scale and translation parameters, respectively.

3.4   Integration of Probability Densities

In our proposed camera network system, the likelihood $p(\mathbf{Y}_{i,t}^{s}|H_{i,t})$ in each of the camera node computers is integrated with the other likelihoods by the integration node computer to calculate $p(\omega_i, \mathbf{Y}_{i,t})$ in Eq. (7). Face recognition is then performed using the joint p.d.f. $p(\omega_i, \mathbf{Y}_{i,t})$.

In order to calculate the approximation of the joint p.d.f. $p(\omega_i, \mathbf{Y}_{i,t})$, we must first calculate $p(H_{i,t}|\omega_i)$ in Eq. (11), which corresponds to the face tracking process. First, we consider the whole hypothesis space Ω_H, and the division thereof by hypercube C_k:

$$\Omega_H = \bigcup_k C_k. \tag{14}$$

C_H and V_H denote the hypercube containing the hypothesis H and the volume of the hypercube, respectively. The updated occurrence p.d.f. of the hypothesis H can be approximated as follows:

$$p(\hat{H}_{i,t}|\omega_i) \approx \prod_{s \in S_s(C_H)} \frac{K}{NV_H}, \tag{15}$$

where $S_s(C_H)$ is the set of cameras such that their field of view contains the hypercube C_H. K is the weighted average of the number of hypotheses in the hypercube C_H defined as follows:

$$K = \sum_{H_i \in C_H} w_i(H_i). \tag{16}$$

The weight is used to update the likelihood from the observation. In this paper, we use Eq. (13) as the weight since reuse of the weights reduces the computational cost. The flow of the calculation process in our camera system is shown in Fig. 5.

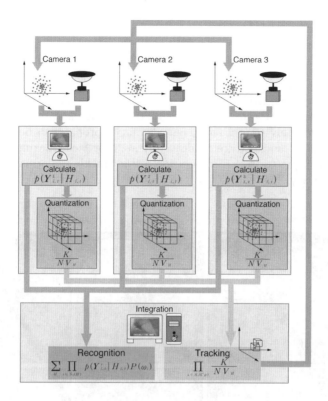

Fig. 5. Calculation process flow

4   Experiments

We conducted experiments to evaluate the efficiency of the proposed method. Five omni-directional cameras were used to acquire an image sequence of three pedestrians. The image size was 1024×768 pixels with a depth of 8 bits gray and the frame rate of the images 15 fps. Facial images of seven individual were used for learning and to construct classifiers for the three individual. For each person, we collected 3000 face images in each orientation. We also collected 21000 non-face images for learning. In addition, we used 300 images from the Softpia Japan face database and 7143 images from the FERET Database. All images were cropped and normalized to 100×100 pixels. For each orientation of a person, 3000 images were used as positive data and the rest as negative data. The width of rectangular filters was 32 and 64 pixels and the features were extracted using parallel transformation every four pixels. We selected 1000 features in each classifier with the false acceptance rate for all classifiers being less than 2%. 3D positional hypotheses were generated using the center coordinate of the top 50 $p(\hat{H}_{i,t}|\omega_i)$ as the average of the normal distribution. 5000 positional hypotheses were generated in each camera.

60   Y. Utsumi, Y. Iwai, and H. Ishiguro

The results of face tracking are shown in Fig. 6 and 7. In Fig. 6, rectangles show the regions with the highest likelihood. The colors of the rectangle denotes the personal ID. In the left image of Fig. 7, red rectangles show the hypotheses with high likelihood generated in the camera while green rectangles show those generated in other cameras. In the right image of Fig. 7, red rectangles show the hypotheses with high likelihood after integration of the likelihood.

As shown in Fig. 6, the proposed method can track and recognize faces appropriately. Not only frontal faces, but also facial profiles can be tracked. The proposed rotation and texture models work well for face tracking in image sequences. According to Fig. 7, integration of the tracking information improves tracking accuracy. This shows that the proposed probabilistic model is effective

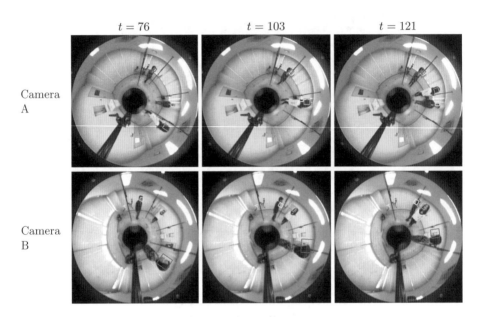

Fig. 6. Tracking results

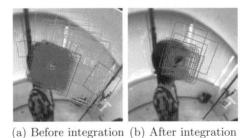

(a) Before integration (b) After integration

Fig. 7. Likelihood integration

$t = 76$ $t = 103$ $t = 121$

Camera
A

Camera
B

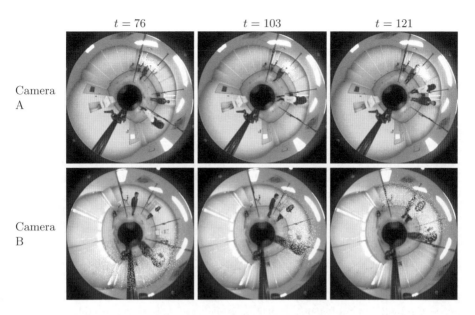

Fig. 8. Likelihood maps of a person

$t = 76$ $t = 103$ $t = 121$

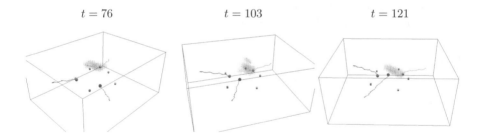

Fig. 9. Hypotheses in 3D space

for face tracking and recognition in multiple image sequences. As shown in Fig 6, there may be hypotheses with high likelihood on a non-face region. We need to use a more adaptive learning algorithm for real image sequences, such as an online learning algorithm, to improve the accuracy of the classifiers.

Likelihood maps are given in Fig. 8. These maps show the existence of the person tracked with red rectangles in Fig. 6. Dots show the hypotheses of facial existence, while the degree of red indicates the strength of likelihood. The hypotheses on faces have high likelihood and the system can calculate likelihood well. However, in camera B, certain hypotheses other than those on faces also have high likelihood. Owing to the integration of the probability density, hypotheses with incorrect likelihood do not affect tracking results, although they may contribute to low tracking accuracy. A more adaptive learning algorithm, such as an online learning algorithm, is needed for real image sequences to improve the accuracy of classifiers.

The hypotheses generated for a person in 3D space are shown in Fig. 9. These hypotheses are generated for the person tracked with yellow rectangles in Fig. 6. Spheres show the positions of faces, while cubes show the positions of the cameras. Blue dots show the hypotheses that have low likelihood, while red dots show those with high likelihood. According to Fig. 9, hypotheses are generated around the tracked face, and a random walk is used as the facial movement model. As shown in Fig. 6, the person was occluded in image $t = 105$ from camera A. Despite the fact that one of the faces was occluded in one camera, the hypotheses could still be generated because the face was not occluded in other cameras and the likelihoods of all cameras are integrated.

5   Conclusion

In this paper, we proposed a face tracking and recognition method based on a probabilistic model with multiple cameras. We used three facial models for the posterior calculation: 3D shape, movement, and texture models. Facial shape is expressed by 3D facial feature positions, while texture is represented by Haar-like features extracted from five different orientations of facial images. Facial movement is expressed by the random walk model. Experimental results confirm that the proposed method can track and recognize a face correctly. In future work, we aim to improve the likelihood function to avoid tracking non-face regions.

References

1. Fan, J., Dimitriva, N., Philomin, V.: Online face recognition system for videos based on modified probabilistic neural network. In: Proceedings of the 2004 International Conference on Image Processing (ICIP 2004), Singapore, October 2004, vol. 3, pp. 2019–2022 (2004)
2. Trivedi, M.M., Huang, K.S., Mikic, I.: Dynamic context capture and distributed video arrays for intelligent spaces. IEEE Transactions on System, Man and Cybernetics–Part A: Systems and Humans 35(1), 145–163 (2005)
3. Kim, M., Kumar, S., Pavlovic, V., Rowely, H.: Face tracking and recognition with visual constraints in real-world video. In: Transactions on IEEE Conference on Computer Vision and Pattern Recognition, pp. 1–8 (2008)
4. Lee, K.C., Ho, J., Kriegman, D.: Acquiring linear subspaces for face recognition under variable lighting. IEEE Transactions on Pattern Analysis and Machine Intelligence 27(5), 1–15 (2005)
5. Park, U., Jain, A.K., Ross, A.: Face recognition in video: Adaptive fusion of multiple matchers. In: Proceedings on IEEE Conference on Computer Vision and Pattern Recognition (CVPR 2007), June 2007, pp. 1–8 (2007)
6. Verma, R.C., Schmid, C., Mikolajczyk, K.: Face detection and tracking in a video by propagating detection probabilities. IEEE Transactions on pattern analysis and machine intelligence 25(10), 1215–1228 (October 2003)
7. Kublbeck, C., Ernst, A.: Face detection and tracking in video sequence using the manifold census transformation. Image and Vision Computing 24, 564–572 (2006)

8. Li, Y., Ai, H., Yamashita, T., Lao, S., Kawade, M.: Tracking in low frame rate video: a cascade particle filter with discriminative observers of different life spans. IEEE Transactions on Pattern Analysis and Machine Intelligence 30(10), 1728–1740 (2008)
9. Leistner, C., Roth, P.M., Grabner, H., Bischof, H., Starzacher, A., Rinner, B.: Visual on-line learning in distributed camera networks. In: Proceedings of Second ACM/IEEE International Conference on Distributed Smart Cameras (ICDSC 2008), Stanford, CA (September 2008)
10. Freund, Y., Schapire, R.E.: A decision-theoretic generalization of on-line learning and an application to boosting. Journal of Computer and System Sciences 55(1), 119–139 (1997)
11. Viola, P., Jones, M.J.: Robust real-time face detection. International journal of computer vision 57(2), 137–154 (2004)
12. Utsumi, Y., Iwai, Y., Yachida, M.: Performance evaluation of face recognition in the wavelet domain. In: Proceedings on IEEE/RSJ International Conference on Intelligent Robots and Systems (IROS 2006), October 2006, pp. 3344–3351 (2006)

Spatiotemporal-Boosted DCT Features for Head and Face Gesture Analysis

Hatice Çınar Akakın and Bülent Sankur

Bogazici University, Electrical & Electronics Engineering Department,
Bebek, Istanbul

Abstract. Automatic analysis of head gestures and facial expressions is a challenging research area and it has significant applications in human-computer interfaces. In this study, facial landmark points are detected and tracked over successive video frames using a robust method based on subspace regularization, Kalman prediction and refinement. The trajectories (time series) of facial landmark positions during the course of the head gesture or facial expression are organized in a spatiotemporal matrix and discriminative features are extracted from the trajectory matrix. Alternatively, appearance based features are extracted from DCT coefficients of several face patches. Finally Adaboost algorithm is performed to learn a set of discriminating spatiotemporal DCT features for face and head gesture (FHG) classification. We report the classification results obtained by using the Support Vector Machines (SVM) on the outputs of the features learned by Adaboost. We achieve 94.04% subject independent classification performance over seven FHG.[1,2]

1   Introduction

Human face is a rich source of nonverbal information. Indeed, not only it is the source of identity information but it also provides clues to understand social feelings and can be instrumental in revealing mental states via social signals. Facial expressions form a significant part of human social interaction [1,2]. While communicating, we express ideas that are visualized in our minds by using words integrated with nonverbal behaviors. Therefore when the body language and verbal messages are used in complementary roles, our messages can be more clear and can be conveyed more accurately. Face then functions as a channel in communicating the emotional content of our messages. Gestures, eye and head movements, body movements, facial expressions and touch constitute the nonverbal message types of our body language. Therefore, empowering computers with the capability to recognize and to respond to nonverbal communication clues is important [3,4,5,6].

In this study, we consider two data representation types, namely facial landmark trajectories and intensity image patches on expressive regions of the face

---

[1] This work was supported by TUBITAK project with number 107E001 and by Bogazici University project with number 09HA202D.

[2] Thanks to Arman Savran for providing his Adaboost code.

A.A. Salah et al. (Eds.): HBU 2010, LNCS 6219, pp. 64–74, 2010.

extracted throughout the video sequences. DCT features are extracted from those face representations for the automatic analysis of facial expressions and head gestures. Adaboost algorithm is exploited in order to reduce the dimensionality of the total features and to obtain more discriminative DCT coefficients for the classification.

The paper is organized as follows. In the next section we briefly review related works. Section 3 describes the data representation types and extracted features. Classification method is explained in Sect. 4. Section 5 gives details of the used dataset and presents implemented classifiers and the experimental results. Finally, conclusions are drawn in Sect. 6.

2   Related Work

Most of the work in the literature on facial expression analysis is focused on the six basic emotions, i.e., happiness, surprise, sadness, fear, anger and disgust [7,8,9,10,5,11,12]. The majority of facial expression recognition systems attempt to identify Facial Action units (FAUs) [13,7,8,14,15,16,12] based on Facial Action Coding System (FACS) [17]. In FACS, the facial behavior is decomposed into 46 action units (AUs), each of which is anatomically related to the individual facial muscles. Although they only define a small number of distinctive AUs, different combinations of AUs can be sufficient for accurately detecting and measuring a large number of facial expressions.

Head displays, sometimes called as emblems [14,18] fulfill a semantic function and provide conversational feedback. Examples of emblems are head nodding (head up and down) and head shaking (head swinging left and right) with or without accompanying facial expressions. In social interactions head and facial displays may convey a message, provide conversational feedback, and form a communicative tool [2,1]. For example, head nod is an affirmative cue, frequently used throughout the world to indicate understanding, approval and agreement [2,1,19,20,21]. On the other hand, head shake is almost a universal sign of disapproval, disbelief, and negation [2,1,19,20,21]. Prediction of frustration and human fatigue detection problems were analyzed by integrating information from various sensory information [22,23,24].

Bartlett et al. [25] used Gabor filters for appearance based feature extraction from the still images. They obtained their best recognition results by selecting a subset of Gabor filters using AdaBoost and then training Support Vector Machines on the outputs of the filters selected by AdaBoost. Shan [11] studied facial representation based on LBP features for facial expression recognition. They examined different machine learning methods, including template matching, SVM, LDA, and the linear programming technique on LBP features. They obtained their best results with Boosted-LBP by learning the most discriminative LBP features with AdaBoost, and the recognition performance of different classifiers were improved by using the Boosted-LBP features.

There are relatively few papers in the literature addressing the FHG detection issue. In Kang et al. [20], location of eyes is detected and tracked in video sequence, and the resulting trajectory is used to recognize head shake and head nod gestures using HMMs. Somewhat similarly, Kapoor and Picard [19] used an active camera with infrared LEDs to track pupils. The position of pupils are used as observations by a discrete HMM pattern analyzer to detect head nods/shakes. Morency et al. [21] investigated how dialog context from an embodied conversational agent can improve visual recognition of user gestures such as head nod and head shakes. For recognizing these gestures, they tracked head position and rotation, then computed head velocity vector and used SVM classifiers. In Aran's study [26] a multi-class classification strategy for Fisher scores was proposed and tested on a hand gesture dataset and a sign language expression dataset [27].

3   Data Representations and Spatiotemporal Features for FHG

Once the facial landmark points are tracked in each FHG video frame, two different data types are extracted: i) Landmark trajectories; ii) Intensity face image patches. Even though, head and facial gestures may differ in total duration they mostly follow a fixed pattern of temporal order. Therefore, in order to process extracted data from face videos, we used both spatial normalization and temporal normalization. The details of the feature extraction process is given in the following subsections.

3.1   Facial Landmark Trajectories

A number (l) of facial landmark points are detected and tracked over successive video frames using an automatic landmark detection and algorithm [28] (Figure 1). The algorithm detects facial landmarks in the initial frame using DCT-features trained with SVM classifiers, and then applies a multi-step tracking method based on adaptive templates, Kalman predictor and subspace regularization for the subsequent frames.

Once the landmark coordinates are detected over the successive frames, the landmark coordinate data of the face video is reduced to a FxT matrix P. Here, each row of the P matrix represents the time sequence of the x or y coordinates of one of the 17 landmarks. In order to obtain landmarks independent from the initial position of the head the first column is subtracted from all columns of P, so that we only consider the relative landmark displacements with respect to the first frame. This presupposes that the landmark estimates in the first frame of the sequence are reliable.

In our work we used 17 ($l = 17$) landmarks as illustrated in Figure 1 which resulted in $F = 34$ coordinates.

3.2   Feature Extraction from Face Image Patches

Deformations occurring on the face during an expression involves changes over whole regions, such as mouth and eye regions. The estimated landmarks enable

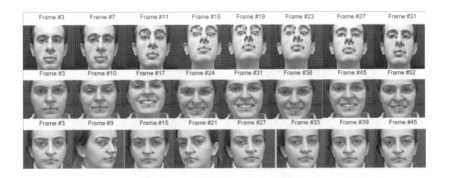

Fig. 1. Illustration of the 17 tracked facial landmarks on sample image sequences

us to parse the face into regions of interest. We have heuristically selected four patches covering the most expressive facial parts, as shown in Figure 3. Patch sizes are chosen large enough to cover a whole expressive face region. Furthermore patches are positioned using the tracked facial landmark locations. In that respect, sizes and semantic positions of the patches do not vary with changes in head orientation.

Extracted patches are scaled into fixed block size as in Table 1. The discriminative features from patches consist of DCT coefficients, not from the whole patch but from the 16x16 non-overlapping blocks tessellating the patch. Since the expressive eye region is critical, it is doubly covered. Beside the eye and eyebrow patches, one larger patch that jointly covers them and that overlaps with the other four (16x16 DCT block) is used in order to better interpret the appearance changes between the eyebrows. We selected the first 20 DCT coefficients (after skipping the DC value) from the zigzag order. All DCT block patterns are then concatenated into a single vector to form the feature vector 20 x (total block number = 15). Since the patch-based, 300-coefficient long appearance feature is extracted from each of the T frames, the gesture video thus generates 300xT dimensioned feature matrix S. As can be seen from Figure 2, the rows of the S matrix represents the temporal changes of the selected DCT coefficients and the columns represents the selected 300 DCT coefficients (spatial features extracted at time k).

$$S = \begin{bmatrix} DCT_1^1 & \cdots & DCT_T^1 \\ \vdots & \ddots & \vdots \\ DCT_1^{300} & \cdots & DCT_T^{300} \end{bmatrix}$$

Temporal Domain ⟶

Spatial Domain ⟶

Fig. 2. Representation of S matrix which is composed of DCT features of image patches

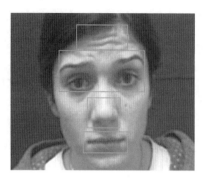

Fig. 3. Facial patches defined on a sample image

Since duration of FHG videos is variable depending on the gesture type and upon the actor, we normalized length of the landmark trajectories and appearance features by using the "resample" function of the Matlab so that all gestures spatiotemporal consisted had length T. Note that "resample" function basically changes the sampling rate of a given sequence to a desired one using a polyphase implementation. The resulting spatiotemporal trajectory matrix P has rows corresponding to landmark coordinates and columns corresponding to normalized time index; similarly appearance feature matrix S has rows corresponding to spatial features (300 DCT coecients) and columns corresponding to normalized time index. In our study we chose T as 60 which is also the average length of the gesture sequences with 11 frames standard deviation.

In order to decrease the dimensionality of P and S matrices, in our case 34x60=2040 for landmark trajectory data and 300x60=18000 for appearance data, respectively, we apply DCT to each row of the data matrix P and S to extract the temporal information of the data matrices. Here rows of the P and S matrix correspond to normalized time domain of the data. We select the first 20 DCT coefficients, by excluding the DC term, and normalize the resulting DCT feature vector to unit norm. DCT is chosen because it is known to have good energy compaction property for highly correlated data and can serve the purpose of summarizing and capturing the data content. Hence we get

Table 1. Facial patch dimensions and sub-block sizes on original intensity frames

Patch Label	Region on the Face	Patch Size	number of 16x16 blocks
1	eyes and eyebrows	16x64	5
2	nose	16x32	2
3	mouth	16x64	4
4	forehead	16x64	4

680x1 (34x20) dimensioned DCT coefficients for trajectory matrix P and 6000x1 (300x20) dimensioned DCT coefficients for appearance features.

4   Classification of FHGs

A set of discriminative and effective features should be selected from the DCT coefficients to construct the FHG classifier. It is known that the motion of certain landmarks are more expressive and hence contain more discriminative information, and this selection depends on the face and head gesture types. Therefore it would pay to pinpoint these more discriminative and effective features per gesture. The Adaboost [29] algorithm seems to be the right tool for optimal feature selection [30,11,31] from the high dimension data. In this paper, we use the Adaboost [29] learning to select 7 to 30 percent of the features from the initial set extracted features.

4.1   Boosting the DCT Features

A sequence of weighted weak classifiers are boosted to form a final strong classifier. A weak classifier is designed by selecting a single feature performance and by setting optimally a threshold such that the best classification performance is achieved. In this study, weak classifiers are chosen as nearest mean classifiers.

4.2   Classification with SVM

We combine Adaboost selected feature with SVM [32] classification. Note that, we run the Adaboost-based feature selection separately for each experiment setup and then SVM is trained for the two-class classification problem. Therefore we formulate C (number of classes) two-class problems, and in each one we separate one of the classes from the ensemble of all other classes. This result in C different SVMs. When a test feature vector arrives, we calculate the output of each SVM classifier for this test data, where the C outputs give the class likelihoods. Then the classifier with maximum probability is declared as the gesture class of the test data. In order to find the parameter setting, we carried out grid-search on the hyper-parameters in the 11-fold cross-validation and selected the parameters with maximum recognition accuracy. Note that, radial basis function is used as an SVM kernel in the implementation of SVM classifier.

5   Experimental Results

5.1   Video Database (BUHMAP)

We tested our FHG recognition algorithm on the BUHMAP video database [27] (http://www.cmpe.boun.edu.tr/pilab/pilabfiles/databases/buhmap/). BUHMAP includes seven non-manual gesture classes (but not including neutral state) selected from Turkish Sign Language (TSL). The details of the gesture

Table 2. Characteristics of the BUHMAP FHG videos

Head and Facial Gesture Classes in BUHMAP DB [27]	
Head shaking (**G1**):	Rotating head left and right sides repetitively
Head up (**G2**):	Tilting the head back while at the same time raising the eyebrows
Head forward (**G3**):	Moving head forward and raising eyebrows
Sadness (**G4**):	Lips turned down, eyebrows down
Head up-down (**G5**):	Nodding head repetitively
Happiness (**G6**):	Smile and expression of joy
Happy up-down (**G7**):	Nodding with smile

Table 3. Test set and experiment setup

Test	Subjects (S)	Class (C)	Repetitions (R)
	11	7 (**G1**, **G2**, **G3**, **G4**, **G5**, **G6**, **G7**)	5
Experiment	Training	Testing	Method
11 fold	10 S, 5 R, 350 videos	1 S, 5 R, 35 videos	Leave-one-S-out cross validation

classes are given in Table 2. Our test set includes seven gesture types acted by eleven subjects, with five repetitions each, hence overall 385 video shots.

The videos are recorded at 30 fps at the resolution of 640x480. Each video starts and ends in the neutral state of the face.

As presented in Table 3 an 11-fold cross-validation scheme is carried out for training and testing any one feature set and classifier combination. For each fold, one subject's gesture samples (7x5=35 gesture samples) are left out as test set and the 350 gesture samples of the remaining subjects are used for training. Thus for each fold, each gesture class has 5 test samples and 50 positive training samples. Notice that, recognition results reported in this study are computed as the average of 11-fold testing.

5.2   Results

The classifiers chosen for the face and head gesture classification problem are given in Table 4. The classification performance of DCT features and boosted-DCT features are given in order to compare the performances of these two feature extraction methods. Table 5 represents the recognition results of the each individual classifier over seven gesture classes. We give the following clarifications for the Tables 4 and 5: Set P denotes the landmark trajectory features and S denotes the sequence of image patch features. Furthermore the superscript indicates the number of features used and the subscript indicates the selection method. Thus for example:

Table 4. Proposed classifiers FHG classification

Classifier	Data / Size	Feature selection / Size/Classification
$P^{200}_{DCT\_ADA}$:	DCT of Trajectory matrix P / 680x1	Adaboost/200/SVM
P^{680}_{DCT} :	DCT of Trajectory matrix P / 680x1	$-$/680/SVM
$S^{400}_{DCT\_ADA}$	DCT of intensity image patches S / 6000	Adaboost/400/SVM
S^{6000}_{DCT}	DCT of intensity image patches S / 6000	$-$/6000/SVM
$(S+P)^{600}_{DCT\_ADA}$	DCT of intensity image patches S + DCT of Trajectory matrix P/ 6680	Adaboost/600/SVM
$(S+P)^{6680}_{DCT}$	DCT of intensity image patches S + DCT of Trajectory matrix P/ 6680	$-$/6680/SVM

Table 5. Proposed classifiers FHG classification (C1:)

Classifier	G1	G2	G3	G4	G5	G6	G7	Total
$P^{200}_{DCT\_ADA}$	96.4	100	89.1	70.9	80	89.1	78.2	86.2
P^{680}_{DCT}	98.2	98.2	89.1	67.3	70.9	87.3	72.7	83.4
$S^{400}_{DCT\_ADA}$	100	92.7	87.3	89.1	100	81.8	94.6	92.2
S^{6000}_{DCT}	96.4	94.6	87.3	90.9	90.9	76.4	85.5	88.8
$(S+P)^{600}_{DCT\_ADA}$	96.4	98.2	89.1	90.9	90.9	80	89.1	93.77
$(S+P)^{6680}_{DCT}$	100	100	87.3	98.2	98.2	83.6	89.1	90.65
$P^{200}_{DCT\_ADA}$ +$S^{400}_{DCT\_ADA}$	100	100	92.7	92.7	92.7	89.1	90.9	94.03

- $P^{200}_{DCT\_ADA}$: 200 DCT coefficients out of 680x1 available DCT coefficients of trajectory matrix P have been selected via Adaboost.
- $(S+P)^{600}_{DCT\_ADA}$: DCT features from the trajectory matrix and image patch sequence have been pooled, and then 600 of them have been selected via Adaboost.

The results show that:

(*i*) Feature selection by Adaboost algorithm improves the classification performance about 3 to 4 percentage points.

(*ii*) 92.22 % best individual classification performance is obtained with boosted-DCT features extracted from face intensity image patches ($S^{400}_{DCT\_ADA}$).

(*iii*) Feature-based fusion of boosted-DCT features of trajectory matrix and boosted-DCT features of intensity image patches ($(S+P)^{600}_{DCT\_ADA}$) surpass the classification performance of boosted-DCT features of intensity image patches.

(*iv*) Best overall classification performance (94.03 % Table 6) is achieved by decision fusion of boosted-DCT features of trajectory matrix ($P^{200}_{DCT\_ADA}$) and and boosted-DCT features of face intensity image patches ($S^{400}_{DCT\_ADA}$).

Table 6. Decision fusion of $P_{DCT\_ADA}^{200}$ and $S_{DCT\_ADA}^{400}$

	G1	G2	G3	G4	G5	G6	G7
G1	**100**	0	0	0	0	0	0
G2	0	**100**	0	0	0	0	0
G3	0	7.3	**92.7**	0	0	0	0
G4	0	0	1.8	**92.7**	1.8	1.8	1.8
G5	0	0	1.8	5.4	**92.7**	0	0
G6	0	0	0	0	0	**89.1**	10.9
G7	0	0	1.8182	0	1.8	5.4	**90.9**

Note that, decision combination is implemented by summing the scores of the classifiers.

6 Conclusion

In this study we have analyzed spatiotemporal feature extraction methods based on accurate tracking of facial landmarks on facial expressions and head gesture sequences. Two types of data representations are investigated, namely facial landmark trajectories and patches of face intensity images. Both modalities have been subjected to DCT transformation for feature extraction. Selection of DCT features is implemented both heuristically using only the low-pass coefficients and algorithmically, using the Adaboost algorithm. The first conclusion is that the proposed classifiers perform satisfactory FHG identification as they achieve scores well above 90 %. In fact, our method surpass significantly the average classification performances reported recently, i.e., 77 % in [26] and 86.4% [28] using the subset of BUHMAP dataset (210 videos of four subjects).

An interesting observation is that sequence and subspace classifiers have very similar performances. While sequence classifiers (e.g. HMM) are designed to compensate for time variations between sequences, the fact that, subspace classifiers with spatiotemporal features have on a par performance can be attributed to the mitigation of this variability by linear time normalization. The best classification result of an individual classifier (without any decision fusion) is achieved for a database with seven gesture classes is 92.2% is state-of-the-art performance. Work is progressing on FHG classification involving a larger set of gestures and mental states.

References

1. Knapp, M.L., Hall, J.A.: Nonverbal communication in human interaction, 6th edn. Wadsworth/Thomson Learning, Belmont (2006)
2. Mehrabian, A., Ferris, S.R.: Inference of attitude from nonverbal communication in two channels. Journal of Counseling Psychology 31(3), 248–252 (1967)
3. Vinciarelli, A., Pantic, M., Bourlard, H.: Social signal processing: Survey of an emerging domain. Image and Vision Computing 27(12), 1743–1759 (2009)

4. Gatica-Perez, D.: Automatic nonverbal analysis of social interaction in small groups: A review. Image and Vision Computing 27(12), 1775–1787 (2009)
5. Sebe, N., Lew, M., Sun, Y., Cohen, I., Gevers, T., Huang, T.: Authentic facial expression analysis. Image and Vision Computing 25(12), 1856–1863 (2007)
6. Zeng, Z., Pantic, M., Roisman, G., Huang, T.: A survey of affect recognition methods: Audio, visual, and spontaneous expressions. IEEE Transactions on Pattern Analysis and Machine Intelligence 31(1), 39–58 (2009)
7. Bailenson, J.N., Pontikakis, E.D., Mauss, I.B., Gross, J.J., Jabon, M.E., Hutcherson, C.A.C., Nass, C., John, O.: Real-time classification of evoked emotions using facial feature tracking and physiological responses. Int. J. Hum.-Comput. Stud. 66(5), 303–317 (2008)
8. Zhang, Y., Ji, Q.: Active and dynamic information fusion for facial expression understanding from image sequences. IEEE Transactions on Pattern Analysis and Machine Intelligence 27(5), 699–714 (2005)
9. Hupont, I., Cerezo, E., Baldassarri, S.: Facial emotional classifier for natural interaction 7(4), 1–12 (2008)
10. Dornaika, F., Davoine, F.: Simultaneous facial action tracking and expression recognition in the presence of head motion. International Journal of Computer Vision 76(3), 257–281 (2008)
11. Shan, C., Gong, S., McOwan, P.: Facial expression recognition based on local binary patterns a comprehensive study. Image and Vision Computing 27(6), 803–816 (2009)
12. Tsalakanidou, F., Malassiotis, S.: Real-time 2d+3d facial action and expression recognition. Pattern Recognition 43(5), 1763–1775 (2010)
13. Wang, T., James Lien, J.J.: Facial expression recognition system based on rigid and non-rigid motion separation and 3d pose estimation. Pattern Recognition 42, 962–977 (2009)
14. Kaliouby, R.A.: Mind-reading machines: automated inference of complex mental states. Technical report, UCAM-CL-TR 636 (2005)
15. Tong, Y., Wang, Y., Zhu, Z., Ji, Q.: Robust facial feature tracking under varying face pose. Pattern Recognition 40, 3195–3208 (2007)
16. Pantic, M., Rothkrantz, L.: Facial action recognition for facial expression analysis from static face images. IEEE Transactions on Systems, Man, and Cybernetics–Part B: Cybernetics 34(3), 1449–1461 (2004)
17. Ekman, P., Friesen, W.: Facial Action Coding System: A Technique for the Measurement of Facial Movement. Consulting Psychologists Press, Palo Alto (1978)
18. Kanaujia, A., Huang, Y., Metaxas, D.: Emblem detections by tracking facial features. In: Conference on Computer Vision and Pattern Recognition Workshop, p. 108 (2006)
19. Kapoor, A., Picard, R.W.: A real-time head nod and shake detector. In: Proceedings from the Workshop on Perspective User Interfaces (2001)
20. Kang, Y.G., Joo, H.J., Rhee, P.K.: Real time head nod and shake detection using hmms. In: Gabrys, B., Howlett, R.J., Jain, L.C. (eds.) KES 2006. LNCS (LNAI), vol. 4253, pp. 707–714. Springer, Heidelberg (2006)
21. Morency, L.P., Sidner, C., Lee, C., Lee, C., Darrell, T.: Contextual recognition of head gestures. In: Proc. of the 7th Int. Conf. on Multimodal Interfaces, pp. 18–24 (2005)
22. Kapoor, A., Burleson, W., Picard, R.W.: Automatic prediction of frustration. International Journal of Human-Computer Studies 65(8), 724–736 (2007)

23. Ji, Q., Lan, P., Looney, C.: A probabilistic framework for modeling and real-time monitoring human fatigue. IEEE Transactions on Systems, Man, and Cybernetics, Part A 36(5), 862–875 (2006)
24. Yang, J.H., Mao, Z.H., Tijerina, L., Pilutti, T., Coughlin, J.F., Feron, E.: Detection of driver fatigue caused by sleep deprivation. Trans. Sys. Man Cyber. Part A 39(4), 694–705 (2009)
25. Bartlett, M.S., Littlewort, G., Frank, M., Lainscsek, C., Fasel, I., Movellan, J.: Recognizing facial expression: Machine learning and application to spontaneous behavior. In: IEEE Computer Society Conference on Computer Vision and Pattern Recognition, vol. 2, pp. 568–573. IEEE Computer Society Press, Los Alamitos (2005)
26. Aran, O., Akarun, L.: A multi-class classification strategy for fisher scores: Application to signer independent sign language recognition. Pattern Recognition 43(5), 1776–1788 (2010)
27. Aran, O., Ari, I., Guvensan, M.A., Haberdar, H., Kurt, Z., Turkmen, H.I., Uyar, A., Akarun, L.: A database of non-manual signs in turkish sign language. In: IEEE 15th Signal Processing and Communications Applications Conference (SIU 2007) (June 2007)
28. Akakin, H.C., Sankur, B.: Analysis of head and facial gestures using facial landmark trajectories. In: COST 2101/2102 Conference, pp. 105–113 (2009)
29. Freund, Y., Schapire, R.E.: A decision-theoretic generalization of on-line learning and an application to boosting. Journal of Computer and System Sciences 55(1), 119–139 (1997)
30. Littlewort, G., Bartlett, M.S., Fasel, I., Susskind, J., Movellan, J.: Dynamics of facial expression extracted automatically from video. Journal of Image and Vision Computing, 615–625 (2004)
31. Yang, P., Liu, Q., Metaxas, D.N.: Boosting encoded dynamic features for facial expression recognition. Pattern Recognition Letters 30(2), 132–139 (2009); Video-based Object and Event Analysis
32. Chang, C.C., Lin, C.J.: LIBSVM: a library for support vector machines (2001), Software available at http://www.csie.ntu.edu.tw/~cjlin/libsvm

Concensus of Self-features for Nonverbal Behavior Analysis

Derya Ozkan and Louis-Philippe Morency

Institute for Creative Technologies
University of Southern California
{ozkan,morency}@ict.usc.edu
http://projects.ict.usc.edu/multicomp/

Abstract. One of the key challenge in social behavior analysis is to automatically discover the subset of features relevant to a specific social signal (e.g., backchannel feedback). The way that these social signals are performed exhibit some variations among different people. In this paper, we present a feature selection approach which first looks at important behaviors for each individual, called self-features, before building a consensus. To enable this approach, we propose a new feature ranking scheme which exploits the sparsity of probabilistic models when trained on human behavior problems. We validated our self-feature concensus approach on the task of listener backchannel prediction and showed improvement over the traditional group-feature approach. Our technique gives researchers a new tool to analyze individual differences in social nonverbal communication.

Keywords: Feature selection, non-verbal behavior analysis, L_1 regularization.

1   Introduction

Nonverbal communication is a highly interactive process, in which the participants dynamically send and respond to nonverbal signals such as speech prosody, gesture, gaze, posture, and facial expression movements. These signals play a significant role in determining the nature of a social exchange. This coherence in communication plays an important role in various areas including contradict resolution [1], psychotherapeutic effectiveness [2], and improved classroom test performances [3]. One of the key challenge in social behavior analysis is to automatically discover the subset of features relevant to a specific social signal [4].

It is well known that culture, age and gender affect people's nonverbal communication [5,6]. The traditional approach for feature selection looks at the most relevant features from all observations (e.g. all human interactions in the dataset). This *group-feature* approach has the potential to select features that are not relevant to any specific individual but only to the average model. This technique is likely to miss some discriminative features which are specific to subset of the population.

A.A. Salah et al. (Eds.): HBU 2010, LNCS 6219, pp. 75–86, 2010.
© Springer-Verlag Berlin Heidelberg 2010

In this paper, we present a feature selection approach which first looks at important behaviors for each individual, called *self-features*, before building a consensus. Figure 1 compares our self-feature concensus approach to the typical group-feature approach. To enable efficient feature selection, we propose a feature ranking scheme based on a sparse regularization method called L_1 regularization [7,8,9]. This scheme is a non-greedy ranking method where two or more features can have the same rank, meaning that these features have joint influence and they should be selected together. Our sparse feature ranking approach can be applied for both group-features and self-features.

We evaluate our approach on the task of listener feedback prediction, to predict the starting points of listener head-nods in a dyadic interaction of two people. We use a sequential probabilistic model, Conditional Random Fields, which is a recently used technique for predicting the backchannels [10]. The experiments are conducted on the RAPPORT dataset from [11] which contains 42 storytelling dyadic interactions.

The following section present related work in nonverbal behavior analysis and feature selection. In Section 3, we describe our self-feature consensus framework. Sparse ranking scheme is described in Section 4. In Section 5, we explain the dataset, features and evaluation metrics used in our experiments, and give the results on the task of listener head-nod prediction. Finally, we conclude with discussion and future work.

2   Related Work

Nonverbal behavior plays an important role in human social interactions. The ability to correctly understand and respond to social signals is considered to be the indicative of social intelligence [12] [13]. Due to it's necessity, social signal processing has became a new domain that aims to automatically sense and understand human social interactions through machine analysis [4] [14]. One of the earliest works in this domain focused on social signal detection for predicting the outcome of dyadic interactions such salary negotiations, hiring interviews, and speed-dating conversations [15]. Second focus of attention has been analysis of social interactions in multimedia recordings. There are three main tasks explored in this context: (1) analysis of interactions in small groups, (2) recognition of roles, and (3) sensing of users interest in computer characters. An extensive list of studies for each domain can be found in [4].

One of the recent approaches in dyadic interactions analysis include recognition [16] and prediction [10] of listener backchannel feedbacks. Earlier, the researchers took a unimodal approach using only either the prosodic features such as pitch and power contours [17] [18], or features like pause duration and trigram part-of-speech frequency [19]. Maatman et al. [11] presented a multimodal approach that combines the prosodic feature based method in [18] with a simple head-nod mimicking method. Later, Morency et al. [10] proposed a multimodal approach to automatically learn a predictive model of listener backchannel feedback.

Feature selection refers to the task of finding a subset of features that are most relevant to the model, and provides a good representation of data. It alleviates the problem of overfitting by eliminating the noisy features. With only the relevant features, a better understanding and analysis of data is facilitated. Based on the gradient-based feature selection method (grafting) in [20], Vail et. al. [21] proposed an incremental feature selection technique for Maximum Entropy Modeling. A Boosting-like method was presented in [22] that iteratively constructs feature conjunctions, which increases the conditional log-likelihood of the model when added. A well known feature selection technique based on L_1 regularization was also applied for conditional random fields in robot tag domain [9].

Although well studied in psychology and sociology [23] [5] [6], individual differences in nonverbal communication have not yet been explored through machine analysis. In this paper, we present a computational approach which enables a better analysis of individual differences in non-verbal behaviors.

3 Concensus of Self-features

Figure 1(a) shows an overview of our self-feature concensus approach. The first step of our algorithm is to find a ranked subset of the most relevant features for each person individually. We refer to this subset as self-features. Section 4 describes our feature ranking algorithm. Figure 1(b) compares our approach to the typical group-feature approach.

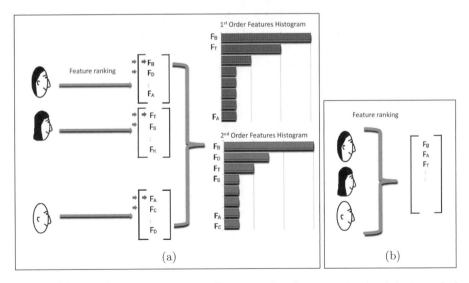

Fig. 1. (a) **Self-feature concensus.** Features of each person in the data is ranked first. Then, we select top n from these ranked list of self-features to construct n^{th} order histogram of feature counts. In this figure, only the 1st and 2nd order histograms are shown. (b) **Group-feature approach.** Features are selected by using all people's observations at once.

Once the ranked lists of self-feature are obtained, we create a consensus over self-features by using only the top n of each list. A concensus is represented by composing an nth order histogram using the top n of each self-feature. This consensus provides a ranking of self-features, and we expect the relevant features to be replicated in these histograms. To remove possible outliers, we apply a threshold on the concensus features to keep only a subset of relevant features. The intuition behind this threshold is that the relevant features are expected to appear frequently in top n of many self-features corresponding to different people, whereas the outlier features would not appear that as often. The minimum required concensus threshold has been selected to be $n+1$ for an nth order histogram in our experiments. Figure 1(a) shows two consensus examples: first and second order histograms.

4   Sparse Ranking

Our feature ranking scheme relies on sparse regularization that applies some constraints on model parameters during training. For a better understanding, we first describe the Conditional Random Fields model used in our experiments and then show how sparse regularization enable feature ranking in a non-greedy manner.

4.1   Conditional Random Fields

Conditional Random Field (CRF) [24] is a probabilistic discriminative model for sequential data labeling. It is an undirected graphical model that defines a single log-linear distribution over label sequences given a particular observation sequence. CRF learns a mapping between a sequence of multimodal observations $\mathbf{x} = \{x_1, x_2, ..., x_m\}$ and a sequence of labels $\mathbf{y} = \{y_1, y_2, ..., y_m\}$. Each y_j is a class label for the jth frame of a video sequence and is a member of a set $\mathcal{Y}$ of possible class labels, for example, $\mathcal{Y} = \{\texttt{head-nod}, \texttt{other-gesture}\}$. Each frame observation x_j is represented by a feature vector $\phi(x_j) \in \mathbf{R}^d$, for example, the prosodic features at each sample.

Given the above definitions, the conditional probability of y is defined as follows:

$$P(\mathbf{y} \mid \mathbf{x}, \theta) = \frac{1}{Z(x)} exp(\sum_\alpha \theta_\alpha F_\alpha(\mathbf{y}, \mathbf{x})) \tag{1}$$

where θ is a vector of linear weights, and $Z(x)$ is a normalization factor over all possible states of $\mathbf{y}$. Feature function F_α is either a state function $s_k(y_j, \mathbf{x}, j)$ or a transition function $t_k(y_{j-1}, y_j, \mathbf{x}, j)$. State function s_k depends on the correlation between label at position j and the observation sequence; while transition function t_k depends on the entire observation sequence and the labels at positions i and i-1 in the label sequence.

Given a training set consisting of m labeled sequences $(\mathbf{x_i}, \mathbf{y_i})$ for $i = 1...m$, training of conditional random fields involves finding the optimum parameter set, θ, that maximizes the following objective function:

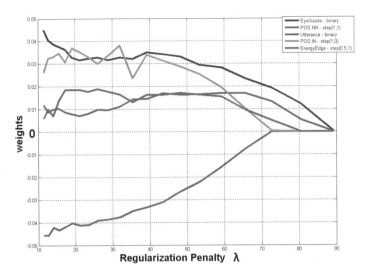

Fig. 2. Sparse ranking using regularization path. As λ goes from higher to lower values, feature weights start to become non-zero based on their relevance to the model.

$$L(\theta) = \sum_{i=1}^{m} \log P(\mathbf{y}_i \mid \mathbf{x}_i, \theta) \tag{2}$$

which is the conditional likelihood of the observation sequence.

4.2   The Method

Our method exploits regularization technique which provides smoothing when the number of learned parameters is very high compared to size of available data. Using a regularization term in the optimization function during training can be seen as assuming a prior distribution over the model parameter. The two most commonly used priors are Gaussian(L_2 regularizer) and Exponential (L_1 regularizer) priors. A Gaussian prior assumes that each model parameter is drawn independently from a Gaussian distribution and penalizes according to the weighted square of the model parameters. An Exponential prior penalizes according to the weighted L_1 norm of the parameters and is defined as follows:

$$R(\theta) = \lambda \parallel \theta \parallel_1 = \lambda \sum_i \mid \theta_i \mid \tag{3}$$

where θ is the model parameters and $\lambda > 0$. In training of conditional random fields, this regularization term is added as a penalty in the log-likelihood function that is optimized. Therefore, Equation 2 becomes:

$$L(\theta) = \sum_{i=1}^{m} \log P(\mathbf{y}_i \mid \mathbf{x}_i, \theta) - R(\theta) \tag{4}$$

L_1 regularization results in sparse parameters vector in which many of the parameters are exactly zero [25]. Therefore, it has been widely used in different domains for the purpose of feature selection [22] [9]. The λ in Equation 3 determines how much penalty should be applied by the regularization term. Larger values indicate larger penalty, thus produces sparser vector parameters.

Figure 2 shows the effect of regularization on feature weights. This regularization path was created by starting with a high regularization penalty λ where all the features are zero and then gradually reduce the regularization until all the features have non-zero values. In this path, if a feature becomes non-zero in earlier stages (i.e., large λ), this signifies that it is an important feature. Our ranking scheme is based on this observation. We rank the features in the order of it's becoming non-zero in the regularization path. The pseudo code for our algorithm is as follows:

> $ranked\_features = empty$
> **for** $\lambda = \infty$ down to 0 **do**
>   train a CRF with current λ
>   **for** all nonzero feature params θ_i **do**
>   **if** θ_i is NOT in selected_features **then**
> $ranked\_features = selected\_features + \theta_i$
>   **end if**
>   **end for**
> **end for**
> **return** $ranked\_features$

5   Experiments

We test the validity of our approach on the multimodal task of predicting listener nonverbal backchannel (i.e., listener head-nods). Backchannel feedback prediction has received considerable interest due to its pervasiveness across languages and conversational contexts [11] [10].

5.1   The Data

We are use the RAPPORT dataset [11] that contains 42 dyadic interactions between a speaker and a listener. Data is drawn from a study of face-to-face narrative discourse ('quasi-monologic' storytelling). In this dataset, participants in groups of two were told they were participating in a study to evaluate a communicative technology. Subjects were randomly assigned the role of speaker and listener. The speaker viewed a short segment of a video clip taken from the Edge Training Systems, Inc. Sexual Harassment Awareness video. After the speaker finished viewing the video, the listener was led back into the computer room, where the speaker was instructed to retell the stories portrayed in the clips to the listener. The listener was asked to not talk during the story retelling. Elicited stories were approximately two minutes in length on average. Participants sat approximately 8 feet apart.

5.2   Multimodal Features and Encodings

We use four different type of multimodal features in our models: prosodic, lexical, part-of-speech, and visual gesture features. **Prosody** refers to the rhythm, pitch and intonation of speech. Several studies have demonstrated that listener feedback is correlated with a speaker's prosody [17]. Listener feedback often follows speaker pauses or filled pauses such as "um" (see [19]). We encode the following prosodic features, including standard linguistic annotations and the prosodic features suggested by Ward and Tsukhara [18]:

– Downslopes in pitch continuing for at least 40ms; regions of pitch lower than the 26th percentile continuing for at least 110ms (i.e., lowness); drop or rise in energy of speech (i.e., energy edge); fast drop or rise in energy of speech (i.e., energy fast edge), vowel volume (i.e., vowels are usually spoken softer), pause in speech (i.e., no speech).

Gestures performed by the speaker are often correlated with listener feedback [26]. Eye gaze, in particular, has often been implicated as eliciting listener feedback. Thus, we encode speaker looking at the listener as our **visual gesture** feature.

Some studies have suggested an association between **lexical** features and listener feedback [19]. Therefore, we include top 100 individual words (i.e., unigrams) that are selected based on their frequency in the data.

Finally, we attempt to capture syntactic information that may provide relevant cues by extracting four types of features from a syntactic dependency structure corresponding to the utterance. Using a part-of-speech tagger [27], we extract the part-of-speech tags for each word (e.g. noun, verb, etc.) as our **Part-of-speech(POS)** features.

We encode our features using 13 different encoding templates as introduced by [10]. The purpose of this encoding dictionary is to capture different relationships between speaker features and listener backchannels. For instance, listener backchannels sometimes happen later after speaker features, or when the speaker features are present for certain amounts of time and its influence may not be constant over time. To automatically obtain these relations, we use three encoding templates in our experiments: **binary encoding** that is designed for speaker features which influence on listener backchannel is constraint to the duration of the speaker feature, **step function** that is a version of binary encoding with two additional parameters: width of the encoded feature and delay between the start of the feature and its encoded version. and **ramp function** that linearly decreases for a set period of time (width parameter). Step and ramp functions are used with 6 different parameters(width and delay): (0.5 0.0), (1.0 0.0), (0.5 0.5), (1.0 0.5), (0.5 1.0), (1.0 1.0) for step, and (0.5 1.0), (1.0 1.0), (2.0 1.0), (0.5 0), (1.0 0), (2.0 0) for ramp.

5.3   Methodology

We performed hold-out testing by randomly selecting a subset of 10 interactions (out of 42) for the test set. The training set contains the remaining 32 dyadic interactions. All models evaluated in this paper were trained with the same training and test sets. The test set does not contain individuals from the training set. Validation of model parameters was performed using a 3-fold strategy on the training set. For L_1 regularization, λ ranged $1000 * 0.95^k, k = [20, 22..170]$. For L_2 regularization, the validated range was $10^k, k = [-3..3]$. The training of CRF models was done using the hCRF library [28].

The performance is measured by using the F-measure, which is the weighted harmonic mean of precision and recall. Precision is the probability that predicted backchannels correspond to actual listener behavior. Recall is the probability that a backchannel produced by a listener in our test set was predicted by the model. We use the same weight for both precision and recall, so called F_1. During validation we find all the peaks (i.e., local maxima) from the marginal probabilities. These backchannel hypotheses are filtered using the optimal threshold from the validation set. A backchannel (i.e., head-nod) is predicted correctly if a peak happens during an actual listener backchannel with high enough probability.

5.4   Results

We ran four experiments: (1) group-feature approach with sparse ranking, (2) effect of the order parameter on self-feature concensus, (3) analysis of selected self-features and (4) comparison of self-feature concensus to group-feature approach.

For the first experiment, we apply our sparse ranking scheme using all the training people in a group-feature manner. To show the effect of sparse ranking, we train a separate CRF for each subset of group-features. For comparison, we trained one CRF using all features (1833 encoded features). All CRFs were retrained using L_2 regularization following previous work on CRF-based backchannel prediction [10]. (L_1 was still used during the sparse ranking step).

Table 1. Group-features with sparse ranking. We incrementally add features as they appear in the regularization path and use for retraining. Each row shows the features added at that stage, therefore the model at this stage is retrained with these new features plus the features above it. Final row shows values for using all the features instead of feature selection.

Features	Precision	Recall	F_1
EyeGazes-binary	0.16469	0.14164	0.1523
... + POS:NN-step(1,.5) **... + VowelVolume**-step(.5,1)	0.15281	0.25903	0.19222
... + Pause-step(1,0) **... + Lowness**-step(1,.5)	0.19818	0.37516	**0.25935**
... + POS:NN-step(1,1)	0.2002	0.1918	0.19591
... + Lowness-step(1,0) **... + VowelVolume**-step(.5,.5)	0.20512	0.1943	0.19956
Baseline: All features *No feature selection*	0.1643	0.6079	**0.2587**

Table 2. Selected features with self-feature concensus using histograms of different orders (after outlier rejection)

$1^{st}Order$	$2^{nd}Order$	$3^{rd}Order$
POS:NN-step(1,1)	**POS:NN**-step(1,1)	**POS:NN**-step(1,1)
Utterence-binary	**POS:NN**-step(1,.5)	**POS:NN**-step(1,.5)
EyeGaze-binary	**Utterence**-binary	**Utterence**-binary
Pause-binary	**EyeGaze**-binary	**EyeGaze**-binary
POS:DT-step(1,.5)	**EyeGaze**-step(1,1)	**Pause**-step(1,0)
Lowness-step(1,0)	**Pause**-binary	**POS:DT**-step(1,.5)
	Pause-step(1,0)	**Lowness**-step(1,0)
	POS:DT-step(1,.5)	**Lowness**-step(1,.5)
	Lowness-step(1,0)	

Precision, recall and F_1 values are given in Table 1. In each row, features are added as they appear in the L_1 regularization path of our sparse ranking scheme. The best performance happens in the third step with five selected features and F_1 value of 0.25935. The last row of Table 1 represents the performance when no feature selection is applied (all features are used). This result shows that sparse ranking can find a subset relevant of features, with performance similar to the baseline model that contain all features.

For the same listener backchannel prediction task, Morency et al. [10] used a greedy-forward feature selection method on the RAPPORT dataset. Although, the experimental set up was slightly different (i.e. different test and train sets were used), the best precision, recall and F_1 values archived with this method were 0.1862, 0.4106, 0.2236, respectively.

Our second experiment studies the effect of the order parameter on self-feature concensus. We constructed feature histograms with orders 1, 2, and 3 by looking at the top 1st, 2nd, and 3rd features in each list. Then, we applied a threshold of 2, 3, and 4 respectively on the histograms for outlier rejection. The list of features for each order is listed in Table 2. This result is really interesting since the same features appear in all three consensus.

For our third experiment, we analyze the features selected for our task of head-nod prediction. It is interesting that some features are selected by both self-feature concensus and group-feature approach, such as *Pause, EyeGaze, Lowness, POS:NN*. *Utterance* and *POS:DT* are the two features selected by self-feature concensus approach that do not appear in the top 20 features from the group-feature approach. *POS:DT* refers to determiners in language, such as *the, this, that*. *Utterance* refers to the beginning of an utterance. Mixed together, these two features represent moments where the speaker starts an utterance with a determiner. To show the relative importance of the *Utterance* and *POS:DT* features, we added these two features to the list of features obtained by group-feature approach and trained a new CRF model. Precision, recall and F_1 values are 0.21685, 0.38653, 0.27783, respectively. We see an improvement over group-feature approach, showing the importance of self-feature concensus.

Table 3. Precision, recall and F_1 values of retrained CRFs with group-feature approach and self-feature concensus

Method	Precision	Recall	F_1
self-feature concensus			
Order 1	0.2192	0.4939	0.3037
Order 2	0.23802	0.48628	**0.3196**
Order 3	0.24449	0.28211	0.26196
group-feature approach	0.19818	0.37516	0.25935
Baseline: all features	0.1643	0.6079	0.2587

Our last experiment compares our self-feature concensus approach to the typical group-feature approach. Using the selected self-features from Table 2, we retrained a L_2 regularized CRFs over all training instances. Precision and recall values for these retrained CRFs of self-feature concensus and group-feature approach (best result from first experiment) are given in Table 3. The best F_1 value achieved with 2nd order histogram is 0.3196. Also, all three self-feature concensus models perform better F_1 than the group-feature approach and the CRF trained with all features (i.e., no feature selection). This results show that using self-features improves listener backchannel prediction.

6 Conclusion

Nonverbal behaviors play an important role in human social interactions and a key challenge is to build computational models for understanding and analyzing this communication dynamic. In this paper, we proposed a framework for finding the important features involved in human nonverbal communication. Our self-feature concensus approach first looks at important behaviors for each individual before building a consensus. It avoids the problem with the group-feature approach which focused on the average model and oversees the inherent behavioral differences among people. We proposed a feature ranking scheme exploiting from L_1 regularization technique. This scheme relies on the fact that adding more penalty on the model parameters will result in sparser results in which only the important features will be promoted.

Our framework was tested on the task of listener head-nod prediction in dyadic interactions. We used the RAPPORT dataset that contains 42 dyadic communications between a speaker and a listener. The results are promising and provides improvement over traditional group-feature approach. In our future work, we plan to use this framework for different prediction tasks, such as gaze aversion and turn-taking prediction.

References

1. Drolet, A.L., Morris, M.W.: Rapport in conflict resolution: Accounting for how face-to-face contact fosters mutual cooperation in mixed-motive conflicts. Journal of Experimental Social Psychology 36, 26–50 (2000)

2. Tsui, P., Schultz, G.: Failure of rapport: Why psychotheraputic engagement fails in the treatment of asian clients. American Journal of Orthopsychiatry 55, 561–569 (1985)
3. Fuchs, D.: Examiner familiarity effects on test performance: Implications for training and practice. Topics in Early Childhood Special Education 7, 90–104 (1987)
4. Vinciarelli, A., Pantic, M., Bourlard, H.: Social signal processing: Survey of an emerging domain. Image and Vision Computing Journal 26, 1743–1759 (2009)
5. Matsumoto, D.: Culture and Nonverbal Behavior. In: The Sage Handbook of Nonverbal Communication. Sage Publications Inc., Thousand Oaks (2006)
6. Linda, L., Carli, S.J.L., Loeber, C.C.: Nonverbal behavior, gender, and influence. Journal of Personality and Social Psychology 68, 1030–1041 (1995)
7. Ng, A.Y.: Feature selection, l-1 vs. l-2 regularization, and rotational invariance. In: International Conference on Machine Learning (2004)
8. Smith, A., Osborne, M.: Regularisation techniques for conditional random fields: Parameterised versus parameter-free. In: Dale, R., Wong, K.-F., Su, J., Kwong, O.Y. (eds.) IJCNLP 2005. LNCS (LNAI), vol. 3651, pp. 896–907. Springer, Heidelberg (2005)
9. Vail, D.L.: Feature selection in conditional random fields for activity recognition. In: IEEE/RSJ International Conference on Intelligent Robots and Systems (2007)
10. Morency, L.P., de Kok, I., Gratch, J.: Predicting listener backchannels: A probabilistic multimodal approach. In: Conference on Intelligent Virutal Agents, pp. 243–255 (2008)
11. Maatman, M., Gratch, J., Marsella, S.: Natural behavior of a listening agent. In: Panayiotopoulos, T., Gratch, J., Aylett, R.S., Ballin, D., Olivier, P., Rist, T. (eds.) IVA 2005. LNCS (LNAI), vol. 3661, pp. 25–36. Springer, Heidelberg (2005)
12. Albrecht, K.: Social intelligence: The new science of success. John Wiley and Sons Ltd., Chichester (2005)
13. Thorndike, E.L.: Intelligence and its use. Harpers Magazine 140, 227–235 (1920)
14. Vinciarelli, A., Pantic, M., Bourlard, H., Pentland, A.: Social signal processing: State-of-the-art and future perspectives of an emerging domain. In: 16th ACM International Conference on Multimedia (2008)
15. Curhan, J.R., Pentland, A.: Thin slices of negotiation: Predicting outcomes from conversational dynamics within the first five minutes (2007)
16. Morency, L.P., de Kok, I., Gratch, J.: Context-based recognition during human interactions: Automatic feature selection and encoding dictionary. In: 10th International Conference on Multimodal Interfaces (2008)
17. Nishimura, R., Kitaoka, N., Nakagawa, S.: A spoken dialog system for chat-like conversations considering response timing. In: Matoušek, V., Mautner, P. (eds.) TSD 2007. LNCS (LNAI), vol. 4629, pp. 599–606. Springer, Heidelberg (2007)
18. Ward, N., Tsukahara, W.: Prosodic features which cue back-channel responses in english and japanese. Journal of Pragmatics 23, 1177–1207 (2000)
19. Cathcart, N., Carletta, J., Klein, E.: A shallow model of backchannel continuers in spoken dialogue. In: European Chapter of the Association for Computational Linguistics, pp. 51–58 (2003)
20. Perkins, S., Lacker, K., Theiler, J., Guyon, I., Elisseeff, A.: Grafting: Fast, incremental feature selection by gradient descent in function space. Journal of Machine Learning Research 3, 1333–1356 (2003)
21. Riezler, S., Vasserman, A.: Incremental feature selection and l1 regularization for relaxed maximum-entropy modeling. In: Conference on Empirical Methods on Natural Language Processing, pp. 174–181 (2004)

22. McCallum, A.R.C.: Efficiently inducing features of conditional random fields. In: 19th Conference on Uncertainty in Artificial Intelligence (2003)
23. Gallaher, P.E.: Individual differences in nonverbal behavior: Dimensions of style. Journal of Personality and Social Psychology 63, 133–145 (1992)
24. Lafferty, J., McCallum, A., Pereira, F.: Conditional random fields: Probabilistic models for segmenting and labelling sequence data. In: International Conference on Machine Learning (2001)
25. Tibshirani, R.: Regression shrinkage and selection via the lasso. Journal of the Royal Statistical Society, Series B 58, 267–288 (1994)
26. Burgoon, J.K., Stern, L.A., Dillman, L.: Interpersonal Adaptation: Dyadic Interaction Patterns. Cambridge University Press, Cambridge (1995)
27. Sagae, K., Tsujii, J.: Dependency parsing and domain adaptation with LR models and parser ensembles. In: Proceedings of the CoNLL Shared Task Session of EMNLP-CoNLL, pp. 1044–1050. Association for Computational Linguistics (2007)
28. hCRF library (2007), http://sourceforge.net/projects/hcrf/

Recognizing Human Action in the Wild

Ivan Laptev

INRIA Paris - Rocquencourt / ENS, France
`ivan.laptev@inria.fr`

Abstract. Automatic recognition of human actions is a growing research topic urged by demands from emerging industries including (i) indexing of professional and user-generated video archives, (ii) automatic video surveillance, and (iii) human-computer interaction. Most applications require action recognition to operate reliably in diverse and realistic video settings. This challenging but important problem, however, has mostly been ignored in the past due to several issues including (i) the difficulty of addressing the complexity of realistic video data as well as (ii) the lack of representative datasets with human actions "in the wild". In this talk we address both problems and first present a supervised method for detecting human actions in movies. To avoid a prohibitive cost of manual supervision when training many action classes, we next investigate weakly-supervised methods and use movie scripts for automatic annotation of human actions in video. With this approach we automatically retrieve action samples for training and learn discriminative visual action models from a large set of movies. We further argue for the importance of scene context for action recognition and show improvements using mining and classification of action-specific scene classes. We also address the temporal uncertainty of script-based action supervision and present a discriminative clustering algorithm that compensates for this uncertainty and provides substantially improved results for temporal action localization in video. We finally present a comprehensive evaluation of state-of-the-art methods for actions recognition on three recent datasets with human actions.

A.A. Salah et al. (Eds.): HBU 2010, LNCS 6219, p. 87, 2010.
© Springer-Verlag Berlin Heidelberg 2010

Comparing Evaluation Protocols on the KTH Dataset

Zan Gao[1], Ming-yu Chen[2], Alexander G. Hauptmann[2], and Anni Cai[1]

[1] School of Information and Communication Engineering,
Beijing University of Posts and Telecommunications, Beijing 100876, P.R. China
[2] School of Computer Science, Carnegie Mellon University, 15213, PA, USA
zangaonsh4522@gmail.com, {mychen,alex}@cs.cmu.edu,
annicai@bupt.edu.cn

Abstract. Human action recognition has become a hot research topic, and a lot of algorithms have been proposed. Most of researchers evaluated their performances on the KTH dataset, but there is no unified standard how to evaluate algorithms on this dataset. Different researchers have employed different test setups, so the comparison is not accurate, fair or complete. In order to know how much difference there is when different experimental setups are used, we take our own spatio-temporal MoSIFT feature as an example to assess its performance on the KTH dataset using different test scenarios and different partitioning of the data. In all experiments, support vector machine (SVM) with a chi-square kernel is adopted. First, we evaluate performance changes resulting from differing vocabulary sizes of the codebook, and then decide on a suitable vocabulary size of codebook. Then, we train the models using different training dataset partitions, and test the performances one the corresponding held-out test sets. Experiments show that the best performance of MoSIFT can reach 96.33% on the KTH dataset. When different n-fold cross-validation methods are used, there can be up to 10.67% difference in the result. And when different dataset segmentations are used (such as KTH1 and KTH2), the difference in results can be up to 5.8% absolute. In addition, the performance changes dramatically when different scenarios are used in the training and test dataset. When training on KTH1 S1+S2+S3+S4 and testing on KTH1 S1 and S3 scenarios, the performance can reach 97.33% and 89.33% respectively. This paper shows how different test configurations can skew results, even on standard data set. The recommendation is to use a simple leave-one-out as the most easily replicable clear-cut partitioning.

Keywords: Action Recognition, training/test data sets, partitioning, experimental methods.

1 Introduction

The problem of data sets and partitioning the data sets has confronted every researcher. Some standard evaluation efforts, such as TRECVID, organized by the U.S. National Institute of Standards (NIST), provide enough data and specify a partitioning of the data into training and testing for all published experiments. While researchers still at times evaluation only subsets of the data that perhaps are most suitable to their approaches, the basic partitioning ensures at least a clear method to duplicate and

A.A. Salah et al. (Eds.): HBU 2010, LNCS 6219, pp. 88–100, 2010.
© Springer-Verlag Berlin Heidelberg 2010

validate any experiments, as well as developing improved methods. The problem is more acute, when there is not enough data for reliable trainings. This is the case with the well-known Weizmann and KTH action data sets, where the data sets have been made public, but no standard has been agreed for evaluation.

The typical research approaches, discussed in more detail in section 2, try multiple folder cross-validation, where some data is used for training, and some held out for testing. In addition, each KTH video includes multiple repetitions of an action, and some papers treat adjacent scenes as separate instances in the data, using one for training and the other for testing, while others partition the data at the complete video file level. Similar choices exist with the same person performing an action in different camera settings, etc. While one might argue that this is unlikely to result in major different, this paper intends to show that the differences are quite significant and we argue for a uniform leave-one-file-out approach in these situations, which is easy to understand and replicate, but also provides a relatively large amount of training data in each iteration.

In general, action recognition has been widely researched and applied in many domains, such as visual surveillance, human computer interaction and video retrieval etc. Many schemes have been proposed for the human action recognition, and we give a brief overview over some of the more frequently cited approaches in the literature.

Aggarwal and Cai [1] give an overview of the various tasks involved in the motion analysis of human body. Hu et al. [2] review the visual surveillance in dynamic scenes and analyze possible research directions. Dollar et al. [3] use sparse spatiotemporal features to perform behavior recognition including human and rodent behavior. Schuldt et al. [4] construct video representations in terms of local space-time features and integrate such representations with SVM classification schemes for recognition. Laptev and Lindeberg [5] build on the idea of the Harris and Forstner interest point operators and detect local structures in space-time. Shechtman and Irani [6] extend the notion of 2-dimensional image correlation into a 3-dimensional space-time volume, thus enabling them to correlate dynamic behaviors and actions. Liu and Shah [8] use the Maximization of Mutual Information (MMI) technique to select the optimal number of words for bag-of-words algorithm.

Laptev et al. [9] address recognition of natural human actions in diverse and realistic video settings. Klaser et al. [13] present a local descriptor based on histograms of oriented 3D spatio-temporal gradients. Wong and Cipolla [12] utilize the global information to yield a sparser set of interest points for motion recognition. Willems et al. [14] present the spatio-temporal interest points that are at the same time scale-invariant (both spatially and temporally). Oikonomopoulos et al. [18] detect the spatiotemporal salient points by measuring changes in the information content of pixel neighborhoods not only in space but also in time. Sun et al[32] exploit what kinds of features are suitable for different action datasets, and fuse local the holistic feature can get much better performance. Bobick and Davis [21] use temporal templates, including motion-energy images and motion-history images to recognize human movement. Gorelick et al. [22] exploit a solution to the Poisson equation to extract various shape properties from images. Wang and Suter [23] learn explicit representations for dynamic shape manifolds of moving humans.

Jia and Yeung [29] use a dimensionality reduction approach called LSTDE to recognize silhouette-based human action. Gorelick et al. [28] regard human actions as three dimensional shapes induced by silhouettes in the space time volume. Weinland et al. [19] use learned 3D exemplars to produce 2D image information to perform view-independent action recognition. Rodriguez et al. [24] use a frequency domain technique, called the Maximum Average Correlation Height (MACH) filter, to recognize single-cycle human actions. Wang et al. [31] use the Discrete Fourier Transform (DFT) and Discrete Wavelet Transform (DWT) to describe silhouette-based image.

The experimental setup of different research papers will be discussed in the section 2. We then briefly describe our MoSIFT algorithm for interest point detection and feature description in section 3. In section 4, we present experimental performance results for the same system on the KTH dataset under different conditions. Finally, we conclude with a summary and discussion.

2 Related Work

The main idea of this paper is to highlight the fact that the performance will be greatly influenced by the different ways and data are used for training and testing. We assume testing will always be done on data not used for training. However, in order to compare fairly and completely, we should have a uniform standard which data is used for training and which for testing. First of all, we will review some related papers that all use different experimental setups. The typical performance evaluation of action recognition uses one of several available action databases, most prominent among those are the Weizmann database [28] and the KTH database (see Fig 2) [4]. Both have been widely used to evaluate action recognition approaches and many results have been reported on them (see Table 3). This is very positive, in that it allows others to judge the difficulty of recognizing actions in this type of video, and perhaps perform their own experiments. Some approaches are evaluated on both databases (e.g. [13, 15, 25-26]) while others either only on the Weizmann (e.g. [27-31, 34]) or the KTH database (e.g. [7-12, 14, 24]). With the Weizmann database, almost all of them (e.g. [27-31, 34]) assess the performance using a leave-one-out setup (See 4.1 in details). Since this is fairly uniform for this dataset in the literature, we will not discuss differences in performance on Weizmann due to methodology. However, on the KTH database, researchers have published widely different kinds of test methods (See Table 3). Some approaches [4, 7, 9, 13, 34] are evaluated on the KTH2 set, but some researchers [8, 10, 12, 14-15, 17, 24-26, 32-33] test their performance on KTH1. Dollar et al. [3] extract selected clips from the KTH data (complete details about KTH, KTH1 and KTH2 will be introduced in section 4.1). Unfortunately, even if researchers use the same basic database, such as KTH1 or KTH2, they often adopt different numbers of folds in the cross-validation. In some papers [4, 7, 13, 34], the authors [7, 13, 34] follow the setting of Schuldt et al [4] using 1-fold cross-validation, but Laptev et al [9] does not adopt this setting, instead a 10-fold cross-validation is used in their experiments. For KTH1, some authors [10, 14, 25] just use 1-fold cross-validation, but 5-fold cross-validation is employed in [15, 24, 26]. Furthermore, some authors [8, 12, 17, 32-33] adopt leave-one-out way to evaluate their performance. From the above analysis, even if the reported performance of some methods is much higher than others, since different experimental settings are employed, the comparison is difficult to trust. Thus, the quality of different methods of performance evaluation for action recognition remains unclear, and people can not compare their approaches fairly and completely. In order to understand how much difference there might be when different test scenarios are employed, we will use our MoSIFT feature and simple SVM classifiers to assess the differences. The following will introduce the MoSIFT feature in brief.

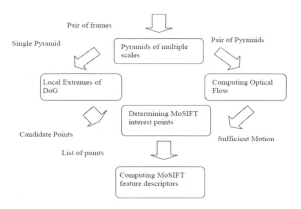

Fig. 1. The MoSIFT framework

3 MoSIFT

Methods based on feature descriptors around local interest points are now widely used in object recognition. This part-based approach assumes that a collection of distinctive parts can effectively describe the whole object. Compared to global appearance descriptions, a part-based approach has better tolerance to posture, illumination, occlusion, deformation and cluttered background. Recently, spatio-temporal local features [4-5, 12-14, 18] have been used for motion recognition in video. The key to the success of part-based methods is that the interest points are distinctive and descriptive. Therefore, interest point detection algorithms play an important role in a part-based approach.

The straightforward way to detect a spatio-temporal interest point is to extend a 2D interest point detection algorithm. Laptev et al. [35] extended 2D Harris corner detectors to a 3D Harris corner detector, which detects points with high intensity variations in both spatial and temporal dimensions. On other words, a 3D Harris detector finds spatial corners with velocity change, which can produce compact and distinctive interest points. However, since the assumption of change in all 3 dimensions is quite restrictive, very few point results and many motion types may not be well distinguished. Dollar et al. [3] discarded spatial constraints and focused only on the temporal domain. Since they relaxed the spatial constraints, their detector detects more interest points than a 3D Harris detector by applying Gabor filters on the temporal dimension to detect periodic frequency components. Although they state that regions with strong periodic responses normally contain distinguishing characteristics, it is not clear that periodic movements are sufficient to describe complex actions. Since recognizing human motion is more complicated than object recognition, motion recognition is likely to require with enhanced local features that provide both shape and motion information, So MoSIFT algorithm[33] are proposed, which detects spatially distinctive interest points with substantial motions. They first apply the well-know SIFT algorithm to find visually distinctive components in the spatial domain and detect spatio-temporal interest points with (temporal) motion constraints. The motion constraint consists of a 'sufficient' amount of optical flow around the distinctive points. The framework is shown in Fig 1. Details of the algorithm can be viewed in [33].

4   Experiments

For the evaluation, we use the KTH database, containing six types of human actions (walking, jogging, running, boxing, hand waving and hand clapping) performed several times by 25 subjects in four different scenarios: outdoors S1, outdoors with scale variation S2, outdoors with different clothes S3 and indoors S4 (see Fig 2). All sequences were taken over homogeneous backgrounds with a static camera with a 25 fps frame rate. The sequences were down-sampled to the spatial resolution of 160*120 pixels and have a length of four seconds in average. To the best of our knowledge, this is the largest video database with sequences of human actions taken over different scenarios that is widely used for research. In our experiments, we will divide the KTH dataset into different training and test datasets in different ways following some of the published papers [4, 7-9, 12-15, 17, 24-26, 32-34], and also evaluate the performance in these different scenarios.

4.1   Experimental Setup

In order to follow the researchers ([4, 7, 9, 13, 34] and [8, 10, 12, 14-15, 17, 24-26, 32-33]), we rename the KTH database in two ways. One is that some person performs the same action three or four times in the same video, named KTH1, the other is that a person just does an action only one time, named KTH2. In KTH1, there are 599 sequences, while the KTH2 database contains 2391 sequences. We examine two kinds of cross-validation that are frequently employed for KTH1 and KTH2 (n-fold and leave-one-out). Leave-one-out cross-validation uses 24 of 25 subjects to build action models and then tests on the remaining subject. Performance is reported as the average accuracy of 25 runs, each with a different person. As for n-fold, we also follow the Schuldt et al [4] in which all sequences were divided with respect to the subjects into a training set (8 persons), a validation set (8 persons) and a test set (9 persons). The classifiers were trained on a training set while the validation set was used to optimize the parameters of each method. The presented recognition results were obtained on the test set. Performance is reported as the average accuracy of n runs. On KTH1 and KTH2, 1-fold, 5-fold, 10-fold, 30-fold, and leave-one-out cross validation are adopted, as done by various authors.

Fig. 2. Examples of sequences corresponding to different types of actions and scenarios

4.2 Experiment 1

Firstly, we extracted around 2 million interest points from the whole KTH dataset with the MoSIFT detector. Since the number of interest points is large, we randomly sample 25% of the interest points to construct a video codebook. Several codebooks with different vocabulary sizes are produced by k-means clustering. Each interest point is mapped into one cluster (i.e. visual word) based on its feature vector. We then aggregate all the visual words over the duration of a single event. Thus, each event is represented by a visual word histogram. We then apply a χ^2 kernel with an SVM classifier because it has been shown to be better for calculating histogram distances. We perform the experiments on the KTH1 dataset with a leave-one-out experimental setup. In this first experiment, we merely want to know how performance changes with different vocabulary sizes, and select a suitable size for future comparisons. Table 1 and 2 show the performance and the confusion matrix for different codebook sizes.

Table 1. Comparison of different vocabulary sizes

KTH1	Codebook Size						
	100	200	600	1000	2000	3000	4000
Accuracy (%)	89.58	0.9382	0.9383	0.9499	0.9567	0.9633	0.9583

Table 2. Confusion matrix of MoSIFT with a 3000 visual-word vocabulary size

	Boxing	Clapping	Waving	Jogging	Running	Walking
Boxing	**0.99**	0.01	0	0	0	0
Clapping	0.01	**0.979**	0.01	0	0	0
Waving	0	0.01	**0.99**	0	0	0
Jogging	0	0	0	**0.93**	0.07	0
Running	0	0	0	0.11	**0.89**	0
Walking	0	0	0	0	0	**1**

Table 1 shows that MoSIFT has good and stable performance when varying the vocabulary size. When the vocabulary size is 100, its accuracy can still reach 89.58%. After the codebook size is above 200, the performance is stable, but the performance still shows some improvement with further increases in vocabulary size.

When the vocabulary size of codebook is 3000, the best performance is achieved, but when the vocabulary size increases further, performance starts to decline. Table2 gives the confusion matrix of MoSIFT with a 3000 word vocabulary size. The most confusion is between jogging and running, and we found that even humans have difficulties distinguishing them. Table 3 presents the comparison of different published results with a variety of methods all evaluated on the KTH dataset. In Table 3 we find that the MoSIFT feature with a 3000 visual word vocabulary size has the best performance when compared to all other published algorithms we have found to date.

Table 3. Comparison of different methods all using the KTH dataset

Method	Avg Accuracy	Dataset	n-fold CV
Schuldt et al[4]	71.72%	KTH2	1-fold
Klaser et al. [13]	91.40%	KTH2	1-fold
Nazli et al. [34]	94.00%	KTH2	1-fold
Mikolajczyk and Uemura [7]	93.20%	KTH2	1-fold
Our Method(600)	85.66%~94.65%	KTH2	1-fold
Our Method(600)	88.49%~93.57%	KTH2	5-fold
Laptev et al[9]	91.80%	KTH2	10-fold
Our Method(600)	89.24%~93.10%	KTH2	10-fold
Our Method(600)	92.45%	KTH2	leave-one-out
Willems et al. [14]	84.30%	KTH1	1-fold
Nowozin et al. [10]	87.00%	KTH1	1-fold
Our Method(600)	90.10%~95.83%	KTH1	1-fold
Rodriguez et al. [24]	88.70%	KTH1	5-fold
Jhuang et al. [15]	91.70%	KTH1	5-fold
Schindler and Gool [26]	92.70%	KTH1	5-fold
Our Method(600)	90.93%~95.04%	KTH1	5-fold
Fathi and Mori [25]	90.50%	KTH1	1-fold 2/3 1/3
Our Method(600)	91.44%~94.56%	KTH1	10-fold
Niebles et al. [17]	81.50%	KTH1	leave-one-out
Wong and Cipolla [12]	86.60%	KTH1	leave-one-out
Sun et al.[32]	94.00%	KTH1	leave-one-out
Liu and Shah et al[8]	94.20%	KTH1	leave-one-out
Chen and Hauptmann [33]	95.83%	KTH1	leave-one-out
Our Method(600)	93.83%	KTH1	leave-one-out
Our Method(3000)	96.33%	KTH1	leave-one-out
Dollar et al. [3]	81.20%	1200 Clip	1-fold

4.3 Experiment 2

In [4, 7, 9, 13, 34] and [10, 14-15, 24-26], all sequences were divided with respect to the subjects into a training set (8 persons), a validation set (8 persons) and a test set (9 persons). Unfortunately, most of these methods do not describe precisely how they split the KTH dataset into training and testing parts. This makes an accurate comparison impossible. A quick calculation shows that there are $C_{25}^{8} \times C_{25}^{8} \times C_{25}^{9} \equiv 2.3899e+018$ choices of partitions. In the next experiments, we will show how performance changes with different training and testing datasets. In order to balance performance and computation, we choose the 600 word vocabulary size for MoSIFT, and all of the following experiments will adopt a 600 word vocabulary. First, we divide the KTH2 database into a training set (8 persons), a validation set (8 persons) and a test set (9 persons) randomly, but perform the experiments 30 times with different randomly selected partitions.

Table 4. Performance comparison of different data partitioning on KTH2

Run#	Random1	Random2	Random3	Top10	Bottom10
#1-3	89.19	90.15	85.66	94.65	85.66
#4-6	90.50	93.35	89.88	93.36	88.64
#7-9	90.27	92.95	89.63	93.35	89.19
#10-12	91.50	92.18	90.20	93.34	89.31
#13-15	90.72	89.31	91.73	93.16	89.63
#16-18	90.01	93.05	94.65	93.05	89.70
#19-21	93.36	93.34	89.70	92.95	89.88
#22-24	90.95	92.18	92.78	92.78	90.01
#25-27	91.26	91.26	88.64	92.18	90.15
#28-30	93.16	91.72	91.00	92.18	90.20
Average	91.09	91.95	90.39	93.10	89.24

Table 5. Performance comparison of different data partitioning on KTH1

Run#	Random1	Random2	Random3	Top10	Bottom10
#1-3	93.49	93.23	93.23	95.83	92.15
#4-6	92.13	90.10	93.72	95.37	92.13
#7-9	91.67	94.24	95.83	94.79	92.13
#10-12	94.42	94.79	90.63	94.79	91.67
#13-15	92.59	93.75	93.19	94.42	91.67
#16-18	94.42	91.67	90.63	94.42	91.67
#19-21	95.37	93.72	92.19	94.27	91.62
#22-24	91.67	92.67	93.75	94.24	90.63
#25-27	92.13	92.15	94.27	93.75	90.63
#28-30	93.06	91.62	94.79	93.75	90.10
Average	93.09	92.79	93.22	94.56	91.44

Table 4 shows that if we have no cross-validation, the performance can vary from a low score of 85.6579% to a high 94.6545%.

The performance varies from 88.487% to 93.57% when an average of 5 sample partitions is used. If we have 10-different partitions, the performance can fluctuate from 89.237% to 93.10%. When using all of our 30 runs, we can get an average accuracy of 91.14%.

The same experiments are performed on KTH1, and Table 5 gives the results. Table 5 indicates that the best and worst performance is 95.83% and 90.10% respectively without cross validation, choosing simply the best or worst single result. When 5 partitioning are average, the performance can range from 90.93% to 95.04%. The fluctuation of averaging 10 partitionings runs from 91.44% to 94.56%.

From Table 4 and 5, we can see that the fluctuation will be small with the increase of n in the n-fold cross validation. Table 3 gives the comparison of different methods using KTH, and the fluctuation also is shown for our method. For example, for testing on KTH2 without cross-validation, if we choose the best performance of our algorithms, it will be 94.65%, which is much better than 91.4% in [13], but the lowest performance of our algorithms is 85.66%, which is much worse than 91.4% in [13]. What is worse, we also do not exactly know what setting was used in [13]. The same situation occurs when we perform the experiments on KTH1 with 5-fold cross-validation. Thus, we cannot draw strong conclusions that our algorithm is much better or worse than that in [13], which is unfortunate. Since we just performed 30 experiments from 2.38993e+18 possibilities, fluctuation could still much bigger than in our experiments. However, for the leave-one-out setup, all experiments have the same setting, so performance can be compared fairly and completely.

4.4   Experiment 3

From the above experiments, we can see that different test designs affect performance, but the leave-one-out way always has the same setting, so in the following experiments, the leave-one-out way will be used. Table 3 shows that the authors [4, 7, 9, 13, 34] evaluate their performance on the KTH2 database, but the KTH1 database is used in experiments by [8, 10, 12, 14-15, 17, 24-26, 32-33], so in this experiment, we will assess the difference between KTH1 and KTH2. In order to evaluate this completely, we will train and test on different scenarios.

In the KTH database, there are four scenarios: outdoors S1, outdoors with scale variation S2, outdoors with different clothes S3 and indoors S4. To analyze the influence of these different scenarios, we perform training on different subsets of {S1}, {S1, S3}, {S1, S3, S4} and {S1, S2, S3, S4}, at the same time, {S1}, {S2}, {S3}, {S4}, and {S1, S2, S3, S4} will be used to test. We perform experiments on the KTH1 and KTH2 respectively. In order to compare fairly and completely, all the settings are otherwise the same. The performance is given in Fig.3 and Fig.4, and the comparison is shown in Table 6.

From Fig.3 and 4, we find that when we train the models and test on different scenarios, the biggest change occurs for the actions of jogging and running, while other actions are relative stable. When we the train the models without the S2 scenario and test on all scenarios, the performance of the S2 scenario is the worst, but when the training database includes the S2 scenario, the performance will increase rapidly.

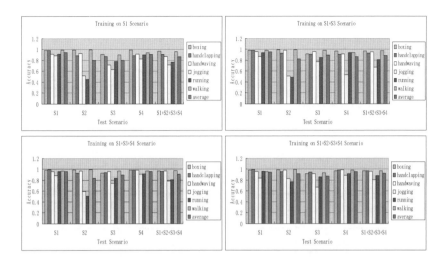

Fig. 3. Each action performance when training and testing on KTH2 in different scenarios

The same effect also can be seen in the S3 and S4 scenarios. In Table 6, we see that when we train the models on the S1 scenario and test on S1, S2, S3, S4, S1+S2+S3+S4 on KTH1 and KTH2, the performance on KTH1 is much better than on KTH2. Similar results occur in other experiments except the red fold in the Table 6. Schuldt et al [4] noted that the S2 scenario was the most difficult to detect as there are scale variations in this scenario. However, the last row in Table 6 shows that its performance is much better than in the S3 scenario on KTH1 and KTH2.

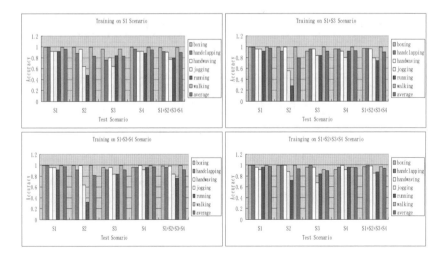

Fig. 4. Each action performance when training and testing on KTH1 in different scenarios

We suspect the reason is that MoSift has better tolerance to scale variation than to appearance variation (remember the S3 scenario is outdoors with different clothes), and the confusion of the S2 and S3 scenario also has some influence on the performance of S3.

Table 6. Average performance of training/testing in different scenarios on KTH1 and KTH2

	Training Scenario							
	S1		S1+S3		S1+S3+S4		S1+S2+S3+S4	
Test Scenario	KTH1	KTH2	KTH1	KTH2	KTH1	KTH2	KTH1	KTH2
S1	0.96	0.95	0.97	0.95	0.97	0.96	0.97	0.95
S2	0.83	0.80	0.79	0.82	0.81	0.83	0.93	0.92
S3	0.83	0.80	0.92	0.90	0.92	0.90	0.89	0.87
S4	0.95	0.91	0.93	0.87	0.97	0.96	0.95	0.95
S1+S2+S3+S4	0.89	0.86	0.90	0.88	0.92	0.91	0.94	0.92

Table 7 gives the performance with different training and testing on KTH1 and KTH2 different scenarios. The biggest difference between KTH1 and KTH2 can reach 5.85%. When we train on S1+S2+S3+S4, and test on S1, S2, S3, S4, S1+S2+S3+S4, the difference is 2.5%, 1.3%, 1.9%, 0.1%, 1.38% respectively. If we are not careful about the cross-validation and database used in our experiments, the total range of performance differences can reach 10.67%.

Table 7. Performance difference of training and testing on KTH1 and KTH2 different scenarios

	Training Scenario			
Test Scenario	S1	S1+S3	S1+S3+S4	S1+S2+S3+S4
S1	0.0134	0.0217	0.0134	0.0250
S2	**0.0300**	0.0250	0.0200	0.0133
S3	0.0251	0.0224	0.0239	0.0190
S4	**0.0367**	**0.0584**	0.0101	0.0016
S1+S2+S3+S4	0.0276	0.0210	0.0084	0.0139

5   Conclusion

In this paper we reviewed existing action recognition approaches' performance on KTH dataset, and found that people evaluated their performances by different test ways. Based on our analysis, we performed the experiments by different test ways and different scenarios. Experiments show that the performance deviations of different n-fold cross-validation can achieve 9%, and the performance diversity of different database can reach 5.85%. What is worse, if we consider the both conditions, the difference can be 10.66%.

To compare the performance fairly and completely, the uniform standard should set up, and the leave-one-out way maybe a good one. In our experiments, we find that the increase of training samples will affect the performance in some cases. We therefore recommend that future research always adopts leave-one-out experimental setups, and that training scenarios be always carefully described to avoid unscientific and confusing comparisons.

Acknowledgements

This material is based in part upon work supported by the National Science Foundation under Grants No. 0624236 and 0751185. Zan Gao is partially supported by the NSFC (No. 60772114 and No.90920001). Any opinions, findings, and conclusions or recommendations expressed in this material are those of the author(s) and do not necessarily reflect the views of the National Science Foundation and the National Science Foundation of China.

References

1. Aggarwal, J.K., Cai, Q.: Human motion analysis: a review. In: IEEE Proceedings of Nonrigid and Articulated Motion Workshop, pp. 90–102 (1997)
2. Hu, W., Tan, T., Wang, L., Maybank, S.: A survey on visual surveillance of object motion and behaviors. In: SMC
3. Dollar, P., Rabaud, V., Cottrell, G., Belongie, S.: Behavior recognition via sparse spatio-temporal features. In: IEEE International Workshop on Visual Surveillance and Performance Evaluation of Tracking and Surveillance, pp. 65–72 (2005)
4. Schuldt, C.L., Caputo, B.I.: Recognizing human actions: a local SVM approach. In: ICPR, vol. (17), pp. 32–36 (2004)
5. Laptev, I., Lindeberg, T.: Space-time interest points. In: ICCV, pp. 432–439 (2003)
6. Shechtman, E., Irani, M.: Space-time behavior-based correlation-OR-How to tell if two underlying motion fields are similar without computing them? PAMI 29(11), 2045–2056 (2007)
7. Mikolajczyk, K., Uemura, H.: Action recognition with motion-appearance vocabulary forest. In: CVPR, pp. 1–8 (2008)
8. Liu, J., Shah, M.: Learning human actions via information maximization. In: CVPR, pp. 1–8 (2008)
9. Laptev, I., Marszaek, M., Schmid, C., Rozenfeld, B.: Learning realistic human actions from movies. In: CVPR, pp. 1–8 (2008)
10. Nowozin, S., Bakır, G.O., Tsuda, K.: Discriminative subsequence mining for action classification. In: ICCV, pp. 1–8 (2007)
11. Gilbert, A., Illingworth, J., Bowden, R.: Scale invariant action recognition using compound features mined from dense spatio-temporal corners. In: Forsyth, D., Torr, P., Zisserman, A. (eds.) ECCV 2008, Part I. LNCS, vol. 5302, pp. 222–233. Springer, Heidelberg (2008)
12. Wong, S.-F., Cipolla, R.: Extracting spatiotemporal interest points using global information. In: ICCV, pp. 1–8 (2007)
13. Klaser, A., Marszałek, M., Schmid, C.: A spatio-temporal descriptor based on 3D-gradients. In: BMVC (2008)

14. Willems, G., Tuytelaars, T., Gool, L.V.: An efficient dense and scale-invariant spatio-temporal interest point detector. In: Forsyth, D., Torr, P., Zisserman, A. (eds.) ECCV 2008, Part II. LNCS, vol. 5303, pp. 650–663. Springer, Heidelberg (2008)

15. Jhuang, H., Serre, T., Wolf, L., Poggio, T.: A biologically inspired system for action recognition. In: ICCV, pp. 1–8 (2007)

16. Liu, J., Ali, S., Shah, M.: Recognizing human actions using multiple features. In: CVPR, pp. 1–8 (2008)

17. Niebles, J.C., Wang, H., Fei-Fei, L.: Unsupervised learning of human action categories using spatial-temporal words. IJCV 79(3), 299–318 (2008)

18. Oikonomopoulos, A., Patras, I., Pantic, M.: Spatiotemporal saliency for human action recognition. In: ICME, pp. 1–4 (2005)

19. Weinland, D., Boyer, E., Ronfard, R.: Action recognition from arbitrary views using 3D exemplars. In: ICCV, pp. 1–7 (2007)

20. Efros, A.A., Berg, A.C., Mori, G., Malik, J.: Recognizing action at a distance. In: ICCV, vol. (2), pp. 726–733 (2003)

21. Bobick, A.F., Davis, J.W.: The recognition of human movement using temporal templates. PAMI 23(3), 257–267 (2001)

22. Gorelick, L., Galun, M., Sharon, E., Basri, R., Brandt, A.: Shape representation and classification using the Poisson Equation. In: CVPR, vol. (2), II-61–67 (2004)

23. Wang, L., Suter, D.: Learning and matching of dynamic shape manifolds for human action recognition. IEEE Transactions on Image Processing 16(6), 1646–1661 (2007)

24. Rodriguez, M.D., Ahmed, J., Shah, M.: Action MACH: a spatio-temporal maximum average correlation height filter for action recognition. In: CVPR, pp. 1–8 (2008)

25. Fathi, A., Mori, G.: Action recognition by learning mid-level motion features. In: CVPR, pp. 1–8 (2008)

26. Schindler, K., Gool, L.v.: Action snippets: how many frames does human action recognition require? In: CVPR, pp. 1–8 (2008)

27. Thurau, C., Hlavac, V.: Pose primitive based human action recognition in videos or still images. In: CVPR, pp. 1–8 (2008)

28. Gorelick, L., Blank, M., Shechtman, E., Irani, M., Basri, R.: Actions as space-time shapes. PAMI 29(12), 2247–2253 (2007)

29. Jia, K., Yeung, D.-Y.: Human action recognition using local spatio-temporal discriminant embedding. In: CVPR, pp. 1–8 (2008)

30. Weinland, D., Boyer, E.: Action recognition using exemplar-based embedding. In: CVPR, pp. 1–8 (2008)

31. Wang, L., Geng, X., Leckie, C., Kotagiri, R.: Moving shape dynamics: a signal processing perspective. In: CVPR, pp. 1–8 (2008)

32. Sun, X., Chen, M.-Y., Hauptmann, A.: Action Recognition via Local Descriptors and Holistic Features. In: CVPR, pp. 58–65 (June 25, 2009)

33. Chen, M.-y., Hauptmann, A.: MoSIFT: Reocgnizing Human Actions in Surveillance Videos. CMU-CS-09-161. Carnegie Mellon University (2009)

34. Ikizler, N., Cinbis, R.G., Duygulu, P.: Human action recognition with line and flow histograms. In: ICPR, pp. 1–4 (2008)

35. Laptev, I., Lindeberg, T.: Space-time interest points. In: ICCV, pp. 432–439 (2003)

3D Mean-Shift Tracking of Human Body Parts and Recognition of Working Actions in an Industrial Environment

Markus Hahn[1], Fuad Quronfuleh[1], Christian Wöhler[2], and Franz Kummert[3]

[1] Daimler AG, Group Research and Advanced Engineering, Ulm, Germany
[2] Image Analysis Group, Dortmund University of Technology, Dortmund, Germany
[3] Applied Informatics, Bielefeld University, Bielefeld, Germany

Abstract. In this study we describe a method for 3D trajectory based recognition of and discrimination between different working actions in an industrial environment. A motion-attributed 3D point cloud represents the scene based on images of a small-baseline trinocular camera system. A two-stage mean-shift algorithm is used for detection and 3D tracking of all moving objects in the scene. A sequence of working actions is recognised with a particle filter based matching of a non-stationary Hidden Markov Model, relying on spatial context and a classification of the observed 3D trajectories. The system is able to extract an object performing a known action out of a multitude of tracked objects. The 3D tracking stage is evaluated with respect to its metric accuracy based on nine real-world test image sequences for which ground truth data were determined. An experimental evaluation of the action recognition stage is conducted using 20 real-world test sequences acquired from different viewpoints in an industrial working environment. We show that our system is able to perform 3D tracking of human body parts and a subsequent recognition of working actions under difficult, realistic conditions. It detects interruptions of the sequence of working actions by entering a safety mode and returns to the regular mode as soon as the working actions continue.

1 Introduction

The efficiency of many industrial production processes can be increased by establishing a close collaboration between humans and machines exploiting their unique capabilities. A safe interaction between humans and industrial robots requires vision methods for 3D pose estimation, tracking, and recognition of the motion of human body parts. A robust method often used for object tracking is the mean-shift algorithm [2,3,5], which searches for a local mode of the empirical density function.

The mean-shift tracking approach introduced in [4] is extended to 3D space in [12]. In the experiments in [12], a large-baseline system consisting of four colour cameras is used. The head of a human is tracked using an ellipsoid model. The large baseline results in a high accuracy of the 3D pose estimation, since in this

A.A. Salah et al. (Eds.): HBU 2010, LNCS 6219, pp. 101–112, 2010.
© Springer-Verlag Berlin Heidelberg 2010

setting relatively small errors of the estimated disparities of the order of a few pixels do not lead to large errors of the depth estimation. Furthermore, in the scenes regarded in [12] the objects and the background can be separated easily as both can be described unambiguously by colour histogram features.

To recognise gestures or actions, many recognition systems use Hidden Markov Models (HMMs) due to their ability to probabilistically represent the variations of the training data. Li et al. [11] use HMMs to classify hand trajectories of manipulative actions and take into account the object context. Black and Jepson [1] present an extension of the CONDENSATION algorithm and model gestures as temporal trajectories of the velocity of the tracked hands.

This study addresses the problem of tracking and recognising the motion of humans in a working environment, which is a precondition for a close collaboration between human workers and industrial robots. As an imaging system, we use a small-baseline trinocular camera sensor similar to that of the SafetyEYE protection system (www.safetyeye.com) which is used in production processes to protect human workers. In the context of this application, we are restricted to the small-baseline configuration and therefore cannot make use of the advantages of the multi-view setup described in [12]. Small disparity errors may thus lead to large depth errors, and it is often difficult to distinguish the tracked object from the cluttered background. Hence, the extension of the 3D mean-shift tracking approach proposed in this study relies on grey value histograms and 3D point cloud data generated by stereo image analysis. The subsequent action recognition stage consists of a particle filter based non-stationary HMM framework.

2   3D Tracking Stage

The idea behind our tracking approach is to extract the motion of all moving objects in the observed scene with a 3D mean-shift tracking algorithm and a simple ellipsoid model. At each time step the recognition stage then determines the relevant object (e.g. the hand) which performs the working actions, and recognises the current working action with a particle filter based matching of a non-stationary HMM.

2.1   Clustering and Object Detection

Object detection and 3D tracking are based on a scene flow field. We use a combination of dense optical flow and sparse correlation-based stereo. The dense optical flow algorithm described in [14] is used to determine the object motion in the image sequence. We combine the optical flow field with the 3D points from the stereo algorithm to obtain the scene flow field (cf. Fig. 1). The velocity component parallel to the depth axis is not computed.

At each time step, a graph based clustering stage extracts all moving objects from the scene flow field, essentially separating moving objects from the (stationary or differently moving) background. The computed clusters are approximated as ellipsoids and the 3D ellipsoid pose $\Phi = [c_x, c_y, c_z, \beta]^T$ is determined

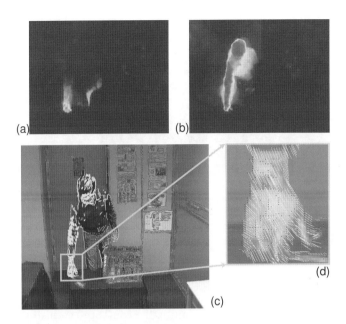

Fig. 1. Dense optical flow computed according to [13]. (a) Horizontal component. (b) Vertical component. Warmer colours denote larger values of the components. (c) Reprojected sparse scene flow field. (d) Enlarged section of the sparse scene flow field.

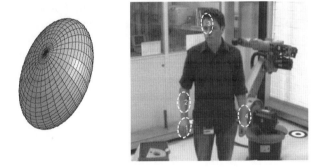

Fig. 2. Left: Ellipsoid model used for tracking arbitrary objects or object parts in the 3D point cloud. Right: Reprojection of four tracked objects.

(cf. Fig. 2). Only the 3D centre $\mathbf{c} = [c_x, c_y, c_z]^T$ of the ellipsoid and the rotation angle β around the depth axis are part of the pose vector $\mathbf{\Phi}$, since we assume that the approximated objects are parallel to the image plane. The 3D pose update of all tracked objects is based on a two-stage 3D extension of the mean-shift algorithm [3,5]. If a tracked object is not moving for more than 5 time steps it is deleted.

Fig. 3. Two-stage mean-shift procedure. Projected search region (left), 3D probability grid (middle), final result (right).

2.2   Target Model

The target model $\widehat{\mathbf{q}}_{(id)}$ with the object index id is computed based on the first 3D ellipsoid pose $\mathbf{\Phi}^{(id)}$ and is updated at every time step. It consists of a one-dimensional histogram of greyscale values. To compute the histogram $\widehat{\mathbf{q}}_{(id)}$ we place a grid on the surface of the ellipsoid, the resolution of which is equal to the pixel resolution at the current depth. Every 3D point on the surface grid of the ellipsoid is projected into the images of all three cameras. The histogram bin of a 3D-point $\mathbf{p}$ is obtained with the lookup function $iBin(\mathbf{p}) = \frac{1}{3}\left(I_{uv}^{C_1} + I_{uv}^{C_2} + I_{uv}^{C_3}\right)$, where $I_{uv}^{C_c}$ is the greyscale value in the image from camera c at the projected position (u, v) of the 3D point $\mathbf{p}$. With all 3D points on the surface grid of the ellipsoid a one-dimensional histogram of the object appearance is computed. We employ a convex and monotonically decreasing kernel profile g which assigns a smaller weight to locations that are farther away from the centre of the ellipsoid. A normalisation of the histogram yields the relative frequency of each greyscale value on the ellipsoid surface, which is interpreted as a probability.

2.3   Image-Based Mean-Shift

In the first stage, the mean-shift procedure is applied to a search region, a 3D plane parallel to the image plane centred at the last object position. Similar to [2] in 2D, we use the target model $\widehat{\mathbf{q}}_{(id)}$ as a look-up table to compute the probability value for all 3D points in the search region. The lookup function $iBin$ is used to obtain a probability value for each 3D point on the grid. Fig. 3 (left) depicts the projected search region in the image of one camera and Fig. 3 (middle) shows the inferred 3D probability grid. The 3D centre point $\widetilde{\mathbf{c}}$ is estimated with the mean-shift procedure using a geometric ellipse model. The ellipse orientation β is computed similar to [2]. This mean-shift stage allows only for an update of the lateral pose of the tracked ellipsoid, since the probability grid is parallel to the image plane. No information from the scene flow field is used, such that a pose update of the ellipsoid is computed even if there is no new 3D information available.

2.4   Point Cloud Based Mean-Shift

In this stage all moving 3D points of the scene flow field are used to update the 3D pose of the tracked ellipsoid. At the first iteration $j = 1$ of the mean-shift procedure the ellipsoid centre $\mathbf{c}_{j=1}$ is initialised with the estimated 3D centre point $\widetilde{\mathbf{c}}$ of the image-based mean-shift stage. For all subsequent iterations, the ellipsoid model is moved to the new position

$$\mathbf{c}_{j+1} = \frac{\sum_{n=1}^{N} \mathbf{s}_n \cdot g\left(\mathbf{s}_n, \mathbf{c}_j\right) \cdot \widehat{\mathbf{q}}_{(id)}(iBin(\mathbf{s}_n))}{\sum_{n=1}^{N} g\left(\mathbf{s}_n, \mathbf{c}_j\right) \cdot \widehat{\mathbf{q}}_{(id)}(iBin(\mathbf{s}_n))}, \tag{1}$$

where $\mathbf{c}_j$ is the previous centre position. In the mean-shift procedure we use a truncated Gaussian kernel [3] with a smaller weight $g\left(\mathbf{s}_n, \mathbf{c}_j\right)$ assigned to 3D points $\mathbf{s}_n$ farther away from the ellipsoid centre $\mathbf{c}_j$. Our mean-shift based 3D tracking approach incorporates an appearance weighting $\widehat{\mathbf{q}}_{(id)}(iBin(\mathbf{s}_n))$ obtained by looking up the appearance probability of the moving 3D point $\mathbf{s}_n$ in the target model $\widehat{\mathbf{q}}_{(id)}$, such that a 3D point with an appearance similar to the target appearance is assigned a higher weight. Fig. 3 (right) depicts all moving 3D points and the final result of the two-stage mean-shift procedure for 3D tracking.

3   Action Recognition Stage

The working action recognition stage is based on a 3D trajectory classification and matching approach. The tracking stage yields continuous data streams of the 3D poses of all tracked objects in the scene. The trajectories are given by the 3D motion of the centre point of the tracked ellipsoid. The cyclic sequence of working actions in an engine assembly scenario is known to our system. However, it may be interrupted by "unknown" motion patterns. To allow an online action recognition, we apply a sliding window approach.

Due to the fact that our system is designed for safe human–robot interaction, we implemented a recognition stage with two levels (Fig. 4). At the first level, a decision is made whether the human worker performs a known working action (regular mode) or an unknown motion (safety mode) based on a set of trajectory classifiers [8]. In the safety mode (level 1), the system may prepare to slow down or halt the industrial robot. The regular mode (level 2) defines the cyclic working process performed by the human worker. It is implemented as a HMM in which the hidden state is continuously estimated by a particle filter.

3.1   Trajectory Classifiers

The state of level 1 according to Fig. 4 is determined by a set of classifiers [8] based on features extracted from the trajectory data in the sliding window of size $W = 8$ time steps for all tracked objects. Movements between two working actions (transfer motion) are recognised by a transfer classifier. Since it is known where the worker has to tighten a screw or to fit a plug, a second classifier

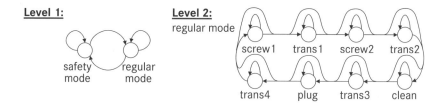

Fig. 4. Two-level architecture of the action recognition stage

(working action classifier) is used for recognising working actions by incorporating spatial context for the actions "screw 1", "screw 2", "clean", and "plug". The reference locations are obtained based on the known 3D pose of the engine. A third classifier (distance classifier) is applied to the result of the working action classifier and decides whether the recognised working action is a known one, since such motion patterns can only occur close to the 3D object associated with that action. The combination of the three classifiers, resulting in an output discriminant vector for the six classes "unknown", "transfer", "screw 1", "screw 2", "clean", and "plug", is described in detail in [8].

3.2   Recognition of the Sequence of Actions

The decision whether the system is in safety mode or in regular mode is made based on the result of the distance classifier and the matching accuracy of the particle weights in level 2, where the observed trajectories are analysed with respect to the occurrence of known working actions. Similar to [11] we apply a particle filter based matching of a non-stationary HMM in order to recognise the sequence of working actions. The HMM of level 2 (cf. Fig. 4) is derived from the known cyclic working task, defined by a parameter set $\lambda = (S, A, B, \Pi)$ where S denotes the set of hidden states, A the non-stationary (time-dependent) transition probabilities, B the probabilities of observing the visible state v_k given the hidden state s_i, and Π the initial probability of state s_i. We assigned a set of reference trajectories to each hidden state $\{q_1, \ldots, q_n\}$ based on the associated working action. Our approach relies on a small number of reference trajectories which are defined by manually labelled training sequences.

The CONDENSATION algorithm is used to estimate the state of the HMM based on temporal propagation of a set of N weighted particles $((\mathbf{s}_t^{(1)}, w_t^{(1)}), \ldots, (\mathbf{s}_t^{(N)}, w_t^{(N)}))$ with the particle state $\mathbf{s}_t^{(i)} = (q_t^{(i)}, \phi_t^{(i)}, id_t^{(i)})$. The particle $\mathbf{s}_t^{(i)}$ contains the hidden state $q_t^{(i)}$, the current phase $\phi_t^{(i)}$ in this hidden state, and the index $id_t^{(i)}$ of the relevant object. The phase indicates the fraction by which the working action has been completed. The resampling step reallocates a certain fraction of the particles with regard to the predefined initial distribution Π and the currently tracked objects. The propagation of the weighted particles over time consists of a prediction, selection, and update step as follows:

Select: Selection of $N - M$ particles $\mathbf{s}_{t-1}^{(i)}$ according to their respective weight $w_{t-1}^{(i)}$ and random distribution of M new particles over all other states in the HMM.

Predict: The current state of each particle $\mathbf{s}_t^{(i)}$ is predicted based on the selected particles, the HMM structure (cf. Fig. 4), the current phase $\phi_t^{(i)}$, and the object index $id_t^{(i)}$. The transition probabilities denoted by A are not stationary but depend on the current phase $\phi_t^{(i)}$ of the particle. The phase is always restricted to the interval $[0, 1]$. A high phase value indicates that the reference trajectories are almost traversed and that there is an increased probability to proceed to the next state.

Update: To compute the weight $w_t^{(i)}$ of a predicted particle $\mathbf{s}_t^{(i)}$, the 3D data in the current sliding window are matched with the current sub-trajectory of all reference trajectories of the hidden state $q_t^{(i)}$. The current sub-trajectory in a hypothesis trajectory is defined by its phase $\phi_t^{(i)}$ and length W. The final weight is given by the Levenshtein distance on trajectories (LDT) measure [7] of the best matching reference trajectory multiplied by the discriminant value associated with the corresponding action class of the hidden state $q_t^{(i)}$.

4   Experimental Evaluation

We evaluate the proposed tracking and action recognition system using real-world image sequences acquired with a trinocular camera system with a horizontal and vertical baseline of 150 mm. The time interval between subsequent image triples amounts to 71 ms. In each test sequence, a person performs a pre-defined sequence of working actions. The background is fairly cluttered, the contrast between the persons and the background tends to be low, and the persons are wearing various kinds of clothes e.g. with long and short sleeves and with and without work gloves.

4.1   Evaluation of the 3D Mean-Shift Tracking Stage

The metric evaluation of the tracking stage of our system is performed on nine test sequences with five different test persons. Sequences 1–5 display various persons working in an office environment, while sequences 6–9 show persons working in a typical industrial production environment. Each sequence consists of at least 300 image triples. The average distance of the test persons to the camera system varies from 2.7 m to 3.3 m. As required by the envisioned application scenario we use greyscale images. The ground truth data consist of the coordinates of three reference points in the world coordinate system, which correspond to the fingertip, the wrist, and the upper forearm. To extract the ground truth data, three markers were attached to the hand-forearm limb. The positions of the markers in the images were measured with a chequerboard corner localisation routine [10], and their 3D coordinates were determined based on bundle adjustment.

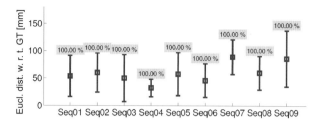

Fig. 5. Positional error of the mean-shift tracking stage (Euclidean distance with respect to ground truth data (GT)) for the nine test sequences. The "100%" labels indicate that the method is able to track the hand performing the working actions completely across all test sequences.

For the image sequences and ground truth data, see http://aiweb.techfak.uni-bielefeld.de/content/hand-forearm-limb-data-set.

In the test sequences, an average number of 6.3 objects are tracked simultaneously by the mean-shift method. These objects always comprise the right hand of the person (which performs the working actions). The ellipsoid associated with the right hand is indicated manually once for the first image of the sequence. When tracking fails and the hand gets lost, the corresponding ellipsoid is re-initialised based on the ellipsoid located closest to the last known hand position. The average Euclidean distances between the estimated hand position and the ground truth data (here: the coordinates of the wrist point) along with the corresponding standard deviations are depicted for each test sequence in Fig. 5. Due to the re-initialisation step, our system is able to track the hand performing the working actions completely across all test sequences, as indicated by the labels on top of the error bars in Fig. 5. The average Euclidean distance corresponds to 45–90 mm, the standard deviation to 16–50 mm. The metric accuracy of the hand position estimated by the 3D mean-shift approach is thus comparable to the accuracy of the wrist point estimated by the model based shape flow method [9] on the same data set. In the latter work, however, the full 3D pose of the articulated hand-forearm limb, including internal degrees of freedom, is determined along with its temporal derivative.

Fig. 6 illustrates the results of the mean-shift tracking approach for four test sequences. In part, large values of the Euclidean distance between the estimated hand position and the ground truth data may result from the fact that the centre of the ellipsoid associated with the hand does not necessarily correspond to the wrist but rather to the middle of the hand (cf. second example in Fig. 6).

The average runtime of our Matlab implementation of the 3D mean-shift tracking algorithm corresponds to 260 ms per tracked ellipsoid on a 2.4 GHz Core 2 Duo processor. For a C++ implementation we thus expect frame rates around 10 fps, which is at least an order of magnitude higher than the frame rate achievable with the model-based approach described in [9]. In our experiments, the stereo and optical flow information was determined offline but is computable nearly in video real-time using graphics hardware (cf. e.g. [6,13]).

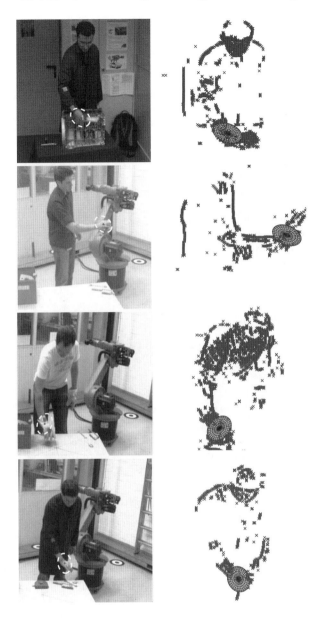

Fig. 6. Example results of the mean-shift tracking algorithm for four test sequences. Left column: Reprojected ellipsoid associated with the person's right hand. Right column: Moving 3D points in the scene along with the 3D tracking result.

4.2   Evaluation of the Action Recognition Stage

The action recognition stage of our system is evaluated by analysing 20 trinocular real-world test sequences acquired from different viewpoints. The sequences

Table 1. Action recognition results in terms of the average action recognition rate (RR), the average word error rate (WER), and the average and standard deviation of the temporal offsets

	screw1	screw2	clean	plug
total [#]	26	27	31	33
correct [#]	24	26	29	31
duplicate[#]	2	2	3	3
deletion [#]	2	1	2	1
substitution [#]	0	0	0	1
insertion [#]	1	2	0	0
recognition rate (RR) [%]	92.3	96.3	93.5	93.9
word error rate (WER) [%]	11.5	11.1	6.5	6.1
temporal offset (begin):				
mean [ms]	−324	116	625	−31
std [ms]	754	826	1192	1262
temporal offset (end):				
mean [ms]	−71	78	−461	572
std [ms]	822	1060	1458	1707

contain working actions performed by eight different test persons in front of a complex cluttered working environment. The distance of the test persons to the camera system amounts to 2.2–3.3 m. For training, only two sequences in which the working actions are performed by two different individuals were used. Only these two individuals (teachers) are well trained. The teacher-based approach is motivated by our application scenario, in which workers are generally trained by only a few experts. We assigned ground truth labels manually to all images of the training and test sequences. All results were obtained with a total number of $N = 500$ particles and $M = 100$ uniformly distributed particles. Table 1 shows that the system achieves an average action recognition rate (RR) of more than 90% on the test sequences. The average word error rate (WER), which is defined as the sum of insertions, deletions, and substitutions, divided by the total number of test patterns, amounts to less than 10%. The action recognition results in Table 1 are similar to those achieved in [8], where the model-based tracking approach described in [9] is used to extract the trajectory data. In contrast to [8] where a single object is analysed, objects performing known actions are extracted out of a multitude of tracked objects in this study.

Beyond the recognition of working actions, our system is able to recognise disturbances, occurring e.g. when the worker interrupts the sequence of working actions by blowing his nose. The system then enters the safety mode and returns to the regular mode as soon as the working actions continue. Fig. 7 (top) depicts the tracked objects and the recognition history of the relevant object. Fig. 7 (bottom) shows the final action recognition result compared to the ground truth data (GT) (red: screw 1; black: screw 2; green: clean; brown: plug; blue: transfer). On the average, our system recognises the working actions with a temporal offset of several tenths of a second when compared to the manually defined beginning

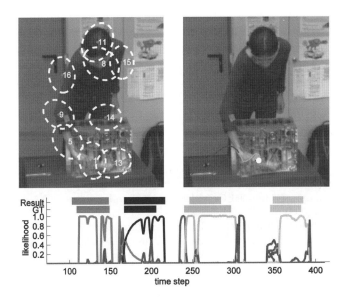

Fig. 7. Recognition of working actions for an example image sequence. Upper left: All objects tracked by the mean-shift algorithm. Upper right: Trajectory of the object assigned to known working actions by the action recognition stage. Bottom: Likelihoods of the individual actions for a complete sequence, recognition result, and manually labelled ground truth (GT) (red: screw 1; black: screw 2; green: clean; brown: plug; blue: transfer).

of an action, where the standard deviations are always larger than the mean values. One should keep in mind, however, that our manually assigned action labels are not necessarily perfectly accurate.

The computation time per image of the action recognition stage amounts to less than 1 s in our Matlab implementation, such that we expect less than 100 ms per image for a C++ implementation.

5   Summary and Conclusion

In this study we have introduced a method for 3D trajectory based recognition of and discrimination between different working actions. A two-stage mean-shift algorithm is used for detection and 3D tracking of all moving objects in the scene. Sequences of working actions have been recognised with a particle filter based non-stationary HMM framework, relying on the spatial context, a trajectory classification, and a similarity matching between observed 3D trajectories and a set of reference trajectories. For our test sequences, the average Euclidean distance between the estimated position of the hand performing the working actions and the ground truth data corresponds to 45–90 mm and the standard deviation to 16–50 mm. The action recognition stage of the system is able to extract the relevant object from a multitude of tracked objects. The average word error rate on the real-world data set amounts to less than 10%. The action recognition results are comparable to those achieved using a computationally much more complex model-based tracking approach. Our system is able to detect interruptions of the sequence of working actions by temporarily entering a safety mode. The evaluation results render our system a promising, computationally efficient approach to 3D body tracking and action recognition in complex real-world environments.

References

1. Black, M.J., Jepson, A.D.: A probabilistic framework for matching temporal trajectories: Condensation-based recognition of gestures and expressions. In: Burkhardt, H.-J., Neumann, B. (eds.) ECCV 1998. LNCS, vol. 1406, pp. 909–924. Springer, Heidelberg (1998)
2. Bradski, G.R.: Real time face and object tracking as a component of a perceptual user interface. In: Workshop on Appl. of Computer Vision, pp. 214–219 (1998)
3. Cheng, Y.: Mean shift, mode seeking, and clustering. IEEE Trans. Pattern Anal. Mach. Intell. 17(8), 790–799 (1995)
4. Comaniciu, D., Ramesh, V., Meer, P.: Real-time Tracking of Non-Rigid Objects Using Mean Shift. In: IEEE Conf. on Computer Vision and Pattern Recognition, vol. 2, pp. 142–149 (2000)
5. Comaniciu, D., Ramesh, V., Meer, P.: Kernel-based object tracking. IEEE Trans. Pattern Anal. Mach. Intell. 25(5), 564–577 (2003)
6. Gehrig, S.K., Eberli, F., Meyer, T.: A Real-Time Low-Power Stereo Vision Engine Using Semi-Global Matching. In: Fritz, M., Schiele, B., Piater, J.H. (eds.) ICVS 2009. LNCS, vol. 5815, pp. 134–143. Springer, Heidelberg (2009)
7. Hahn, M., Krüger, L., Wöhler, C.: 3D action recognition and long-term prediction of human motion. In: Gasteratos, A., Vincze, M., Tsotsos, J.K. (eds.) ICVS 2008. LNCS, vol. 5008, pp. 23–32. Springer, Heidelberg (2008)
8. Hahn, M., Krüger, L., Wöhler, C., Kummert, F.: 3D action recognition in an industrial environment. In: Ritter, H., Sagerer, G., Dillmann, R., Buss, M. (eds.) Proc. 3rd Int. Workshop on Human-Centered Robotic Systems, Cognitive Systems Monographs, vol. 6, pp. 141–150. Springer, Heidelberg (2009)
9. Hahn, M., Krüger, L., Wöhler, C., Sagerer, G., Kummert, F.: Spatio-temporal 3D Pose Estimation and Tracking of Human Body Parts in an Industrial Environment. In: Oldenburger 3D-Tage (2010)
10. Krüger, L., Wöhler, C.: Accurate chequerboard corner localisation for camera calibration and scene reconstruction. Submitted to Pattern Recog. Lett. (2009)
11. Li, Z., Fritsch, J., Wachsmuth, S., Sagerer, G.: An object-oriented approach using a top-down and bottom-up process for manipulative action recognition. In: Franke, K., Müller, K.-R., Nickolay, B., Schäfer, R. (eds.) DAGM 2006. LNCS, vol. 4174, pp. 212–221. Springer, Heidelberg (2006)
12. Tyagi, A., Keck, M., Davis, J.W., Potamianos, G.: Kernel-Based 3D Tracking. In: IEEE Conf. on Computer Vision and Pattern Recognition (2007)
13. Wedel, A., Pock, T., Zach, C., Bischof, H., Cremers, D.: An improved algorithm for TV-L1 optical flow computation. In: Dagstuhl Visual Motion Analysis Workshop (2008)
14. Wedel, A., Rabe, C., Vaudrey, T., Brox, T., Franke, U., Cremers, D.: Efficient dense scene flow from sparse or dense stereo data. In: Forsyth, D., Torr, P., Zisserman, A. (eds.) ECCV 2008, Part I. LNCS, vol. 5302, pp. 739–751. Springer, Heidelberg (2008)

Feature Representations for the Recognition of 3D Emblematic Gestures

Jan Richarz and Gernot A. Fink

Intelligent Systems Group, Robotics Research Institute
TU Dortmund University, Dortmund, Germany
{jan.richarz,gernot.fink}@udo.edu

Abstract. In human-machine interaction, gestures play an important role as input modality for natural and intuitive interfaces. The class of gestures often called "emblems" is of special interest since they convey a well-defined meaning in an intuitive way. We present an approach for the visual recognition of 3D dynamic emblematic gestures in a smart room scenario using a HMM-based recognition framework. In particular, we assess the suitability of several feature representations calculated from a gesture trajectory in a detailed experimental evaluation on realistic data.

Keywords: 3D dynamic gesture recognition, human-machine interaction, smart rooms, time-series analysis.

1 Introduction

In building interfaces for Human-Machine-Interaction (HMI), different facets of natural inter-human interaction should be taken into account to realize intuitive interfaces. This includes the analysis of speech and gesture, as well as gaze, facial expression and body language. While some of these modalities may be very subtle and subject to considerable variations between users, speech and gestures are much more explicit. Thus, they have been studied extensively as important cues for interpreting user intents and realizing human-centered interfaces. In this publication, we focus on the automatic visual recognition of dynamic arm gestures. For natural interaction, there should be as few constraints as possible imposed on the user. In particular, users should be able to interact with the interface from anywhere in the environment, which requires view- and position-invariant recognition. To achieve this, we aim at recognising gestures in 3D space using a (potentially arbitrary) multi-camera setup.

Since the term gesture has been used in very different meanings (including fingertip motion and full-body actions), some clarification is needed. In linguistics and semiotics, a variety of gesture taxonomies exist (cf. eg. [1]). Generally, three major classes of gestures can be identified, with speech-accompanying subconscious gesticulation at one end of the spectrum, artificial well-defined sign languages at the other, and emblems in between. The first is inherently multimodal [2] and difficult to interpret due to its subconscious nature. Sign language typically lacks intuitiveness and requires special user training.

A.A. Salah et al. (Eds.): HBU 2010, LNCS 6219, pp. 113–124, 2010.
© Springer-Verlag Berlin Heidelberg 2010

Emblems are gestural actions that are well-defined and convey a certain meaning on their own, but are understood intuitively since they are established within a certain cultural region. Therefore, they are especially suited for natural HMI. We focus on one-armed emblems performed by cooperative users.

Dynamic arm gestures are defined by subsequent movements of a few prominent points (e.g. joint positions) relative to the body. Thus, given a spatio-temporal track of these points, recognition is a problem of time-series or trajectory analysis. Results from other work on gesture analysis (cf. Sec. 2) suggest that, for emblems, this problem reduces to analysis of the hand trajectory. Indeed, measurements like in [3] indicate that, for simple stroke-like arm movements the trajectories of the joints and hand are qualitatively similar. Furthermore, analyzing typical emblematic gestures shows that they tend to be composed of a relatively small set of basic movements. This suggests strong similarities to the field of on-line handwriting recognition, where the track of one point (the pen tip) is recognized based on basic units (characters or strokes) and some features describing their general spatio-temporal evolution (cf. e.g. [4]).

Accordingly, we exploit findings from this field and investigate whether 3D emblematic arm gestures can be recognized using approaches inspired by on-line handwriting recognition. Since the latter is a 2D problem, the concepts must either be transferred to 3D, or the 3D gesture trajectory has to be projected to some appropriate 2D frame. We will investigate both possibilities in the following. In particular, we propose representing a gesture by projection on its principal plane of motion, which we call the action plane. For the acquisition of gesture trajectories, we build upon our previous work on 3D pointing gesture recognition [5] and saliency-based view selection in multi-camera setups [6].

2   Related Work

The relevance of gestures for natural HMI – either as exclusive cue or as part of multi-modal systems – is undisputed. However, most work in the field focuses either on the recognition of specially crafted artificial gesture alphabets and sign language [7,8] or on the interpretation of full-body movements, generally referred to as action recognition (cf. e.g. [9] for a recent survey, [10,11]). While the shortcomings of artificial gesture alphabets regarding their intuitiveness have already been mentioned, full-body action recognition is related closely to emblematic gesture analysis, but typically operates on a higher level of abstraction: Instead of creating an input modality for HMI, it rather aims at analysing human behavior in surveillance settings, or for scene understanding. Approaches from the field may, however, also be suitable for gestural interfaces.

Regarding the classification of emblematic dynamic gestures, the dominant approach is to represent gestures as trajectories in some reference frame and classify them with probabilistic graphical models encoding temporal relationships. In particular, (Hidden) Markov Models ((H)MM) have been used extensively. Good results have been achieved on gestures representing arabic digits [12] using only trajectory orientation information. In [13], bimanual movements are classified by combining the trajectory with a shape descriptor of the hand, whereas [14] use the centroid positions of hand candidates and their mean optical flow. [15] transform the spatiotemporal trajectory to discrete symbols with a Self-Organizing Map, and classify the symbol sequence together with optical flow features in a MM framework. Combinations of 2D hand trajectories and associated inertial sensor data have also been used [16,17]. Gaussian density features extracted at visual interest points are applied in [18], and gestures are classified using a protocol learning strategy.

In on-line handwriting recognition (cf. [4] for an overview of the field), state of the art recognizers are typically either also based on HMM [19] or on connectionist approaches [20]. However, the features used to describe time-series of points are much more diverse. Examples include velocity and curvature along with shape-describing features of short trajectory segments [20] or Hu moments [21]. [22] and [19] use pen pressure, vicinity, curliness and features relating the trajectory to the baseline. Appearance-based descriptors and higher-level structural features, like ascenders, descenders and crossings, are also frequently combined with online trajectory features (e.g. in [20][19]). Some of these features lack a straightforward resemblance for the task of gesture recognition. E.g., pen pressure is not available, and features referring to a baseline (like ascenders and descenders) are difficult to apply, since, opposed to handwriting, it is not clear what the baseline of a gesture should be. However, a multitude of interesting features for trajectory representation remain, and impressive results have been published in the field. To the best of our knowledge, no previous work exists applying similar features to 3D dynamic arm gesture recognition, and we will demonstrate their suitability in this work.

3   Visual Recognition of 3D Emblematic Gestures

As stated before, our goal is the automatic recognition of one-armed dynamic emblems performed by cooperative, but untrained users. Restricting the interaction space to a predefined area or camera setup, as well as requiring the user to wear markers or tracking gear, would impose severe limitations on the general applicability of such a system. Furthermore, the pose or orientation of the user with respect to the interface should not be restricted. Therefore, we aim at a 3D recognition framework based on visual cues utilizing off-the-shelf cameras in a principally arbitrary multicamera setup. Figure 1 shows an overview of the proposed approach. We will describe the individual components in the following.

The key assumption is that emblematic arm gestures may be analysed using the trajectory of the active hand alone, which means that no expensive full-body model tracking is required. While this seems like a strong assumption, its validity is indicated by the good results reported in the related literature. The first step is the extraction of 2D spatiotemporal hand and head trajectories in the individual camera images. These are then combined to a 3D trajectory. Also, the estimation of the action plane from the trajectory points and the representation of projected trajectories is shown. The main contribution lies in the assessment of different

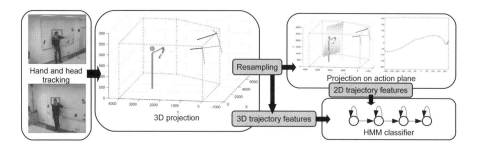

Fig. 1. Overview of the proposed approach

alternate feature representations inspired by on-line handwriting recognition, which will be done in a detailed experimental evaluation on a realistic data set. We conclude with a discussion of the results.

3.1   2D Trajectory Acquisition

In order to extract gesture trajectories, persons and their gesturing hands have to be detected first. We apply a detector based on Histograms of oriented Gradients (HoG) and a Multi-Layer Perceptron classifier which does not rely on skin color or face structure, but uses the shape of the head-shoulder line instead. Therefore, it is able to detect persons under a large variety of poses and viewing angles. The centers of the detection rectangle in subsequent frames form the head trajectory. Hand candidates are found combining motion detection with a personalized skin color model trained on-line [5]. The result is a series of spatial image coordinates for head and hands, along with temporal information. These are postprocessed using Gaussian smoothing to eliminate detection jitter, and short tracks of duplicate points are removed.

3.2   3D Combination

Given spatiotemporal trajectories from at least two cameras, the original 3D gesture trajectory can be reconstructed. First, the individual trajectories have to be aligned. We use a simple greedy aggregation algorithm taking into account temporal differences and reconstruction errors of pairs of data points. For the somewhat idealised data we use here (cf. Sec. 5.1), this is sufficient. Note that, in a multi-camera setting, a view selection algorithm can be applied choosing the two "best" views according to some global criteria [6]. Aligned trajectory points are then projected to 3D by ray casting.

It should be pointed out that our cameras are not synchronised. Therefore, and because of detection inaccuracies and the discretization of the image plane, the rays will generally be skewed. Thus, the projection is calculated as follows: Given two aligned points $\mathbf{p}_i^t = (p_{xi}^t, p_{yi}^t)$, $\mathbf{q}_j^t = (p_{xj}^t, p_{yj}^t)$ from cameras i and j at time t (we omit these indices in the following for readability), their corresponding

3D rays $\mathbf{r}_p = \mathbf{c}_i + \gamma\mathbf{p}'$ and $\mathbf{r}_q$ are obtained by backprojection using the camera calibration matrices. Here, $\mathbf{c}_i$ is the projection center of camera i, $\mathbf{p}'$ is the ray's directional vector, and similar for $\mathbf{r}_q$. The two directional vectors along with one of the projection centers define a plane $\mathcal{P} : \mathbf{n}^T\mathbf{x} - \mathbf{n}^T\mathbf{c}_i = 0$ with $\mathbf{n} = \mathbf{p}' \times \mathbf{q}'$. It contains one of the rays and is parallel to the other with distance d. Let $\mathbf{v}$ be the intersection point calculated after translating both rays into the plane. The reconstructed 3D point $\mathbf{u}$ is then given by linear interpolation

$$\mathbf{u} = (1 - \frac{\alpha_i}{\alpha_i + \alpha_j}) \cdot \mathbf{v} + (1 - \frac{\alpha_j}{\alpha_i + \alpha_j}) \cdot (\mathbf{v} + d\mathbf{n}) \tag{1}$$

where α_i and α_j are some confidence measures for the point positions in the individual images. Setting them to equal values yields the mean point along the direction of $\mathbf{n}$ where the two rays are closest. Candidate selection or rejection can be done based on d. The resulting 3D trajectory finally is resampled and smoothed using curvature-aware impulse resampling [22].

3.3   The Action Plane

Classifying gesture trajectories without seriously limiting the amount of allowed variation according to, e.g., viewpoint, gesturing speed or spatial expansion, cannot be performed reliably on raw spatial coordinates. Normalization to some common reference and abstraction from the absolute positions is necessary. A simple approach to achieve this are derivative features that do not encode the absolute values of trajectory points, but their consecutive changes. However, these may still depend on the external alignment of the trajectory in 3D space.

Another possibility we investigate here arises from our observation that, for most natural emblems, the 3D trajectory exhibits an inherent planar characteristic. This suggests that 3D emblem trajectories may be represented without too much loss of information by projecting them on an appropriate plane. A similar assumption has been made in [16] to compensate for camera pan and tilt. Opposed to them, however, in our setup the plane may be oriented arbitrarily in space, and will only rarely coincide with any of the image planes. We call this concept the action plane in the following, and show how an estimation of such a plane can be derived and used as a common reference for normalization.

Suppose we have a 3D trajectory $\mathbf{T} = [\mathbf{t}_1...\mathbf{t}_n]$ with n points $\mathbf{t}_i = (t_{xi}, t_{yi}, t_{zi})$. We seek a plane $\mathcal{P} : \mathbf{n}^T\mathbf{x} - \lambda = 0$ that best approximates $\mathbf{T}$. This can be formulated as a least-squares regression problem with the objective function

$$f(\mathbf{n}) = \sum_{i=1}^{n} (n_x t_{xi} + n_y t_{yi} + n_z t_{zi} - \lambda)^2 \to Min \tag{2}$$

assuming that $\mathbf{n}$ is normalized to unit length. This is a well-known problem, and the sought plane normal $\mathbf{n}$ is given by the Eigenvector corresponding to the smallest Eigenvalue of $\mathbf{\Psi} = \mathbf{M}^T\mathbf{M}$, $\mathbf{M} = \{t_{x,i} - \bar{t}_x \quad t_{y,i} - \bar{t}_y \quad t_{z,i} - \bar{t}_z\}$, with the data mean $\bar{\mathbf{t}} = \frac{1}{n}\sum_{i=1}^{n} \mathbf{t}_i$.

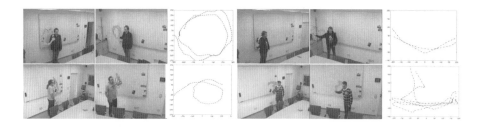

Fig. 2. Examples of action plane projections. Original images with overlaid hand trajectories and their 2D representations for "circle" (left) and "horizontal wave" (right)

Calculating a regression plane in this way may result in a solution strongly influenced by outlier points. Therefore, the above procedure is carried out on the concensus set obtained from RANSAC. Since $\mathbf{n}$ and $-\mathbf{n}$ correspond to the same global orientation of the plane and the sign depends on the choice of points, $\mathbf{n}$ is forced to always point towards the mean of head detections. In our experiments, this yields a good estimate of a gesture's principal plane of motion. When the above procedure is applied incrementally to online data, a smoothness constraint should be applied to the orientation of $\mathbf{n}$ to avoid abrupt changes. One possibility is adding a penalty term taking into account the angle between two consecutive plane normals in the model selection phase of RANSAC.

Projecting $\mathbf{T}$ onto $\mathcal{P}$ requires an 2D orthonormal coordinate system in $\mathcal{P}$. An obvious choice are the remaining two Eigenvectors of $\mathbf{M}$. This results also in a normalization of the global gesture orientation, which may not always be intended. Therefore, we also evaluate a solution where one coordinate axis is forced to be parallel to the ground plane. The trajectory mean $\bar{\mathbf{t}}$ is chosen as coordinate origin. Figure 2 shows some projection results.

3.4   Classification with Hidden Markov Models

HMMs are a popular tool for time-series analysis because of their ability to model temporal relationships between samples in a sound probabilistic framework and provide an integrated approach for segmentation and classification. Their properties are well understood and efficient algorithms exist for training and decoding. Therefore, they have been widely used, and their discriminative power has been demonstrated on a wide variety of tasks.

We use an open source HMM toolbox [23] to train one model for each gesture. The number of states in each model is initialised automatically according to the minimum observation length of the respective gesture class. Emission probabilities are modelled by Gaussian mixture densities with diagonal covariances. The resulting codebook is shared among models and states, i.e. we have semi-continuous HMMs. Classification is done according to the maximum path probability calculated by Viterbi alignment.

4 Trajectory Features

The features used for representing gesture trajectories are mostly motivated by [20]. Some changes are made to adapt them to the different characteristics of the data. In order to increase robustness against noise and detection errors, the features are calculated in a sliding window scheme. Let w be the window size, and let $\mathbf{O}_i = \mathbf{o}_i, ..., \mathbf{o}_{i+w-1}$ be the trajectory points in the ith sliding window and $\mathbf{o}_i^m$ the median point. Then, the features are calculated as follows:

Raw trajectory: Mean point of the window: $\bar{\mathbf{O}}_i = \frac{1}{w}\sum_k \mathbf{o}_k, k = i...i + w - 1$

Normalized trajectory: $\hat{\mathbf{O}}_i = \bar{\mathbf{O}}_i/\bar{h}$, where $\bar{h}$ is the average height of the person calculated from the trajectory of head positions.

Normalized polar trajectory: $\mathbf{P}_i = \{|\mathbf{r}_i|, \phi_i\}$. For the 3D case,
$\mathbf{r}_i = (\bar{\mathbf{O}}_i - \bar{\mathbf{H}}_i)/\bar{h}$, $\phi_i = \arctan(\sqrt{r_{xi}^2 + r_{yi}^2}/r_{zi})$, i.e. the radius between mean trajectory and mean head point inside the window normalized by the person's height and the elevation angle of their connecting line. Note that the azimuth angle would correspond to the global orientation of the person, so it is not included. For 2D, $|\mathbf{r}_i|$ and ϕ_i are polar coordinates in the plane relative to the coordinate origin.

Velocity: The mean velocity of data points in the window, i.e.
$\mathbf{v_i} = \frac{1}{w}\sum_{k=i+1}^{i+w-1}(\mathbf{o}_k - \mathbf{o}_{k-1})/(t_k - t_{k-1})$ where t_k is the time associated with $\mathbf{o}_k$. The mean length of the velocity vectors is also included.

Curvature: Curvature is defined as the cosine and sine of the angle between the vectors from $\mathbf{o}_i^m$ to $\mathbf{o}_i$ and $\mathbf{o}_{i+w-1}$.

Vicinity: These features are intended to describe the general shape of a feature window. Let $\mathbf{d_i} = \mathbf{o}_{i+w-1} - \mathbf{o}_i$ be the vector connecting the window boundaries. The vicinity features comprise the vicinity aspect $\alpha = (d_{yi} - d_{xi})/(d_{yi} + d_{xi})$ for 2D data and three values with permutations of the vector components for 3D data, the cosine and sine of the angle between $\mathbf{d}_i$ and the x-axis or ground plane, respectively, the normalized trajectory length $l_i = \sum_{k=i+1}^{i+w-1} |\mathbf{o}_k - \mathbf{o}_{k-1}|/|\mathbf{d}_i|$ and the average sum of squared distances between trajectory points and $\mathbf{d}_i$.

Orientation change: For two subsequent windows $\mathbf{O}_i$ and $\mathbf{O}_j$, the orientation change is calculated as the cosine and sine of the angle between $\mathbf{d_i}$ and $\mathbf{d_j}$.

Head distance: The mean distance between points in $\mathbf{O}_i$ and the mean head position $\bar{\mathbf{H}}_i$, normalized by $\bar{h}$. This feature encodes some very weak representation of the spatial relation between gesturing hand and head.

All features together yield 20 and 25-dimensional feature vectors for 2D and 3D points, respectively, and twice the size including derivative features.

5 Experiments

The main goal of this publication is the investigation of alternative features regarding their applicability to gesture trajectory recognition, in order to derive a richer representation and optimize recognition results. To this purpose, we have conducted a detailed experimental evaluation on a realistic dataset.

Fig. 3. Selected (cropped) examples of the gesture set with original trajectories overlaid. Gestures marked with (R) are repetitive, (r) indicates a gesture that may or may not be repetitive. From left to right: "circle"(r), "come here"(r), "down", "go away"(r), "pointing", "stop", "up", "horizontal wave"(R) and "vertical wave"(R).

5.1   Experimental Setup and Data

The evaluation took place in a realistic setup inside a smart conference room equipped with several Sony EVI D70P pan-tilt-zoom cameras. The cameras are mounted on the ceiling and are calibrated, but not synchronized. Throughout the experiments, the same pair of cameras was used. In neutral position, their principal axes form an angle of approximately 90°, but their orientations were changed several times during data recording.

A set of nine emblematic command gestures was chosen such that they either represent natural gestures that are commonly used, or their meaning can be understood intuitively. Some examples are shown in Fig. 3. The potential meanings they convey can be used in a variety of scenarios, e.g. directing a mobile robot, steering computational attention, or controlling services of the smart room. The set contains short one-stroke as well as more complicated repetitive gestures, and gestures that can be both. Note that the pointing gesture is not purely emblematic, since it can only be interpreted with additional context.

Short sequences of still images were recorded from 17 different people each performing one to three instances of each gesture with their right as well as their left arm. The sequences were captured with a resolution of 378 by 278 pixels at 20 Hz. No instructions on gesture speed, absolute or relative position, etc., were given. The subjects were allowed to move freely inside the cameras' fields of view, including their orientation with respect to the cameras. Thus, the dataset is quite challenging since it contains multiple viewpoints as well as considerable variations in gesture appearance, speed and trajectory diameter. In total, it contains 51217 images and 799 gesture instances.

The positions of hands and heads were annotated semi-automatically. First, the 2D head and hand detection algorithm was applied. The generated hypotheses were then inspected manually. Missing detections were added and erroneous hypotheses were corrected. In general, if a hypothesis from the detector was remotely correct, it was kept. The gesture instances were furthermore segmented manually, with considerable variations in starting and end points as well as number of repetitions. From the 2D trajectories obtained in this way, the 3D projections were computed using the described algorithm. The resampled trajectory lengths vary between 16 and 364 data points.

Table 1. Classification accuracy in % for single features (left) and respective derivative (Δ) features (right). The best results for each trajectory type are highlighted.

Feature	3D	2D-Ground	2D-PC	Δ3D	Δ2D-Ground	Δ2D-PC
Raw trajectory	59.3	65.0	59.4	**85.1**	62.7	**61.1**
Norm. cart. trajectory	80.0	**65.8**	57.1	44.2	21.3	23.7
Norm. polar trajectory	81.9	61.8	58.8	73.7	**66.5**	60.6
Curvature	40.3	40.3	39.8	48.6	48.2	47.1
Headdistance	61.3	61.3	**61.3**	27.0	27.0	24.2
Orientation change	44.6	46.7	45.6	48.6	48.2	49.9
Velocity	**83.0**	61.5	59.2	76.8	55.9	50.9
Vicinity	74.7	59.7	61.2	71.1	53.2	57.7

5.2   Results

First, each feature type is evaluated separately in order to assess the performance of individual features. Two types of HMM topologies (Linear left-right and Bakis) with different parameter sets were trained and evaluated using 17-fold cross-validation. In each iteration, 16 persons were used for training, and the remaining one for testing. Thus, the reported results are user-independent. For feature extraction, sliding window sizes of 5, 7 and 9 were applied, with 50% window overlap. Table 1 summarizes the best results for 3D trajectory features and 2D projection features using both described coordinate system choices (first coordinate axis parallel to ground plane, denoted as "Ground", and first axis chosen according to first principal component, denoted as "PC").

The best classification results in all cases were achieved using a Bakis model and a window size of five. For the 3D case, using the derivative of the raw trajectory yields a classification accuracy of 85.1%. Compared to this, the 2D features perform poorly, with best results of 66.5% and 61.3%, respectively. This may indicate that our assumption about the inherent planar nature of 3D emblematic gestures is invalid. On the other hand, this assumption is backed up by the low average reconstruction error of the projection (Tab. 2). Thus, the performance loss is more likely to be caused by the loss of positional information in relation to the body as a result of the projection and normalization. This is further indicated by the fact that choosing the 2D coordinate system according to the principal components of the 2D trajectory, thereby normalizing out the trajectory's global orientation, further degrades performance. In this case, the only feature type that encodes some weak relative positional information, the head distance, performs best.

For the remaining two trajectory types, the best results are achieved with derivative representations of the hand trajectory. This, on the one hand, confirms that classifying gestures based on their trajectory alone is indeed a suitable approach, on the other hand it shows that some abstraction from the raw trajectory is needed. As mentioned before, using derivatives of the trajectory is a very simple possibility of abstracting from the absolute spatial positions. Using

Table 2. Average reconstruction errors for projected 2D gesture trajectories

Gesture	RError (mm)	Gesture	RError (mm)	Gesture	RError (mm)
circle	18.8	comehere	15.2	down	15.0
goaway	13.7	pointing	9.6	stop	9.1
up	9.3	hor. wave	22.3	ver. wave	28.6

Table 3. Classification accuracy of feature combinations in %. Feature combinations are: FC1: Δ Raw traj. + velocity + vicinity + headdist; FC2: Δ Raw traj. + vel.; FC3: Δ Raw traj. + vic.; FC4: Δ Norm. polar traj. + vel. + vic.; FC5: Δ Norm. polar traj. + vel.; FC6: Δ Norm. polar traj. + vic.; FC7: vel. + vic.

Features	FC1	FC2	FC3	FC4	FC5	FC6	FC7
3D	82.4	84.4	82.2	83.1	**85.5**	80.4	81.0
2D Ground	64.0	**65.6**	63.0	64.8	**65.6**	62.7	65.0
2D 1st PC	63.3	64.2	62.5	63.7	**65.0**	62.7	63.2

the raw trajectory results in a severe performance loss (59.3% classification accuracy) for the 3D case, while in the 2D case, where the "raw" trajectory is already normalized due to the projection, the results are close to the best. Considering the alternative feature representations, the velocity profile and vicinity features also yield promising results on our data, while orientation change and curvature seem less suited for the task.

Following these findings, combinations of the best-performing trajectory representations with velocity and vicinity features were evaluated, along with the head distance, which seems to be beneficial in the 2D case. The results are summarized in Tab. 3. No improvement in classification accuracy could be achieved, and the results of most combinations are comparable. This suggests that the different feature types are highly correlated. Furthermore, the increased dimensionality of the features leads to a higher complexity of the model, and much more data is needed to accurately estimate the parameters, which may be detrimental to the classifier's performance. Indeed, opposed to the previous experiment, the best results were achieved with Linear models and bigger window sizes (7 for 2D Ground, 9 for the others), which corresponds to simpler models with less states.

This raises the question whether better performance can be achieved by decorrelating the features. In order to assess this, a third experiment was carried out. After normalizing the features to zero mean and unit variance in order to account for the different feature dynamics, Principal Component Analysis (PCA) was applied to the complete feature representation (all feature types + derivatives) of the data, and classifiers were trained using different numbers of Principal Components. Table 4 summarizes the results.

Using PCA features indeed resulted in a substantial improvement in classification accuracy. The best result was again achieved using the first 10 PC of 3D features, which yielded 90.4% correct classifications, a relative improvement

Table 4. Classification accuracy for PCA features in %

No. of PC	1	2	3	4	5	6	7	8	9	10	12	15
3D		60.3	74.5	79.5	83.4	85.4	86.6	88.7	88.0	89.7	**90.4**	89.5	88.6
2D		48.7	63.1	69.3	71.5	72.1	73.2	73.1	76.0	76.5	76.7	76.3	**78.1**
2D+3D		48.1	65.8	76.3	83.0	83.6	83.7	84.4	86.6	86.0	85.6	85.4	**87.0**

of 6.2%. The 2D features still perform substantially worse, with 78.1% accuracy (17.4% relative improvement). However, these findings clearly indicate that emblematic gesture recognition can benefit from the incorporation of alternative feature representations. Surprisingly, combining 2D and 3D features yielded worse results compared to 3D only. A possible reason for this is the high dimensionality (90) of the combined feature space. The amount of available data may not be sufficient for estimating reliable statistics.

6 Summary

We presented an approach to hand-trajectory based 3D emblematic arm gesture recognition for Human-Machine Interaction in a smart room. In particular, we evaluated several alternative feature representations inspired by approaches in on-line handwriting recognition, and demonstrated their suitability for the task in a detailed experimental evaluation on realistic data. It could be shown that the incorporation of the additional features indeed improved the recognition results, and very promising overall results were achieved. The experiments were conducted with offline data, but all presented concepts and algorithms can be applied incrementally to online data in a straightforward way. We plan to extend the recognition approach to a hierarchic system building on strokes or subgesture units, aiming for a more powerful and flexible recognizer.

Furthermore, we suggested that natural emblematic gestures have an inherent planar nature, and proposed representing them by projection on an estimate of this inherent plane. While the recognition results for the projected data were inferior in our experiments, the estimated plane might serve as a cue for inferring the addressee of a gesture – a question we will investigate in our future research.

References

1. Kendon, A.: Current Issues in the Study of Gestures. In: The Biological Foundation of Gestures. Motor and Semiotic Aspects, pp. 23–47. Lawrence Erlbaum Assoc., Mahwah (1986)
2. Eisenstein, J., Davis, R.: Visual and linguistic information in gesture classification. In: Proc. Int. Conf. on Multimodal Interfaces, pp. 113–120 (2004)
3. Atkeson, C.G., Hollerbach, J.M.: Kinematic features of unrestrained vertical arm movements. Journal of Neuroscience 5(9), 2318–2330 (1985)

4. Plamondon, R., Srihari, S.N.: On-line and off-line handwriting recognition: A comprehensive survey. IEEE Trans. Patt. Anal. Mach. Int. 22(1), 63–84 (2000)
5. Richarz, J., Plötz, T., Fink, G.A.: Real-time detection and interpretation of 3d deictic gestures for interaction with an intelligent environment. In: Proc. Int. Conf. on Pattern Recognition (2008)
6. Schauerte, B., et al.: Multi-modal and multi-camera attention in smart environments. In: Proc. Int. Conf. on Multimodal Interfaces and Workshop on Machine Learning for Multi-Modal Interaction (2009)
7. Ong, S., Ranganath, S.: Automatic sign language analysis: A survey and the future beyond lexical meaning. IEEE Trans. Patt. Anal. Mach. Int. 27(6), 873–891 (2005)
8. Wang, Q., et al.: Viewpoint invariant sign language recognition. Computer Vision and Image Understanding 108, 87–97 (2007)
9. Turaga, P., Chellappa, R., Subrahmanian, V.S., Udrea, O.: Machine recognition of human activities: A survey. IEEE Trans. on Circuits and Systems for Video Technology 18(11), 1473–1488 (2008)
10. Thurau, C., Hlavac, V.: Pose primitive based human action recognition in videos or still images. In: Proc. Int. Conf. on Computer Vision and Pattern Recog. (2008)
11. Rapantzikos, K., Avrithis, Y., Kollias, S.: Dense saliency-based spatiotemporal feature points for action recognition. In: Proc. Int. Conf. on Computer Vision and Pattern Recognition, pp. 1454–1461 (2009)
12. Elmezain, M., et al.: A hidden markov model-based continuous gesture recognition system for hand motion trajectory. In: Proc. Int. Conf. on Pattern Recog. (2008)
13. Shamaie, A., Sutherland, A.: Bayesian fusion of hidden markov models for understanding bimanual movements. In: Proc. Int. Conf. on Automatic Face and Gesture Recognition (2004)
14. Alon, J., et al.: A unified framework for gesture recognition and spatiotemporal gesture segmentation. IEEE Trans. Patt. Anal. Mach. Int. 31(9), 1685–1699 (2009)
15. Caridakis, G., et al.: SOMM: Self organizing markov map for gesture recognition. Pattern Recognition Letters 31, 52–59 (2010)
16. Rett, J., Dias, J.: Gesture recognition using a marionette model and dynamic bayesian networks (DBNs). In: Campilho, A., Kamel, M.S. (eds.) ICIAR 2006. LNCS, vol. 4142, pp. 69–80. Springer, Heidelberg (2006)
17. Calinon, S., Billard, A.: Recognition and reproduction of gestures using a probabilistic framework combining PCA, ICA and HMM. In: Proc. Int. Conf. on Machine Learning, pp. 105–112 (2005)
18. Kirishima, T., Sato, K., Chihara, K.: Real-time gesture recognition by learning and selective control of visual interest points. IEEE Trans. Pattern Analyis and Mach. Int. 27(3), 351–364 (2005)
19. Schenk, J., Kaiser, M., Rigoll, G.: Selecting features in on-line handwritten whiteboard note recognition: SFS or SFFS? In: Proc. Int. Conf. on Document Analysis and Recognition, pp. 1251–1254 (2009)
20. Graves, A., et al.: A novel connectionist system for unconstrained handwriting recognition. Trans. Pattern Analyis and Mach. Int. 31(5), 855–868 (2009)
21. Daifallah, K., Zarka, N., Jamous, H.: Recognition-based segmentation algorithm for on-line arabic handwriting. In: Proc. Int. Conf. on Document Analysis and Recognition, pp. 886–890 (2009)
22. Fink, G.A., Wienecke, M., Sagerer, G.: Video-based on-line handwriting recognition. In: Proc. Int. Conf. on Document Analysis and Recognition, pp. 226–230 (2001)
23. Fink, G.A., Plötz, T.: Developing pattern recognition systems based on markov models: The ESMERALDA framework. Pattern Recognition and Image Analysis 18(2), 207–215 (2008)

Types of Help in the Teacher's Multimodal Behavior

Francesca D'Errico[1], Giovanna Leone[2], and Isabella Poggi[1]

[1] Dipartimento di Scienze dell'Educazione – Università Roma Tre – Via del Castro Pretorio 20, 00185 Roma, Italy
fderrico@uniroma3, poggi@uniroma3.it
[2] Dipartimento di Sociologia e Comunicazione - Sapienza Università di Roma – Via Salaria 113, 00185 Roma, Italy
giovanna.leone@uniroma1.it

Abstract. Psychological and social researches of last decades suggest that studying helping relationships may offer important suggestions for a better understanding of human behavior. In this work we present a study on the over-helping behaviors of teachers in their interaction with pupils, which may deepen our knowledge on how prosocial conducts can eventually produce unexpected effects over social interaction and cognitive development. To differentiate between helping and over-helping, we propose a taxonomy of communicative and non-communicative behaviors of teachers towards their pupils (Section 3), and an annotation scheme aimed to detect both helping and over-helping in teacher-pupil dyads (Sect. 4). Results of the study show how the annotation scheme presented allows to classify the different types of helping behavior, provides a reliable basis for the analysis of the teacher's behaviors, and suggest hints useful to empower teachers' self-reflection, in view of an improvement of the teacher-pupil relationship and of the pupils' learning processes.

Keywords: helping and over-helping, multimodal analysis.

1 Help and Over-Help

Within research on altruistic behavior, an intriguing issue is the role of helping in social relationships. According to Nadler [1] and Leone [2], help can convey the meaning of a caring intention of the helper, but it also has a dark side, at least in two senses. On the one hand, the helped person may feel in debt with the helper, and on the other hand the very fact of being helped may perpetuate the asymmetry of the relationship. To occur, in fact, any helping presupposes a power asymmetry between the helper and the helped one. This is why, from the point of view of the receiver, help offers a solution, but also makes socially visible the helped person's lack of autonomy and competence. If help is denied, autonomy is not at stake, but the joint solution is not reached, leading to a situation of under-help. If help is given, the solution is offered, but autonomy is threatened. Anyhow, although help always implies ambivalent consequences and is a turning point for the social relationship between helper and the helped person [2], it is important to arrive to distinguish help from over-help. Here, three questions are crucial:

A.A. Salah et al. (Eds.): HBU 2010, LNCS 6219, pp. 125–139, 2010.
© Springer-Verlag Berlin Heidelberg 2010

1. Is the problem to be solved possibly manageable by the helped one?
2. May a humiliating intention (vs. a caring one) be inferred from the helping behavior?
3. Do the consequences of the helping behavior increase (vs. decrease) the power asymmetry needed for the help to occur?

Over-help occurs when the answer to at least one of these questions is positive. If answer to n.2 is negative, then over-help is in good face, and we may speak of a *benevolent over-help*; if positive, we may label it as *malevolent over-help* [2].

Reviewing the literature on helping, we find very few contributions on over-helping, mostly focussed on malevolent over-helping (see for instance [3]).

Our contribution aims to describe the much less explored *benevolent over-help,* addressing our attention to teacher-pupil relationships. But, just because of the crucial importance of this relationship in shaping the future development of children's social competences in giving, asking and receiving help, we may not simply import the theoretical assumptions used to design empirical research on helping relationships between adults. In this case, in fact, the educational function of the adult implies a specific helping process that Lev Vygotskij, in the pioneering works he conducted in the somehow isolated context of Soviet psychology, defined as *"scaffolding"* [4; 5]. According to this classic theoretical framework, adults bearing an educational responsibility are expected to help children when they cope with a problem that lies in the zone of their proximal development (ZPD), defined by "the distance between what children can do by themselves and the next learning that they can be helped to achieve with competent assistance" [6]. The scaffolding concept implies therefore to *slow down helping behavior*, as soon as the child interiorizes the adult's help. The ultimate goal of scaffolding is, in fact, that the learner should to master the task autonomously, and the more knowledgeable other could withdraw [7].

In the adult-child relationship, therefore, the adult over-helps anytime s/he is not able to perceive that the child, having interiorized the knowledge and skills originally received by the adult him/herself, can produce an autonomous problem-solving. This misperception may be due to the "noise" of other distractive stimulations, as for instance a particularly high degree of anxiety of the adult, making it difficult for him/her to wait for a spontaneous problem-solving on the part of the child [2]. In this situation, the adult can exceedingly perseverate in helping behaviors for problems that are no longer comprised in the child's ZPD, not only interfering with, but also intruding upon the child's autonomous action. This difference between help and over-help can be clearly assessed by putting the adult-child dyad in a situation in which the child confronts a problem-solving s/he could easily overcome autonomously; such a situation makes it easier to see when the adult's help is a scaffolding, or when it is rather an intrusion into a plan of action that the child already masters. In a previous work, we used this research technique (for an overall comment on these methodological choices, [8]) to compare the over-helping tendencies of mothers of chronically ill children vs. mothers of healthy children. Results showed not only a significant increase of over-help for mothers of chronically ill children [9], but also a relevant role of the coping with negative emotions experienced by these mothers during problem solving activities performed by their chronically ill children [10]. Further elaborations made it clear that among these emotions mothers' anxiety was the crucial predictor for intrusive helping to occur [11]. A similar increase in over-help was evident for teacher-pupil dyads of an Italian primary school, when comparing interactions involving pupils of a socially stigmatized group (Rumanians) with interactions involving Italian children [12].

2   Help and Over-Help in the Teacher's Behavior: An Observational Study

In the previously quoted works, over-helping behavior has been shown to occur more for mothers of children with chronic disease mothers as opposed to mothers of healthy children and for teachers interacting with pupils of a stigmatized culture as opposed to teachers interacting with pupils of their own culture. Anyway, more fine-grained observations were needed, to further distinguish between different types of help and over-help. Hence, the goal of this work is to propose a way to better assess which type of help is being provided, through a careful analysis of multimodal behavior of teachers interacting with a pupil of a stigmatised culture.

2.1   Research Issue

The issue we address in this study is to distinguish the various types of helping and over-helping behaviors in teacher – pupil interaction, and to test whether the types of behaviors hypothesised can actually be found in teacher – pupil dyads. To do so we propose a taxonomy of helping behaviours provided by teachers to pupils, to cope with a problem the child could already solve autonomously. In this kind of interaction we could observe both helping and over-helping behaviours, therefore arriving to give more fine-grained examples of subtle differences distinguishing these two kinds of effective vs. superfluous scaffolding interactions [13]. We maintain in fact that a better assessment of the occurrence of helping or over-helping behaviours, through a very detailed analysis of two fragments of highly intrusive vs. low intrusive adult-child interactions, may offer a reliable method for the extraction of multimodal behaviour characterising adult-child helping interactions. In our opinion, this extraction could be later applied to more molar units of scaffolding interactions, so better distinguishing effective helping from unsuccessful over-helping. We propose therefore an annotation scheme for the analysis of the teacher's verbal and nonverbal, communicative and non communicative behaviour, from which is possible to recognize, in the continuum of adult-child interactions, some meaningful signals either of effective helping or of counter-productive over-helping.

2.2   Procedure

The study presented here is part of a larger study about helping and over-helping behavior, which analysed the interaction between Italian teachers and their Italian and Rumanian pupils. Rumanians are in fact, in the region where the study was conducted (Rome and its immediate surroundings), a numerous and negatively stigmatised immigrant group [15]. In that study [11], 21 teacher-pupil dyads were observed in an Italian Primary school, 9 teachers interacting with Rumanian pupils and 12 with Italian pupils, all children being between 6 and 8 years old, balanced for pupil gender.

All dyadic interactions were videotaped during a game simulation, designed to imply some crucial helping interactions, where the teacher could choose how and if help their pupils. The Scenario of the game was the Primitive village of the Flintstones family: the pupil acted as Bam Bam or Pebbles (the Flintsones' little boy or little girl), and the teacher as Wilma, the adult who knows all the secrets of the village. After introducing the scenario, the Master (the dinosaur Dino, played by the experimenter who conducted the game) explained that the village was threaten by a magic spell. In order to gain the magic formula breaking the spell, the child had to solve a riddle; in this step Wilma could choose to help (providing some hints), to over-help (telling how to make the complete picture) or not to help at all. This "helping warm-up" leaded to the next step of the game, where the crucial help sequence could be observed. The child had to solve a puzzle, that when completed showed a magical sentence "Hocus pocus...", and *this task was easy enough to be coped with autonomously by the child.* The teacher-Wilma was free to choose how and if help the child. When the child, thanks to the solution of the puzzle, pronounced the magic formula, the master finally declared the successful end of the game.

2.3 Helping and Over-Helping Teachers

In the study quoted above [11] we measured how much teachers help their pupils. Results showed that they tend to over-help more Rumanian pupils than Italian ones. Moreover, large differences were found between teachers in their helping strategies, leading to distinguish "high intrusive" teachers from "low intrusive" ones.

In this work we focus to a more fine-grained analysis only on two teacher-pupil dyads, already assessed by the previous research as a good example of "high intrusive" or "low intrusive" teacher.

To answer our research issue of a more fine-grained description of multimodal behaviours signalling either helping or over-helping interactions, it is first necessary to distinguish different types and forms of help and over-help. Moreover we have to describe and analyse the behaviors of teachers and pupils, to detect which of them imply a goal to help, and possibly to quantify the kind of help given. In order to this, we built a taxonomy of helping behaviors (Sect. 4) and an annotation scheme for the analysis of teachers' and students' behaviors (Sect. 5).

3 A Taxonomy of Helping and Over-Helping Behaviors

In this section we propose a taxonomy of helping and over-helping behaviors in teacher-pupil interaction. But before distinguishing them we must wonder what can we define as help and what as over-help.

In general, help can be defined as an action – or a deliberate non-action – of a person T which is aimed at favouring another person P, that is, at fulfilling some goal P has – even if P herself is not aware of having it. According to a view of learning as an active process, as seen in the above Vygotskian view of scaffolding, teaching can be conceived of as a series of behaviors aimed at providing a person with permanent capacities that make her autonomous, that is, potentially able to solve her own problems, to achieve her goals, by herself. In this sense, when a teacher is helping a pupil to complete some task, we can say she is providing an adequate level of help if she gives him partial – though useful – hints for task execution, or if she takes advantage of it to teach him general principles he could eventually transfer to future tasks; on the other hand, if she does the pupil's job herself when the child could already autonomously achieve the solution, she is over-helping him. More generally, a teacher is over-helping when she definitely tells the pupil what to do, while she is adequately helping when she sets the conditions for the pupil to understand what to do. From this point of view, a teacher's behaviors can be classified as to its level of help toward the student.

Table 1 below shows different possible types of helping and over-helping behaviors, distinguished along two dimensions, cutting across each other: Teacher's behavior and Pupil's processes. The former dimension refers to what the teacher does, while the latter refers to the processes, in the pupil's mind, to which the teacher's action or non-action is aimed, that is, the processes which, if favoured by the teacher's intervention, should have an impact over task performance. As to the dimension of Teacher's behavior, both help and over-help can be performed through *communication, non-communicative action*, or finally even by *non-action*. Obviously, we count as non-action only "deliberate non-action", that is, cases in which a teacher *could* have done something, but apparently *decided not to do* what she could have done. Within all three cases we can distinguish *technical, cognitive* and *affective* help or over-help, as to the dimension of the Pupil's process affected by the Teacher behavior. So we speak of *technical* help/over-help when an action or deliberate non-action directly allows or induces the pupil to perform some moves; of *cognitive* help/over-help if it provides information or cognitive strategies useful for task completion; of *affective* help/over-help if it induces affective states that may have an impact over task performance.

Starting from COMMUNICATIVE ACTIONS, typical cases of **technical help** are the communicative actions of providing information, hints, suggestions, but also criticism. Criticising may be seen as a form of adequate help to the extent to which, at least indirectly, it provides positive information as to how to do something. On the other hand, orders, directions, prohibitions can be seen as **technical over-help**. Here our definition of over-help can be specified. We classify as over-help those cases in which the helper is intruding into the helped person's free choice and autonomy. If I tell you: *"there is a nice piece here"*, I give you a chance to decide yourself whether or not to place it into the puzzle, while if I tell you *"put this there"*, I do not. Cases of **cognitive help** are those communicative actions that provide not specific solutions but reasoning strategies: for instance, when the teacher puts general questions to make the pupil reason, when she explains processes or proposes doubts in case the pupil is making mistakes. Moreover, if a teacher not only corrects the pupil's move, but explains why it is incorrect, making him reflect over his mistaken process of thought, we have a good example of cognitive help. On the other and, we consider **cognitive over-help** the cases of communication in which the teacher reveals specific moves or strategies the pupil could discover by himself.

Again, one can provide both help and over-help through "affective" communication, that is, communicative acts inducing or preventing emotions that could either favour or hinder the helped person's action. Cases of **helping affective communication** are the communicative actions of encouraging, inciting, praising, confirming, reassuring, sharing emotions with the pupil, and finally minimising his possible negative emotions; while a case of **over-helping affective communication** occurs, for example, if the teacher expresses compassion, or if she hurries the pupils, or simply induces stress in the pupils through the leaking of her own anxiety.

Let us come to **non-communicative actions**. Some of the movements a teacher may perform while assisting a pupil are not aimed at communicating but nonetheless they are helping – or over-helping – actions. Some can be seen as **technical helping behaviors** in that they fulfil the physical conditions for the pupil to do things well: for example, if the teacher prepares the game table, or places a lamp in the right place to let him see better. On the other hand, the teacher performs **technical over-helping** through non-communicative actions when she is substituting herself for the pupil by making the moves the pupil should do: for instance, handing the right piece of the puzzle or placing it herself. But she is over-helping also if she undoes his incorrect move, or corrects the pupil's move, by taking away a piece he put into the wrong slot, without telling him why it is incorrect.

A **non-communicative action** providing **cognitive help** occurs when the teacher does something to put the condition for some cognitive process to take place in the pupil's mind. A typical case is when the teacher turns the pieces of the puzzle in the right direction, so the pupil can better see how to place them. In this case, she is not communicating anything, but simply does something that in the pupil might trigger the insight for his problem solving.

A **non-communicative cognitive over-help** occurs if the teacher prevents the pupil from making a mistake, for instance by taking the piece away from his hand, or else if she undoes the pupil's error – say, by removing a piece placed by him – without an explanation. In an active view of learning that aims at developing the learner's autonomy, errors are an important step towards competence. So, if the teacher, after the pupil has made a mistake, corrects his move and explains why it is an incorrect move, this is adequate help; but if she prevents him from making errors, or if, in any other way, she does not give him the chance of understanding why an error is an error, this is over-help.

Finally, the teacher's action may also fulfil the affective conditions of the pupil's work, by influencing the pupil's emotional state. Thus, it provides **affective help** if it makes the environment warm, motivating or relaxing. Strangely enough, though, it is difficult to find examples of the corresponding affective over-help in the domain of non-communicative action. If for example the teacher's anxiety inadvertently leaks, thus inducing stress in the pupil, we consider this a case of – even unconscious – communication [15]. On the other side, if anxiety simply leads the teacher to do the pupil's moves herself, we consider this a technical over-help, albeit caused by the teacher's emotional state. In this case, her emotion is not communicated but directly *acted out* by performing (intruding and over-helping) actions.

Sometimes a right way to help is **non-action**. In fact, if the teacher for example hurries the pupil, this could make him anxious and perform worse. The opposite of this communicative affective over-help, and sometimes the best kind of help, is waiting, that is, refraining from action. In such cases it is clear how non-action implies a deliberate decision not to act. For example, if the teacher is moving her hand toward the puzzle, but then she refrains and puts it behind her hip, she is just trying not to intervene. We consider this a case of **affective help** through **non-action**. Of course, sometimes a teacher might stay there doing nothing while the pupil actually would need her help. This is a case of *lack of help*, that should be clearly distinguished from deliberate non action. So it is just when you detect movements of inhibition that you can speak of deliberate non-action.

Another non intruding way to help are **epistemic actions**, that is, cognitive actions aimed at acquiring knowledge about how the task is being performed. A typical epistemic action is looking at the pupil's behavior attentively in order to check if he is performing well. Checking, or controlling, can be defined as an epistemic action of acquiring knowledge about how some process is proceeding, in order to be able to re-direct it if something is going badly. Thus epistemic action may be considered, though indirectly a case of help, because it is a step before possibly deciding whether to help, and whether to provide technical, cognitive or affective help. Epistemic action may precede – and hence be indirectly – either technical or cognitive or affective help. For instance, if observing the pupil I see he is almost having the insight, but lacks a crucial information, I can provide it, thus giving cognitive help; if I see he is discouraged, I can decide to encourage, providing affective help. On the other hand, the non-action of refraining from doing is most typically a case of affective help, being a way to leave the pupil reflect without hurry or anxiety.

Table 1. A taxonomy of helping behaviors

Teacher's behavior	Pupil's process	Help	Over-help
COMMUNI-CATION	Technical	provides or reminds information, suggestion, hints, soft criticism	orders, directs, forbids
	Cognitive	puts general questions to make the pupil reason and find the solution, explains the process, how one should do, proposes doubts in case of likely mistakes; explains errors	reveals specific moves or strategies
	Affective	encourages, incites, reinforces, confirms, reassures, share and model emotions, minimizes child's negative emotions	expresses compassion, insists in hurrying up, shows anxiety
ACTION	Technical	fulfils technical conditions: pre-pares game table, put light in the right place	makes pupil's moves substitutes herself for the child
	Cognitive	fulfils cognitive conditions: performs actions to induce insight (turns pieces)	prevent pupil's errors (takes a piece away from the child's hand) or undo pupil's errors (takes pieces put by the child away) without explanation
	Affective	fulfils affective conditions: makes the environment motivating: relaxation, amusement, empow-erment, gratification	
NON-ACTION	Technical Cognitive Affective	refrain from action: waits, inhibits own action	
		epistemic action only: look, check, control	

4 An Annotation Scheme of the Teacher's Multimodal Behavior

The taxonomy above allows to classify general categories of action/non-action. But to analyse our videorecorded data of the teacher-pupil dyads we need to assess the specific concrete behaviors performed by teachers, and classify them as belonging to one or the other of the categories above.

To detect which of them imply a goal to help, to quantify the amount of help or over-help given, and to assess whether and what types of help or over-help are provided it is necessary to describe and analyse the behaviors of teachers and pupils in a detailed manner. So we elaborated a specific annotation scheme based on the model of multimodal communication of Poggi [15].

According to this model action has a hierarchical structure: any action – or deliberate non-action – is aimed at a conscious or unconscious goal, and possibly at a supergoal, a further goal for which the former goal is a means. Communication is a social action whereby a Sender S has the goal of having an Addressee A assume some belief B, and in order to this produces a communicative act – a sentence, gesture, facial expression, gaze, posture, body movement – that conveys belief B as its meaning. Each communicative act has a goal, and possibly one or more supergoals, with a supergoal being a meaning that the Sender wants the Addressee to understand through inference.

The annotation scheme is divided into 6 columns (see Tables 2 and 3).

- Column 1 contains the time in the video of the behavior under analysis.

- Columns 2 and 3 contain a description, respectively, of the teacher's verbal and nonverbal behavior.

- In col. 4 we write the goal of the communicative or non-communicative behaviors in columns 2 and / or 3. For the verbal behavior written in col. 2, its goal is by definition a communicative goal, while for the action written in col. 3 the goal to be written in col. 4 may be either a communicative goal (for the so called non-verbal communicative signals) or not (for those behaviors through which the Agent does not intend to have the other Agent know something). The goal in col. 4, as well as in the following col. 5, is phrased as a sentence of the first person (the teacher) addressed to the second person (the pupil)

- Further, since an action – whether communicative or not – besides its direct goal may aim at one or more supergoals – other goals for which the direct goal is a means – in col. 5 we write the possible supergoal of the actions in 2 or 3. For a non-communicative action a supergoal is some further effect the agent wants to bring about through the goal of col. 4. For instance, if a teacher turns the pieces of the puzzle on the right side, she may do this to check the location of pieces better, hence to know herself where they should go. For a communicative act, the supergoal is an inference the Sender wants the Addressee to draw from that communicative act: so, if the teacher points at the place in the puzzle where the piece belongs, her communicative supergoal is to suggest the pupil to put it there.

- In col. 6 we classify the goal of col. 4 (or the supergoal written in col 5., when there is one) in terms of the taxonomy of help and over-help above (Table 1).

Let us see two fragments of our analysis.

In Table 2, at line 1, time 7.09 (Col.1), teacher n. 2 places the two posts of the game in front of the child and orients them toward her (col. 3). The direct goal of this nonverbal action is for the child to pay attention and concentrate to start the game (col.4). This is a Communicative Cognitive Help (col. 6). Immediately after (line 2, time 7.10), the teacher bends her head in a head canting posture (3), a posture of welcome, of non-dominance, which means: "I put myself at your level" (4). This is then a Communicative action that provides Affective Help of making the child feel welcome (6). At line 3, time 7.11, the teacher asks the child if she has ever done a puzzle. Her goal is to ascertain if the prerequisites hold for the child to play the game. This is, on the teacher's side, a benevolent goal, aimed at fulfilling the cognitive conditions for game playing; but it may result in over-help, since it is not plausible that the pupil has never done a puzzle. Moreover her hypothesis unmasks a presupposition that in the child's culture such kind of game is not used as an educational tool, and the teacher's act may sound as an indulgent attitude toward a person that is worth compassion, which might possibly have a negative effect on the pupil's affective state. So we classify this as Communicative Affective Over-help. (Col. 6).

Table 2. Annotation scheme. The high intrusive teacher.

1. Time	2. Speech	3. Action	4. Goal	5. Supergoal	6. Type of Help/ Over-help
1 7.09		*Places both posts and orients them toward the child*	Pay attention here and concentrate, let's start the game		C Cognitive Help
2 7.10		*Head canting*	I put myself at your level. I welcome you as a mother with her child		C Affective Help
3. 7.11	*L'hai mai fatto un puzzle?* Have you ever done a puzzle?		I ask you to confirm if the prerequisites are fulfilled for you to do this game	I am very indulgent with your possible flaws	C Affective Over-help

Legenda: A = Action; C = Communicative Action; -A = Deliberate Non-Action

Table 3 shows the other teacher's behavior, which is more rarely over-helping.

On lines 1 and 2, time 48.46, she says (col. 2): "Come on, Bam Bam, c'mon let's start". Wnile calling the pupil as the character of the story (line 1, col.4), she incites him to start (line 2, col.4). The supergoal of the former communicative act is to have the child put himself into the character's shoes (line 1,col.5), thus inducing a playful attitude; with the latter (line 2, col.5) she encourages him to start the game. Both acts provide communicative affective help.

Then (line 3) she puts the pieces closer to the child (col.3), to set the conditions for him to start (4), thus making the start easier (5): a non-communicative Action of Technical Help.

After he has put some pieces and some letters appear in the puzzle, at time 48.50 (line 4) she asks him: "What will be written there?". The literal goal of the question is to ask what is written in the puzzle (col.4), but its supergoal is to teach the child a general method to solve problem: to ask questions to himself (col.5). Thus she is performing a Communicative Action that provides Cognitive Help. Moreover, the epistemic future tense used to phrase the question, "what *will* be written there?", with its goal of inducing the pleasant emotion of curiosity, aims at making the game more motivating, thus providing Communicative Affective Help.

At 48.53 (line 5), the teacher says "Let us start there" and at the same time points at an area of the puzzle. She is suggesting where to start from (col.4): a Communicative Technical help.

Then (line 6), she withdraws her hand as if she did not want to point too precisely (col.4), not to be too suggestive and thus develop the pupil's reasoning (5): a deliberate Non-action of Cognitive Help. At the same time, though (line 7), she smiles at the pupil (col.3), meaning she is friendly to him (4), with he supergoal to encourage him (5): a Communicative Affective Help. Then (line 8) she puts her left hand on the nape

Table 3. Annotation scheme. The low intrusive teacher.

1. Time	2. Speech	3. Action	4. Goal	5. Supergoal	6. Type of Help/Over-help
1. 48.46	*forza **Bam Bam**,* c'mon **Bam Bam**,		I call you Bam Bam	By letting you put in the Character's shoes, I induce a playful attitude	C Affective Help
2. 48.46	*dài iniziamo.* C'mon let's start		I incite you to start	I encourage you to start	C Affective Help
3. 48.46		She puts the pieces closer to the child	I make the pieces available for you to start	I make it easier for you to start	A Technical Help
4. 48.50	*Cosa ci **sarà** scritto?* What **will be** written here?		I ask you what might be written there I want to induce curiosity in you	I teach you what kind of questions you should put yourself I elicit a pleasant emotion	C Cognitive Help C Affective Help
5. 48.53	*Cominciamo di là* Let us start there	With left index f. she points at the area where to start	I suggest you where to start		C Technical Help
6. 48.53		She withdraws her hand	I don't want to point at it too precisely	I don't want to suggest too much, I want you to understand it by yourself	A Cognitive Help
7. 48.53		She smiles	I am friendly to you		C Affective Help
8. 48.54		She puts her hand on the nape of her neck	I refrain from helping more	I want you to proceed by yourself	A Cognitive Help
9. 48.54		Looks at the pieces the child is placing	I check if you are putting the pieces well	But I don't let you alone to make mistakes	A Affective Help

of her neck (col.3) to refrain from pointing more (col.4), in order to let him find the solution by himself (5). A Non-action aimed to Help Cognitive development, and a good example of how, strangely enough, one can help by non-helping! At the same time (line 9), though, she leans forward to look at the pieces the child is placing (col.3) to check if he is putting them well (col.4), not to let him alone should he make mistakes (5): a Non-action (namely, epistemic action) aimed at Affective Help.

5   Results

The total timing of the two observations was 13 minutes 31seconds (7.27 for the High intrusive teacher, from minute 7.09 to 14.36, and 6.04 for the Low intrusive teacher, from minute 48.35 to 54.39), balanced for the two teacher. The helping behaviors computed through the annotation scheme confirm the results of the previous study [11] as to the level of help and over-help given. A chi-square test revealed a significant difference between the low and the high intrusive teacher regarding the general type of help, be it performed through communication, action, or non-action [χ^2 (1, 221)= 40,11; p<0.001]. Table 4 shows that the level of help provided by the two teachers during the game simulation follows an inverse behavior pattern: the high intrusive teacher over-helps more than the low intrusive one (55% vs 15%, respectively); while the low intrusive teacher mostly helps adequately (85% vs 45%).

Table 4. Help vs. over-help (percentage and standard errors)

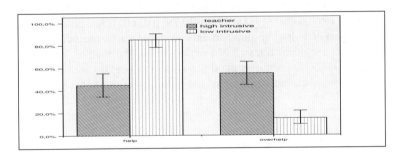

The analysis on the types of help also revealed a significant difference [χ^2 (4, 253)= 44.53; p<0.001]. In particular (see Table 5), the type of help given by the low intrusive teacher is mostly communication (71% for help and 12% over-help) while she presents a very low amount of non-communicative action (6 % for help and 2% over-help). She also presents a very low percentage (9%) of help through deliberate non action (in our annotation scheme we distinguish the cases of help through non action from other forms of the teacher's relaxation or distraction that are not aimed at helping). This could mean that (her) most adequate way of helping is mainly through communication rather than through simply acting or even barely controlling. On the other hand, the high intrusive teacher's communication is equally distributed between help (33%) and over-help (32%), but she also exhibits over-help thought action (14%). That the high intrusive teacher tends to over-help mainly through non-communicative action could confirm the interpretation already proposed for the mothers of children with chronical disease. Over-help could be seen as a "buffering behavior" that responds to the helper's anxiety – due, for instance, to her feeling judged by the experimenter, or to her being worried because the child is slower than she wants–, rather than a long term strategy in favour of recipient [10]. Moreover, the high intrusive teacher helps the pupil through non-action – mainly epistemic action – almost twice as much the low intrusive teacher (17% vs 9%): she checks and looks at the pupils' action more frequently, and she displays a more controlling attitude. This could be another form of expression of the teacher's anxiety.

Table 5. Type and modality of help

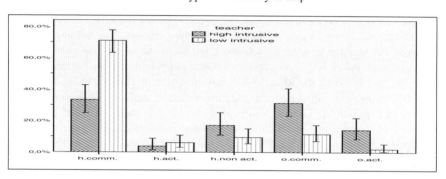

The analysis of the teachers' helping behavior shows that the particular processes of the pupil (affective, cognitive and technical) to which help is directed differ significantly for the two teachers $[\chi^2 (5, 190)= 30.79; p<0.001]$. As shown in Table 6, the low intrusive teacher helps the pupil mainly in an *affective* manner (44%), but she also tries to offer technical hints (23%) or to explain the method and the rationale behind the task (13%), taking the pupil's cognitive processes into account. On the other hand, the over-helping behavior of the high intrusive teacher is primarily of a *technical* type (45%), and essentially aimed at replacing the child's action. She also helps affectively (23%), by encouraging the pupil, and, in fewer cases, she helps cognitively (9%) and technically (11%).

The taxonomy of help and over-help in Table 7 displays the complete helping pattern of the teachers in the two different conditions (low and high intrusiveness), revealing significant differences $[\chi^2 (11, 253)= 55.24; p<0.001]$. First of all it is interesting to notice that the low intrusive teacher chooses a communicative modality of help, giving preference to the *affective communication* (38%), next to the technical (21%) and cognitive one (12%).

The behavior pattern of the high intrusive teacher is oriented mostly to *technical over-help*, both communicated (25%) and acted (14%), but she also tends to help the pupil by communicating in an affective way (19%). The broad spectrum allows to observe that the two teachers differ in help through deliberate non action. The general bias towards "over-action" of the high intrusive teacher and her tendency to intrude into the pupil's action even occurs in the epistemic actions, since the comparison between the two teachers shows that high intrusiveness is correlated to a higher *controlling* attitude during interaction (13% vs 4%).

Table 6. Helped processes

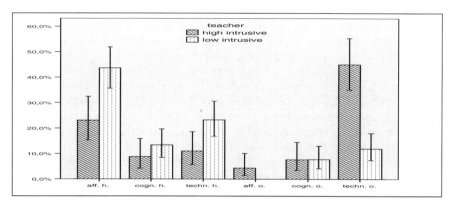

Table 7. Taxonomy of help

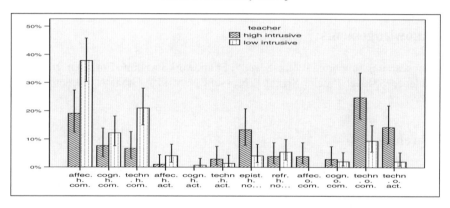

6 Conclusion

In this work we have proposed a taxonomy of helping and over-helping behaviors and an annotation scheme to assess if a teacher, while interacting with her pupil, helps or over-helps him/her, and what kind of help she is providing. The detailed observation carried on thanks to these tools allowed us to deepen our understanding of the over-helping behaviors of teachers that interact with pupils of a socially stigmatised group [11]. According to the data presented above, most interestingly, the high intrusive teacher showed a significantly higher percentage both of deliberate non-action and of acted over-help, while the low intrusive teacher showed a higher percentage of help through communicative action. This *shortcut to action* that affects more the high intrusive teacher may be interpreted, referring to the Vygotskian concept of scaffolding [4, 5] broadly discussed above, as linked to a less frequent use of a strategy of "wait and see". This does not allow the highly intrusive teacher to perceive the actual degree of competence already mastered by the child. On the contrary, the *communicative strategy* of interaction with the pupil more often adopted by the low intrusive teacher allows her to more accurately perceive it. Let apart the high frequency of affective communication, that could also be linked to the early age of the children observed, the inverse relationship between action and communication could be referred, in more general terms, to a particular deficit in scaffolding for the high intrusive teacher, made clear by her over-helping actions, that makes it difficult for her to pay the due attention to the spontaneous capabilities of the child. The very detailed analysis led by the annotation scheme proposed opens to new research directions. More studies have to be conducted, testing, among others, the different *effects* of these two kinds of helping and over-helping (both benevolent in teachers' intentions) on the child's autonomous problem-solving. Due to the different implications for the child of helping vs. intruding interference by the adult, we expect that only the effects of over-help linked to this *shortcut to action* should lead, if repeated in time, to a lower autonomous problem solving of the child. The whole device of over-help and its motives, though, cannot be caught but through an analysis of teachers' and pupils' behavior that takes into account all the nuances of their multimodal communication, and that succeeds in extracting out of it the very bulk of their attitude toward the other.

Acknowledgements

This research is supported by the Seventh Framework Program, European Network of Excellence SSPNet (Social Signal Processing Network), Grant Agreement Number 231287.

References

1. Nadler, A.: Autonomous and dependent help seeking: Personality Characteristics and the seeking of help. In: Sarason, B., Sarason, I., Pierce, R.G. (eds.) Handbook of personality and social support, pp. 258–302. Plenum, New York (1997)
2. Leone, G. (ed.): Le ambivalenze dell'aiuto. Teorie e pratiche del dare e del ricevere. Unicopli, Milano (2009)
3. Gilbert, D., Silvera, D.: Over-helping. Journal of Personality and Social Psychology 70, 678–690 (1996)
4. Vygotskij, L.S.: Mind in society. In: The development of higher psychological processes. Harvard University press, Cambridge (1978)
5. Vygotskij, L.S.: The genesis of higher mental functions. In: Wertsch, J.V. (ed.) The Concept of Activity in Soviet Psychology. M.E. Sharpe, Armonk (1981)
6. Raymond, C.E.: Cognitive Characteristics. In: Learners with Mild Disabilities, pp. 169–201. Allyn & Bacon, A Pearson Education Company, Needham Heights (2000)
7. Hartman, H.: Scaffolding & Cooperative Learning. In: Hartman, H. (ed.) Human Learning and Instruction, pp. 23–69. City College of City University of New York, New York (2002)
8. Mastrovito, T.: Giochi di simulazione e video-feedback: una proposta metodologica. In: Leone, G. (ed.) Le ambivalenze dell'aiuto. Teorie e pratiche del chiedere e del ricevere, pp. 69–112. Unicopli, Milano (2009)

9. D'Errico, F., Leone, G.: Giocare ad aiutare. L'uso di un gioco di simulazione come possi-
bilità di osservazione e di auto-valutazione del sovra-aiuto materno in presenza di una
malattia cronica infantile. In Psicologia della salute 1, 91–106 (2006)
10. D'Errico, F.: Il sovraiuto materno nella malattia cronica infantile: aspetti comportamentali,
emozionali e autoriflessivi. In: Leone, G. (ed.) Le ambivalenze dell'aiuto. Teorie e pratiche
del dare e del ricevere, pp. 113–172. Unicopli Editore, Milano (2009)
11. D'Errico, F., Leone, G., Mastrovito, T.: The paradox of over-help. When teacher's intervention makes an immigrant child more dependent. In: Berg, W. (ed.) Multicultural
classes. Verlag GmbH, Wies-baden (in press)
12. Poggi, I., D'Errico, F.: Social Signals and the action – cognition loop. The case of over-
help and evaluation. In: Proceeding of IEEE International Conference on Affective Computing and Intelligent Interaction, New York (2009)
13. Leone, G.: Interpersonal, social and societal signals in successful and unsuccessful scaffolding. In: Social Signal Foundation. An Outline. International Meeting of the SSPNet,
Rome, December 3-5 (2009)
14. Rapporto Caritas-Migrantes. Dossier statistico immigrazione. Idos- Centro studi e ricerche,
Roma (2007)
15. Poggi, I.: Mind, hands, face and body. In: Goal and belief view of multimodal communication. Weidler, Berlin (2007)

Honest Signals and Their Contribution to the Automatic Analysis of Personality Traits – A Comparative Study

Bruno Lepri, Kyriaki Kalimeri, and Fabio Pianesi

FBK-irst
via Sommarive 18 Povo, Italy
+39-0461-314570
{lepri,kalimeri,pianesi}@fbk.eu

Abstract. In our paper we focus on the usage of different kind of "honest" signals for the automatic prediction of two personality traits, Extraversion and Locus of Control. In particular, we investigate the predictive power of four classes of speech honest signal features (Conversational Activity, Emphasis, Influence, and Mimicry), along with three fidgeting visual features by systematically comparing the results obtained by classifiers using them.

Keywords: Personality Modeling, Social Signal Processing, Human Behavior Analysis, Support Vector Machine.

1 Introduction

Personality is the complex of all the attributes — behavioral, temperamental, emotional and mental — that characterize individual dispositions. Humans have the tendency to understand, explain and predict other humans' behavior in terms of stable properties — personality traits — that are variously assorted on the basis of the observation of everyday behavior.

In folk-psychological practice, the personality of a person is assessed along several dimensions: we are used to talk about an individual as being (non-)open-minded, (dis-)organized, too much/little focused on herself, etc. Several existing theories have formalized this folk-psychological practice to model personality by means of multi-factorial models, whereby an individual's 'objective' personality is described in terms of a number of more fundamental dimensions known as traits. A well known example of a multi-factorial model is the Big Five [1] which owes its name to the five traits it takes as constitutive of people's personality: Extraversion, Emotional Stability, Agreeableness, Conscientiousness, Openness to Experience.

In our work we limit ourselves to the extraversion-introversion dimension of the Big Five. The choice of the this trait was due to the fact that of the Big Five traits, Extraversion is the one that shows up more clearly in, and has the greater impact on, social behaviour [2].

Besides models, as the Big Five, that attempt to provide a comprehensive assessment of people personality, others have privileged specific dimensions, possibly useful to characterize specific dispositions in specific domains. An example is the so-called Locus of Control (LoC) [3], which measures whether causal attribution [4] for

A.A. Salah et al. (Eds.): HBU 2010, LNCS 6219, pp. 140–150, 2010.

one's behavior or beliefs is made to oneself or to external events or circumstances. It consists of a stable set of belief about whether the outcome of one's actions is dependent upon what the subject does (internal orientation) or on events outside of her control (external orientation) [3]. For example, college students with a strong internal locus of control may believe that their grades were achieved through their own efforts, while students with a strong external locus of control may believe that their grades are the result of good or bad luck; hence, they are less likely to expect that their own efforts will result in success and are less likely to work hard for high grades.

The work described in this paper intends to contribute to the task of the automatic recognition of people's personality investigating the predictive power of four acoustic feature sets (Conversational Activity, Emphasis, Influence and Mimicry) and one set of visual features, Bodily Activation, by systematically comparing the results obtained by classifiers using them.

2 Previous and Related Work

Personality traits have been broadly studied in psychology over the last years, as well as their association with particular behavioral markers. Scherer [5; 6] has found extroversion to be associated with shorter latency, fewer silent pauses and fewer "filled" brief pauses. Moreover, he has shown that extroversion attributions correlate significantly with voice quality indicators such as high pitch and variations in the fundamental frequency [6]. Other studies on the differences between the communication styles of introverts and extroverts suggest that the latter speak more and more rapidly, with fewer pauses and hesitations [7].

To the best of our knowledge, the first work addressing the automatic recognition of personality was [8], who used the relative frequency of function words and of word categories based on Systemic Functional Grammar, to train Support Vector Machines for the recognition of Extraversion and Emotional Stability. The data concerning the two personality traits were based on self-reports. Oberlander and Nowson [9] trained Naive Bayes and Support Vector Machines for four (Neuroticism, Extraversion, Agreeableness, and Conscientiousness) of the Big Five traits on a corpus of personal weblogs, using n-gram features extracted from the dataset. Also their personality data were obtained through self-reports. A major finding of theirs is that the model for Agreeableness was the only one to outperform the baseline. Mairesse et al. [10; 11] applied classification, regression and ranking models to the recognition of the Big Five personality traits. They also systematically examined the usefulness of different sets of (acoustic and textual) features suggested by the psycholinguistic and psychosocial literature. As to the personality data, they compared self-reports with observed data. Mairesse et al. [10] showed that Extraversion is the easiest personality trait to be modeled from spoken language, since prosodic features play a major role, while their results were closer to those based on observed personality than on self-reports.

In a recent work, Olguín and colleagues [12] collected various behavioral measurements of the daily activities of 67 professional nurses in a Hospital. The data were collected by means of the sociometer badge [13], a wearable device integrating a number of sensors (an accelerometer, a microphone, and an infrared sensor) measuring aspects such as physical and speech activity, a number of face-to-face interactions with other people, the level of proximity to relevant objects (people, but also beds, etc.) and some social networks parameters. Although the authors' goal was not to predict personality traits from those signals, by exploiting simple correlation analysis they were able to prove that the signals they targeted can provide quite a lot of information about people's personality.

3   The Mission Survival Corpus

For this study, we used the multimodal corpus of Mission Survival II (MS2), which is based on the so-called Mission Survival Task (MST), frequently used in experimental and social psychology to elicit decision making processes in small groups [14]. The MST task comprise in reaching a decision on ranking a list of 12 items, in descending order, according to their contribution in surviving after a plane crash. The MS2 corpus consists of twelve multi-party meetings, with a total duration of 6 hours, of four participants each (see [15] for a more comprehensive description) that involve in a social interaction in which each participant expresses his/her own personal opinion and then the group reaches a consensus mutual decision.

Two modalities were included in this corpus, audio and video. Audio streams were recorded from close-talk microphones as well as one omni-directional microphone placed in the middle of the table. Video streams were recorded from four cameras placed at the corners of the room.

All participants were asked to complete a standard questionnaire validated on the Italian language that corresponds to the Italian version of Craig's Locus of Control (LOC) of Behavior scale [16], as well as the part of Big Marker Five Scales related to the Extraversion dimension [17]. LOC's questionnaire was composed by 17 items, with a rating scale from 0 to 5 points, while the Extraversion's questionnaire was composed by 10 items, with a rating scale from 1 to 7. To the best of our knowledge, the MS2 dataset is the only multimodal data collection, in which the individuals are interacting in a meeting scenario, while at the same time there is available a systematic data collection of the participants' personality traits.

The personality traits of each participant, were characterized from the individual LoC and Extraversion scores. The LoC's mean scores was $\mu = 27$ (standard deviation $\sigma = 7.67$; variance $\sigma^2 = 58.86$), while for the Extraversion the mean is $\mu = 46$ (standard deviation $\sigma = 8.02$; variance $\sigma^2 = 64.30$). Both are consistent with Italian distribution reported by the validation studies above.

4   Framework – Honest Signals

In Pentland's view [18] that we use as reference framework in this paper, some human social signals are reliable because they are too costly to fake. In human-human interaction the non verbal behavior is a great source of reliable signals which give information about emotions, mental states, personality, attitudes, preferences, and other traits of people [19]. De Paulo [20] affirmed that these expressive non-verbal behaviors are harder to suppress and to fake in comparison with verbal behaviors and are more accessible to the external observers. Hence, the lack of control and of accessibility of expressive behavior implies that such behaviors provide the observer with a relatively sound source of information regarding the internal states and the dispositions of the other subjects. A related implication is that the attempts of intentionally manipulating and faking these expressive behaviors during self-presentations are usually unsuccessful. In fact, expressive behavior could be more revealing of communicative intentions and internal states than what is being consciously and verbally communicated [21].

In this work, our goal is to explore how four different sets of acoustic honest signals (Conversational Activity, Emphasis, Influence, and Mimicry) and a set of visual ones related to the bodily activation contribute to the recognition of personality traits during a social interaction.

4.1 Acoustic Features

For the automatic extraction of the acoustic features the toolbox developed at the Human Dynamics group at Media Lab[1] was used. The relevance of these specific features for the analysis of human behavior in social setting was discussed by [18]. Previous works, ([22] and [23]), grouped them into the following four subsets:

Emphasis includes the following relevant features: formant frequency, confidence in formant frequency, spectral entropy, values of the larger autocorrelation peaks, number of the larger autocorrelation peaks, location of the larger autocorrelation peaks, time derivative of energy in frame. Emphasis is considered as a measure of the strength of the speaker's motivation. The consistency of emphasis (the lower the variations, the higher the consistency) is a signal of mental focus, while variability may signal an openness to influence from other people.

Conversational Activity consists of the following features: energy in frame, length of voiced segments, length of speaking segments, fraction of time speaking, and voicing rate. It is usually an indicator of interest and engagement.

Influence measures the amount of influence each person has on another one in a social interaction, by estimating the ratio of overlapping speech segments to the total. Influence is a signal of dominance. Moreover, its strength in a conversation can serve as an indicator of attention.

Mimicry, meant as the un-reflected copying of one person by another during a conversation (i.e. gestures and prosody of one are "mirrored" by the other), is expressed by short interjections (e.g. "yup", "uh-huh",) or back-and-forth exchanges consisting of short words (e.g. "OK?", "done!"). Usually, more empathetic people are more likely to mimic their conversational partners: for this reason, mimicry is often used as an unconscious signal of empathy. Mimicry is a complex behavior and therefore difficult to computationally measure. A proxy of its measure is given by the z-scored frequency of these short utterances (< 1 second) exchanges.

4.2 Visual Features

Regarding the visual context, we have mainly focused on few features related to the energy (fidgeting) associated with head, hands and body movements.

The fidgeting features were automatically annotated by employing the MHI (Motion History Images) techniques [24], which use skin region features and temporal

---

[1] http://groupmedia.media.mit.edu/data.php

motions to detect repetitive motions in the images and associate such motions to an energy value in such a way that the higher the value, the more pronounced the motion.

All these visual features were extracted and tracked for each frame at a frequency of three hertz.

5 Comparing Feature Sets Predictive Power

Our overall goal is to model and predict personality traits by considering the behavior of a subject in 1-minute temporal windows; a task similar to that of a psychologist, asked to assess personality traits based on thin slices of behavior [25].

Here, we will investigate the predictive power of the 5 feature sets (4 audio + 1 video) discussed above by systematically comparing the results obtained by classifiers using them. As in past work [26; 27], we assign much importance to the possibility that, once targeting a given subject in a meeting, the *Target,* knowledge of the behavior of the other participants of the meeting, the *Others*, could help in predicting the Target's personality. This position reflects the idea that Target's behavior is jointly determined by its personality and the social context is in. Hence, besides an across the board comparison of the various feature sets used to characterize Target's behavior, we will systematically exploit those very same feature sets to model the Others' behavior, which essentially forms the social context.

As in [26], the task was modeled as a classification one, with the scores on the two personality traits divided into three classes of (approximately) equal numerosity.

For classification, we used an Support Vector Machine with a Radial Basis Function (RBF) kernel [28]. The cost parameter C and the kernel parameter γ were estimated through the grid technique by cross-fold validation using a factor of 10.

The baseline is represented by the naïve classifier that works on the basis of the prior class probabilities, with accuracy=0.33.

5.1 Experimental Design

Given our purposes, the study was based on a repeated measure design, with two dependent variables – accuracy in predicting Extraversion and accuracy in predicting LoC –and two within factors:

- **Target**, with five levels corresponding to the five feature sets discussed above: ACT (Activity), EMP (Emphasis), MIM (Mimicry), INF (Influence) and FID (Fidgeting).
- **Others**, with six levels, five of which are the same as with Target with the sixth is No_Feat, corresponding to a condition where no information about the context at all is used in personality prediction.

The resulting 5x6 design was analyzed by means of two repeated measures analysis of variance on the accuracy scores obtained from leave-one-subject-out cross-validation runs.

6   Results

Table 1 reports the average accuracy (with SDs) for Extraversion for each conditions, along with the marginal ones.

A first relevant observation is that in most cases the results are well above the baseline. All effects are significant: Target (F1.440, 47=31.709, p<.0001), Others (F2.236, 47=19.810, p<.0001) and the Target*Others interaction (F20, 47=6.267; p<.0001). Concerning Target, all the marginal means are pairwise statistically different (p<.05, with Bonferroni correction for multiple comparisons) except the following pairs: <MIM, INF>, <MIM, FID>, <INF, FID>. Hence, the best performing feature set for Target is Emphasis, followed by Activity, that lies quite lower, and then by Mimicry, Influence and Fidgeting that are even lower and forming a group with similar effects on Target.

Table 1. Mean accuracy scores for Extraversion

<table>
<tr><td></td><td></td><td colspan="7" align="center">Others</td></tr>
<tr><td></td><td></td><td>No_Feat</td><td>ACT</td><td>EMP</td><td>MIM</td><td>INF</td><td>FID</td><td>marginals</td></tr>
<tr><td rowspan="10">Target</td><td rowspan="2">ACT</td><td>0.48</td><td>0.83</td><td>0.84</td><td>0.56</td><td>0.54</td><td>0.58</td><td>0.64</td></tr>
<tr><td>(0.26)</td><td>(0.27)</td><td>(0.29)</td><td>(0.30)</td><td>(0.29)</td><td>(0.25)</td><td></td></tr>
<tr><td rowspan="2">EMP</td><td>0.75</td><td>0.83</td><td>0.85</td><td>0.56</td><td>0.78</td><td>0.78</td><td>0.76</td></tr>
<tr><td>(0.27)</td><td>(0.31)</td><td>(0.31)</td><td>(0.31)</td><td>(0.28)</td><td>(0.29)</td><td></td></tr>
<tr><td rowspan="2">MIM</td><td>0.32</td><td>0.50</td><td>0.52</td><td>0.39</td><td>0.38</td><td>0.46</td><td>0.43</td></tr>
<tr><td>(0.45)</td><td>(0.46)</td><td>(0.46)</td><td>(0.35)</td><td>(0.37)</td><td>(0.32)</td><td></td></tr>
<tr><td rowspan="2">INF</td><td>0.35</td><td>0.52</td><td>0.55</td><td>0.39</td><td>0.43</td><td>0.45</td><td>0.45</td></tr>
<tr><td>(0.45)</td><td>(0.42)</td><td>(0.43)</td><td>(.034)</td><td>(0.39)</td><td>(0.31)</td><td></td></tr>
<tr><td rowspan="2">FID</td><td>0.32</td><td>0.59</td><td>0.59</td><td>0.40</td><td>0.45</td><td>0.53</td><td>0.48</td></tr>
<tr><td>(0.41)</td><td>(0.39)</td><td>(0.39)</td><td>(0.34)</td><td>(0.37)</td><td>(0.29)</td><td></td></tr>
<tr><td>marginals</td><td>0.44</td><td>0.65</td><td>0.67</td><td>0.46</td><td>0.52</td><td>0.56</td><td></td></tr>
</table>

Turning to Others, all the pairwise comparisons are statistically different (p<.05, with Bonferroni adjustment), except for <No_Feat, MIM>, <ACT, EMP>, <MIM, INF>, <INF, FID>. Hence, there are two best performing conditions for Others: Activity and Emphasis.

Concerning the Target*Others interaction, the more noticeable aspect is that when Target=Emphasis performances are uniformly high, even with Others=No_Feat (accuracy=0.75); in other words, just by observing the Emphasis features of the target subject it is possible to reach 0.75 mean accuracy. The only exception is the condition <EMP, MIM>, where performance has a sharp decrease; see Table 1 and Figure 1.

Figure 1 suggest the existence of a monotonically increasing dependency of accuracy on the size of the feature sets employed both for Target and for Others (with the exception of <EMP, MIM>). Polynomial contrast analysis confirms this impression, revealing significant linear and quadratic contrasts for Target, quadratic for Others and linear*quadratic and quadratic*linear contrasts for the Target*Others interaction.

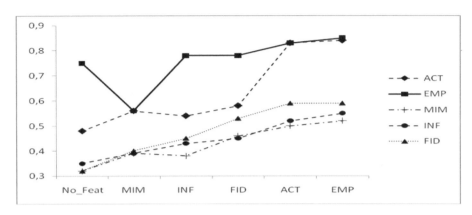

Fig. 1. Extraversion - Average accuracy per conditions, with Others' levels on the X axis

Descriptively, the comparisons of the lines for Target=ACT and Target=EMP in Figure 1 shows a low growth rate of Target=EMP when greater feature sets are considered for Others (the growth rate remains significant, though). The situation is different when Target=ACT, with a higher sensitivity of the growth rate on feature set size.

The best accuracy results are obtained by the conditions <EMP, ACT>, <EMP, EMP>, <ACT, ACT> and <ACT, EMP>, which are pairwise non statistically different (t-test, p<.-05 with Bonferroni correction). For the sake of completeness, Table 2 reports the results for Macro Precision, Macro Recall and Macro F for the four best conditions.

Table 2. Macro-P, Macro-R and Macro-F for best performing conditions on Extraversions

	Macro P	Macro R	Macro F
ACT, ACT	0.825	0.829	0.825
ACT, EMP	0.838	0.839	0.835
EMP, ACT	0.835	0.838	0.834
EMP, EMP	0.849	0.849	0.845

Finally, we ran two more training-test session using the complete feature set discussed above for Target and no features/ the complete feature set for Others. The average accuracy for <ALL, No_Feat> is 0.82 while that for <ALL, ALL> is 0.84. These results do not statistically differ from those seen above for <ACT, ACT>, <ACT, EMP>, <EMP, ACT> AND <EMP, EMP>. Average accuracy scores for LoC are reported in Table 3.

Target and Others main effects are both significant (Target: $F1.539, 47=18.572$, $p<.0001$; Others: $F1.549, 47=10.178$, $p<.0001$). Pairwise comparisons on marginal averages for Target shows that EMP produces the highest performance, followed by ACT and then by MIM, INF and FID, the latter three having pairwise statistically non different values. The Target*Others interaction goes close to significance ($F3.434$, $47=2.515, p=0.052$).

Table 3. Mean accuracy scores for LoC

Target \ Others	No_Feat	ACT	EMP	MIM	INF	FID	marginals
ACT	0.54 (0.31)	0.83 (0.26)	0.83 (0.29)	0.61 (0.28)	0.59 (0.30)	0.67 (0.25)	0.68
EMP	0.74 (0.28)	0.85 (0.31)	0.86 (0.30)	0.61 (0.27)	0.77 (0.28)	0.79 (0.29)	0.77
MIM	0.50 (0.46)	0.58 (0.46)	0.60 (0.46)	0.47 (0.37)	0.46 (0.38)	0.54 (0.30)	0.52
INF	0.46 (0.45)	0.57 (0.45)	0.57 (0.47)	0.46 (0.39)	0.48 (0.38)	0.52 (0.33)	0.51
FID	0.48 (0.336)	0.63 (0.38)	0.65 (0.37)	0.48 (0.32)	0.47 (0.37)	0.56 (0.29)	0.55
marginals	0.54	0.69	0.70	0.53	0.55	0.62	

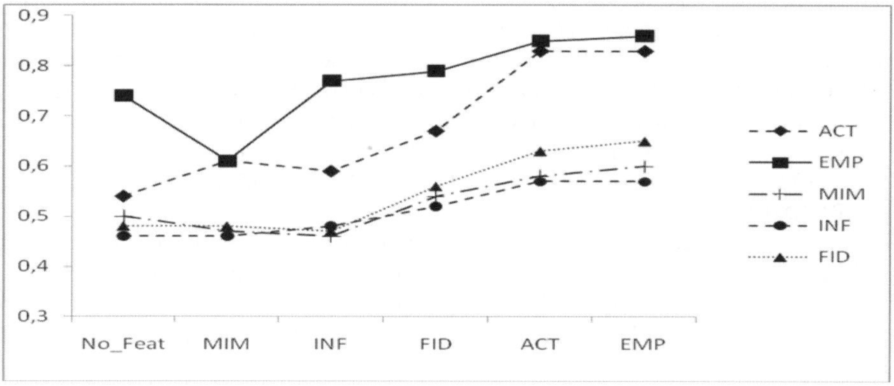

Fig. 2. LoC - Average accuracy per conditions, with Others' levels on the X axis

The results for LoC are very similar to those seen for Extraversion. In both cases Target=Emphasis provides performance that are higher or comparable to those of the other conditions. A similarly low growth rate is noticed (with the exception of <EMP, MIM>) for Target=EMP, starting, however, from much higher values when no features are used for the context. As with Extraversion, the best results are obtained in conditions exploiting the biggest feature sets: <ACT, ACT>, <ACT, EMP>, <EMP, ACT> and <EMP, EMP>. The figures for Macro-R, Macro-P and MACRO-F are reported in Table 4.

The values of accuracy for the additional conditions <ALL, No_Feat> and <ALL, ALL. Are 0.82 and 0.40, respectively. As with Extraversion, these values do not statistically differ from those obtained for the best conditions just discussed.

Table 4. Macro-P, Macro-R and Macro-F for best performing conditions on LoC

	Macro P	Macro R	Macro F
ACT, ACT	0.806	0.805	0.805
ACT, EMP	0.830	0,829	0.830
EMP, ACT	0.844	0.844	0.843
EMP, EMP	0.855	0.855	0.855

7 Discussion and Conclusions

Both for Extraversion and for LoC the conditions performing better are those where Activity and Emphasis features are used either for characterizing the target subject or the other participants. The Emphasis set has the additional property that it works pretty well also when no contextual information is provided. Given the different size of our feature sets, our results also show a dependence on the amount of information (number of features) each set contains, with the two larger ones performing better. Notice, however, that the <EMP, MIM> low results and the comparison with the two conditions where the entire feature sets are used suggest that the dependence on the mere size of the feature sets is not absolute. In particular, when all the features are used for the target there are no differences (either for Extraversion or for LoC) according to whether all or no features at all are used for characterizing the context; moreover, the accuracies for <ALL, No_Feat> and <ALL, ALL> are never statistically different from those for <ACT, ACT>, <ACT, EMP>, <EMP, ACT> and <EMP, EMP>.

All these data taken together seem to point to the idea that the two personality traits addressed here (Extraversion and Locus of Control) are such that consideration of the simple behavior of the target subject is enough to obtain reasonably high performances, provided that the larger feature sets (EMP and ALL) are used. Completeness of information about the subject can be traded off with information concerning the other participants, as with <ACT, ACT>, <ACT, EMP>, <EMP, ACT> and <EMP, EMP>.

Future work involves improving the modelling of the social context, extending it by introducing an index of visual attention received/given by a person, and its relation to his/her specific personality traits. According to psychologists social context has a major impact on one's ability to to process social signals. Furthermore, considering also the remaining personality traits of Big Five's scale would enlarge the scope of the context explored beyond the social one. It is well known, in fact, that traits such as Extraversions are more deeply involved in social behaviour than others, such as Conscientiousness.

References

1. John, O.P., Srivastava, S.: The Big five trait taxonomy: History, measurement and theoretical perspectives. In: Pervian, L.A., John, O.P. (eds.) Handbook of personality theory and research. Guilford Press, New York (1999)
2. Funder, D.C.: Personality. Annual Review of Psychology 52, 197–221 (2001)

3. Rotter, J.B.: Generalized Expectancies for Internal versus External Control of Reinforcment. Psychological Monographs 80 (1, Whole N. 609) (1965)
4. Weiner, B.: Achievement motivation and attribution theory. General Learning Press, Morristown (1974)
5. Scherer, K.R.: Personality Inference from Voice Quality: the Loud Voice of Extraversion. European Journal of Social Psychology 8, 467–487 (1978)
6. Scherer, K.R.: Personality markers in speech. In: Scherer, K.R., Giles, H. (eds.) Social Markers in Speech, pp. 147–209. Cambridge University Press, Cambridge (1979)
7. Furnham, D.: Language and Personality. In: Giles, H., Robinson, W. (eds.) Handbook of Language and Social Psychology. Winley (1990)
8. Argamon, S., Dhawle, S., Koppel, M., Pennbaker, J.: Lexical predictors of personality type. In: Proceedings of Interface and the Classification Society of North America (2005)
9. Oberlander, J., Nowson, S.: Whose thumb is it anyway? Classifying author personality from weblog text. In: Proceedings of the Annual Meeting of the ACL, pp. 627–634. Association for Computational Linguistics, Morristown (2006)
10. Mairesse, F., Walker, M.: Automatic recognition of personality in conversation. In: Proceedings of HLT-NAACL (2006)
11. Mairesse, F., Walker, M.A., Mehl, M.R., Moore, R.K.: Using Linguistic Cues for the Automatic Recognition of Personality in Conversation and Text. Journal of Artificial Intelligence Research 30, 457–500 (2007)
12. Olguín, D.O., Gloor, P.A., Pentland, A.: Capturing Individual and Group Behavior with Wearable Sensors. In: Proceeding of AAAI Spring Symposium on Human Behavior Modeling (2009a)
13. Olguin, D., Waber, B., Kim, T., Mohan, A., Ara, K., Pentland, A.: Sensible organizations: technology and methodology for automatically measuring organizational behavior. IEEE Transactions on Systems, Man, and Cybernetics-Part B: Cybernetics 39(1) (2009b)
14. Hall, J.W., Watson, W.H.: The Effects of a normative intervention on group decision-making performance. Human Relations 23(4), 299–317 (1970)
15. Mana, N., Lepri, B., Chippendale, P., Cappelletti, A., Pianesi, F., Svaizer, P., Zancanaro, M.: Multimodal Corpus of Multi-Party Meetings for Automatic Social Behavior Analysis and Personality Traits Detection. In: Proceedings of Workshop on Tagging, Mining and Retrieval of Human-Related Activity Information, at ICMI 2007, International Conference on Multimodal Interfaces, Nagoya, Japan (2007)
16. Farma, T., Cortivonis, I.: Un Questionario sul "Locus of Control": Suo Utilizzo nel Contesto Italiano (A Questionnaire on the Locus of Control: Its Use in the Italian Context), Ricerca in Psicoterapia, vol. 2 (2000)
17. Perugini, M., Di Blas, L.: Analyzing Personality-Related Adjectives from an Eticemic Perspective: the Big Five Marker Scale (BFMS) and the Italian AB5C Taxonomy. In: De Raad, B., Perugini, M. (eds.) Big Five Assessment, pp. 281–304. Hogrefe und Huber Publishers, Göttingen (2002)
18. Pentland, A.: Honest Signals: how they shape our world. MIT Press, Cambridge (September 2008)
19. Richmond, V.P., McCroskey, J.C.: Nonverbal Behavior in Interpersonal Relations, 3rd edn. Allyn & Bacon, Needham Heights (1995)
20. DePaulo, B.M.: Nonverbal behavior and self-presentation. Psychological Bulletin 111, 203–243 (1992)
21. Ekman, P., Friesen, W.V.: The repertoire of nonverbal behavior: Categories, origins, usage, and coding. Semiotica 1, 49–98 (1969)

22. Lepri, B., Mani, A., Pentland, A., Pianesi, F.: Honest Signals in the Recognition of Functional Relational Roles in Meetings. In: Proceedings of AAAI Spring Symposium on Behavior Modelling, Stanford, CA (2009)
23. Pentland, A.: A Computational Model of Social Signaling. In: Proceedings of the 18th International Conference on Pattern Recognition (ICPR 2006), vol. 1(2006), pp. 1080–1083 (2006)
24. Chippendale, P.: Towards Automatic Body Language Annotation. In: Proceedings of the 7th International Conference on Automatic Face and Gesture Recognition - FG 2006 (IEEE), Southampton, UK, pp. 487–492 (2006)
25. Ambady, N., Rosenthal, R.: Thin slices of expressive behaviors as predictors of interpersonal consequences: A meta-analysis. Psychological Bulletin 111, 256–274 (1992)
26. Pianesi, F., Mana, N., Cappelletti, A., Lepri, B., Zancanaro, M.: Multimodal Recognition of Personality Traits in Social Interactions. In: Proceedings of ICMI 2008, International Conference on Multimodal Interfaces, Chania, Crete, Grecia (2008)
27. Lepri, B., Mana, N., Cappelletti, A., Pianesi, F., Zancanaro, M.: Modeling Personality of Participants during Group Interaction. In: Houben, G.-J., McCalla, G., Pianesi, F., Zancanaro, M. (eds.) UMAP 2009. LNCS, vol. 5535, pp. 114–125. Springer, Heidelberg (2009)
28. Cristianini, N., Shawe-Taylor, J.: An Introduction to Support Vector Machines. Cambridge University Press, Cambridge (2000)

Speech Emotion Classification and Public Speaking Skill Assessment

Tomas Pfister and Peter Robinson

University of Cambridge
Computer Laboratory, 15 JJ Thomson Avenue, Cambridge CB3 0FD, UK
{tjp35,pr10}@cam.ac.uk

Abstract. This paper presents a new classification algorithm for real-time inference of emotions from the non-verbal features of speech. It identifies simultaneously occurring emotional states by recognising correlations between emotions and features such as pitch, loudness and energy. Pairwise classifiers are constructed for nine classes from the Mind Reading emotion corpus, yielding an average cross-validation accuracy of 89% for the pairwise machines and 86% for the fused machine. The paper also shows a novel application of the classifier for assessing public speaking skills, achieving an average cross-validation accuracy of 81%. Optimisation of support vector machine coefficients is shown to improve the accuracy by up to 25%. The classifier outperforms previous research on the same emotion corpus and achieves real-time performance.

1 Introduction

Emotions are fundamental for humans, impacting perception and everyday activities such as communication, learning and decision-making. They are expressed through speech, facial expressions, gestures and other non-verbal clues.

Speech emotion analysis refers to analysing vocal behaviour as a marker of affect, with focus on the non-verbal aspects of speech. Its basic assumption is that there is a set of objectively measurable features in voice that reflect the affective state of a person. This assumption is supported by the fact that most affective states involve physiological reactions which modify the process by which voice is produced. For example, anger often produces changes in respiration and increases muscle tension, influencing the vibration of the vocal folds and vocal tract shape, thus affecting the acoustic characteristics of the speech [1].

Discovering which features are indicative of emotional states and consecutively capturing them can be a difficult task. Furthermore, features indicating different states may be overlapping, and there may be multiple sets of features expressing the same emotional state. One widely used strategy is to compute as many features as possible. Optimisation algorithms can then be applied to select the features contributing most to the discrimination while ignoring others. This avoids making difficult *a priori* decisions about which features may be relevant.

Previous studies indicate that several emotions can occur simultaneously [2]. Examples of co-occurring emotions include being happy at the same time as

A.A. Salah et al. (Eds.): HBU 2010, LNCS 6219, pp. 151–162, 2010.

being tired, or feeling touched, surprised and excited when hearing good news. Improving upon the inference solution for co-occurring emotions presented by Sobol Shikler [3], the new system proposed in this paper is able to achieve real-time performance and higher classification accuracy.

In this paper, we describe an approach for real-time classification of co-occurring emotions. The classification output is a set of classes rather than a single one, allowing nuances and mixtures of emotions to be detected. Moreover, rather than attempting to make difficult *a priori* decisions about which features may be relevant, our strategy is to compute as many features as possible, and then select those offering the best discrimination. Finally, we present a novel application of the classifier to virtual speech coaching for improving public speaking skills.

2   Implementation Methodology

The design of the classifier considers three main factors: (i) the choice of a training corpus, (ii) the need for real-time performance, (iii) the ability to recognise co-occurring emotions.

For emotion classification we choose the Mind Reading corpus [4] which provides a hierarchical structure between groups with a large number of emotion concepts. It was developed by psychologists at University of Cambridge Autism Research Centre, aiming to help autistic children and adults to recognise both basic and complex emotions. The corpus consists of 2927 acted sentences, covering 442 different concepts of emotions, each with 5-7 sentences. The acting was induced and the labelling was done by ten people in different age groups [5]. The labelling of each sample in the corpus required the agreement of 8 members of a panel of 10 expert assessors. Although the samples are acted, the large number of samples makes the corpus suitable for training an emotion classifier.

The main emotion groups of Mind Reading are shown in Table 1. Each of these is further divided into concepts, giving a total of 422 subgroups. For the classifier, a subset of 9 categories representing a large variety of emotions is chosen. Each category contains samples from the groups as shown in Table 1. These are chosen to minimise the overlap between categories. The categories and samples are the same as those used by Sobol Shikler [3,6], allowing direct comparison of results.

Achieving real-time performance required a careful choice of feature extraction and classification algorithms. Recognising co-occurring emotions needed a method for ranking candidate emotions.

2.1   Support Vector Machines

Several potential classifiers were investigated. In previous work on emotion recognition from speech [3], support vector machines (SVMs) and tree algorithms such as C4.5 have been found to be effective. We also tried other methods such as the Naive Bayesian classifier and Perceptrons using the Weka data mining toolkit [7], but SVMs gave the most promising results.

Table 1. The 24 emotion groups in the Mind Reading corpus [5]. The superscripts indicate the main groups from which a subset of affective states is selected to allow comparison of the results to previous research [3]. These subsets are: absorbed[1], excited[2], interested[3], joyful[4], opposed[5], stressed[6], sure[7], thinking[8] and unsure[9].

afraid	angry	bored	bothered[1]	disbelieving
disgusted	excited[2]	fond	happy[3]	hurt
interested[4,5]	kind	liked	romantic	sad
sneaky	sorry	sure[6]	surprised	think[7]
touched	unfriendly[8]	unsure[9]	wanting	

We create the model by constructing an N-dimensional hyperplane that optimally separates data into two categories. Each data instance i is a tuple $(l_i, \mathbf{f_i})$, where $l_i \in \{1, -1\}$ is a class label, with 1 and -1 indicating the class, and $\mathbf{f_i} \in \mathbb{R}^n$ is a set of feature attributes. Optimality is taken to be the maximal separation between the two classes. Any such hyperplane can be written as the set of points $\mathbf{x}$ satisfying $\mathbf{w} \cdot \mathbf{x} - b = 0$ where $\mathbf{x} = \mathbf{f_i}$, $\mathbf{w}$ is the normal vector perpendicular to the hyperplane, $\|\mathbf{w}\|$ is the Euclidean norm of $\mathbf{w}$, and $\frac{|b|}{\|\mathbf{w}\|}$ is the perpendicular distance from the hyperplane to the origin.

We use a modified version of SVMs [8] that allows for mislabelled examples by choosing a hyperplane as cleanly as possible even if there is no hyperplane that can split the two classes. We measure this degree of misclassification by the variable ξ_i and require the solution of the optimisation problem

$$\min_{\mathbf{w},b,\xi}\{\frac{1}{2}\|\mathbf{w}\|^2 + C\sum_i \xi_i\} \tag{1}$$

under constraints

$$l_i(\mathbf{w} \cdot \mathbf{x_i} - b) \geq 1 - \xi_i \quad 1 \leq i \leq n \tag{2}$$

$$\xi_i \geq 0. \tag{3}$$

where $C > 0$ is the penalty for mislabelled examples and n is the number of data instances in the corpus. This can be solved using Lagrange multipliers.

We use a non-linear classifier, replacing the linear dot product $\mathbf{x}_i \cdot \mathbf{x}_j$ by a kernel function that transforms the original input space into a higher-dimensional feature space, allowing the SVM to potentially better separate the two classes. After trialling several possible kernel function candidates, the Radial Basis Function (RBF) kernel

$$K(\mathbf{x_i}, \mathbf{x_j}) = \exp(-\gamma\|\mathbf{x_i} - \mathbf{x_j}\|^2) \tag{4}$$

with $\gamma > 0$, was found to yield the most promising results.

To generalise SVMs to more than two classes, pairwise classification is used. A single multiclass problem is reduced into multiple binary problems by building a classifier for each pair of classes, using only instances from two classes at a time.

2.2   Training

The training system architecture is shown in Fig. 1. Its main components are discussed below.

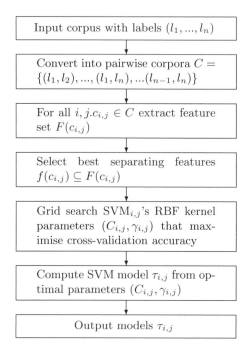

Fig. 1. The training system architecture. $SVM_{i,j}$ represents the support vector for comparing label l_i with l_j.

Feature Extraction. For this work, the openSMILE [9] feature extraction algorithms are used. OpenSMILE provides sound recording and playback via the open-source PortAudio library, echo cancellation, windowing functions, fast Fourier transforms and autocorrelation. Moreover, it is capable of extracting features such as pitch, loudness, energy, mel-spectra, voice quality, mel-spectrum frequency coefficients, and can calculate various functionals such as means, extremes, peaks, percentiles and deviations with a Real-Time Factor $\ll 1$.

Feature Selection. Since a large feature set will be extracted from the speech, it is expected that there are some irrelevant and redundant data that will not improve the SVM prediction performance. Classification algorithms are unable to attain high classification accuracy if there is a large number of weakly relevant and redundant features, a problem known as the *curse of dimensionality* [10]. Algorithms also suffer from computational load incurred by the high dimensional data.

Our approach is to use the predefined openSMILE set `emo_large` with 6552 features, and pick the most relevant ones using feature selection. For choosing relevant features, the Correlation-based Feature Selection (CFS) algorithm [11] is used. It uses a heuristic based on the assumption that good feature sets contain features highly correlated with the class and uncorrelated with each other.

Grid Search. When using the Radial Basis Function SVM kernel, it is important to choose a suitable penalty for mislabelled examples C and the exponentiation constant γ. Because the optimal values are model-specific, a search algorithm is needed for finding a near-optimal set of values.

The goal is to identify good (C, γ) values so that the classifier can accurately predict unseen testing data, rather than choosing them to maximise prediction accuracy for the training data whose labelling is already known. In this work we use v-fold cross-validation. The training set is divided into v equal-sized subsets, with each subset sequentially tested used a classifier trained on the remaining $v - 1$ subsets.

We use a GRID SEARCH algorithm that sequentially tries pairs of (C, γ) in a given range, and picks the one with the highest cross-validation accuracy. Exponentially growing sequences worked well in practice, confirming findings in previous research [12]. The algorithm is run recursively on a shrinking area.

2.3   Classification

The real-time classification system architecture is shown in Fig. 2. Its main components are discussed below.

Segmentation. Real-time analysis of speech requires segmenting the audio. Our static threshold algorithm achieves this by defining three thresholds. First, the silence threshold η defines the threshold for the energy $E = \sum_i^n |s_i|^2 > \eta$, for signals s_i in frame of size n. Second, ρ_{start} sets the number of frames with energy above η that are required until a segment start is detected. Third, ρ_{end} defines the number of frames below η until a segment end is detected. After the audio is segmented, openSMILE is used to extract the features.

Pairwise Fusion Mechanism. Once the audio is segmented and the features are extracted, $n(n-1)/2$ pairwise machines for n classes are run in parallel to predict the class for a segment. In order to determine the most probable class, the probabilities of the multiple binary classifiers are fused.

We propose a fusion method for determining co-occurring emotions. Whereas in traditional single-label classification a sample is associated with a single label l_i from a set of disjoint labels L, multi-label classification associates each sample with a set of labels $L' \subseteq L$. A previous study concluded that the use of complex non-linear fusion methods yielded only marginal benefits (0.3%) over linear methods when used with SVMs [13]. Therefore, three linear fusion methods are implemented:

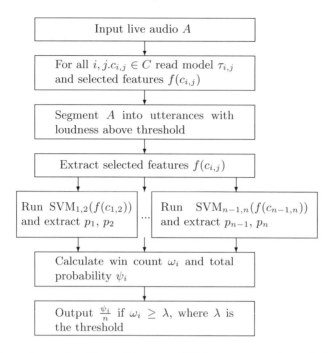

Fig. 2. The real-time classifier architecture. $\text{SVM}_{i,j}$ computes the probabilities p_i and p_j for labels i, j, using features $f(c_{i,j})$.

1. Majority voting using wins from binary classifiers.
2. Maximum combined probability from binary classifiers.
3. Binary classification wins above a threshold.

In the first method we consider all $n-1$ SVM outputs per class as votes and select the class with most votes. Assuming that the classes are mutually exclusive, the *a posteriori* probability for feature vector $\mathbf{f}$ is $p_i = P(\mathbf{f} \in class_i)$. The classifier $\text{SVM}_{i,j}$ computes an estimate $\hat{p}_{i,j}$ of the binary decision probability

$$p_{i,j} = P(\mathbf{f} \in class_i | \mathbf{f} \in class_i \cup class_j) \qquad (5)$$

between classes i and j. The final classification decision $\hat{D}_{voting}$ is the class i for which

$$\hat{D}_{voting} = \arg \max_{1 \le i \le n} \sum_{j \ne i} g(\hat{p}_{i,j}) \qquad (6)$$

where

$$g(p) = \begin{cases} 1 & \text{for } p \ge \frac{1}{2} \\ 0 & \text{otherwise} \end{cases}. \qquad (7)$$

Ties are solved by declaring the class with higher probability to be the winner.

In the second method, the maximum probability $\psi_i = \sum_{p \in S_i} p$ of the binary SVMs is determined. The winner of decision $\hat{D}_{probability}$ is i such that

$$\hat{D}_{probability} = \arg \max_{1 \leq i \leq n} \sum_{j \neq i} \hat{p}_{i,j}. \tag{8}$$

Finally, for detecting co-occurring emotions, the classes are ranked according to the number of wins. The classes with wins above a threshold λ are returned, with the classification decision $\hat{D}_{threshold}$ being the set of classes

$$\hat{D}_{threshold} = \{i \mid \sum_{j \neq i} g(\hat{p}_{i,j}) \geq \lambda\}. \tag{9}$$

We set $\lambda = \lfloor (\mu + \sigma)n \rfloor$ where μ is the mean win count, σ is the standard deviation and n is the class cardinality to allow comparison with Sobol Shikler [3].

3   Application for Public Speaking Skill Assessment

We present a novel application of the classifier for assessing the quality of public speaking skills.

In persuasive communication, the non-verbal clues a speaker conveys require special attention. Untrained speakers often come across as bland and lifeless. Precisely analysing the voice is difficult for humans and is subjective. By using a similar approach as for detecting emotions, our system enables more objective assessment of public speaking skills.

We retrain our classifier using six labels describing public speaking skills shown in Table 2. Following the requirements by Schuller et al. [14], we use non-acted, non-prompted, realistic data with many speakers, using all obtained data. An experienced speech coach was asked to label 124 one-minute-long samples of natural audio from 31 people attending speech coaching sessions. The chosen six labels are the ones that the professional is accustomed to using when assessing the public speaking skills of clients. The samples are labelled on a scale 4–10 for each class. We then divided the samples of classes into higher and lower halves according to the score. The upper half represents a positive detection of the class (e.g. *clear*), and the lower half represents a negative detection (e.g. *not clear*).

One binary SVM per class is used to derive a class-wise probability. If a pairwise approach similar to that in emotion classification had been used, the same samples would have existed in several classes, making separating the classes intractable. As a result, unlike in emotion detection where the most prominent labels describing the speech are selected, for speech quality assessment all classes are detected, each labelled with a probability. This allows users to attempt to maximise all class probabilities, a goal which is more useful for speech coaching.

The results of public speaking skill assessment are shown in Table 2. All classes can be accurately detected. The classes *competent* and *dynamic* present slightly lower detection accuracies, perhaps due to the smaller variation in scores resulting from a small corpus size. Overall, however, the speech quality assessment

Table 2. Detection accuracies in percentages for assessing public speaking skills

Class	10-fold cross-validation	Training samples
clear	80	66
competent	74	49
credible	80	42
dynamic	77	45
persuasive	82	79
pleasant	93	73
Mean	**81**	**59**

accuracies are high (average 81%) and may provide useful feedback to speakers. In future work, performance using alternative evaluation metrics such as those specified by Schuller et al. [14] will be investigated.

4   Evaluation

In this section we evaluate the overall classification results.

The result of applying grid search is shown in Table 3. The optimisation is done on the training data, with the testing data kept unseen. A significant improvement, between 10% and 25%, was observed. As the optimisation maximises the cross-validation accuracy of the training data instead of the training data classification accuracy, the optimisation did not result in overfitting of the model.

The average latency in milliseconds of the classification stage is shown in Fig. 3. It was measured as the time between the detection of the end of a segment and the output of the result. As shown in the figure, normal sentences (1–15 s) are classified in 0.046–0.110 s, making the delay barely noticeable. Improving upon Sobol Shikler's inference solution [3], this allows real-time classification.

The ten-fold cross-validation results for the pairwise SVMs are shown in Table 4. All accuracies are greater than the values obtained in previous research using the same classes and corpus. The results are constantly above 80%, in contrast to the lower bound 60% obtained previously.

A summary of the accuracies for the three different fusion methods is shown in Table 5. The average accuracies are higher than or equal to the results achieved

Table 3. Detection accuracies in percentages with a 70–30% training/testing split for the three fusion methods, with and without grid search

Type of data	Threshold	Max probability	Max wins
Grid search	86	72	70
No grid search	76	47	48

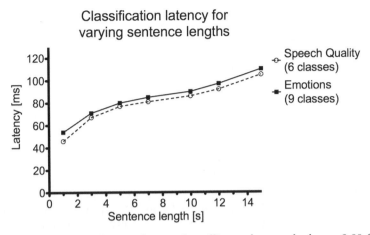

Fig. 3. Average live classification latency in milliseconds on a dual-core 2.66 GHz PC with 4 GB RAM

Table 4. The 10-fold cross-validation accuracy for pairwise SVMs in percentages. The average accuracy is 89%. For comparison, Sobol Shikler's results [3] are in parentheses.

	excited	interested	joyful	opposed	stressed	sure	thinking	unsure
absorbed	**93** (81)	**87** (82)	**96** (82)	**96** (78)	**89** (87)	**85** (84)	**82** (73)	**84** (64)
excited		**90** (71)	**84** (60)	**81** (71)	**80** (61)	**94** (83)	**90** (72)	**87** (75)
interested			**92** (77)	**92** (75)	**91** (66)	**90** (78)	**90** (84)	**85** (72)
joyful				**86** (71)	**85** (61)	**99** (83)	**95** (72)	**92** (75)
opposed					**93** (84)	**91** (72)	**94** (81)	**92** (79)
stressed						**86** (84)	**88** (75)	**86** (78)
sure							**94** (75)	**88** (78)
thinking								**90** (89)

Table 5. Accuracies in percentages for the three fusion methods. Sobol Shikler's results [3] are shown in parentheses. 2.5 classes were inferred on average with a threshold $\lambda = 6$.

Type of data	Threshold	Max probability	Voting
70–30% training/ testing split	**86** (79)	72	70
Training data	**99** (81)	86	88

previously on the same corpus [3]. Notably, the average accuracy of the maximum probability fusion technique is higher than that achieved by majority voting (72% vs 70%). However, for some classes the majority voting accuracy is higher (e.g. *stressed* and *interested*). A higher average accuracy could be achieved by combining these methods. In future work, more advanced fusion methods such as the ensemble classification presented by Schuller et al. [15] and the tree-based approach by Lee et al. [16] will be investigated.

Confusion matrices for fusion using thresholding and maximum probability are shown in Tables 6 and 7 respectively. Inspection of the confusion matrices reveals that some classes are better detected than others. The classes *opposed* and *sure* present the lowest values using any method. This is reflected by the lower number of training samples (38 and 53 samples, compared to the average of 61) resulting from the categorisation choice to allow comparison to Sobol Shikler [3]. Similarly, the class with most samples (*joyful*, 94 samples) is most frequently mistaken to be the correct class. In future work classes with equal numbers of training samples could be used.

As expected, the thresholding fusion method for co-occurring emotion classification yields highest detection accuracies since several classes can be selected at a time. This, however, also leads to much higher confusion values because of the assumption that more than one emotion can be occurring simultaneously. For example, as shown in Table 7, samples labelled *excited* are detected as *joyful* in 35% of cases, compared to a correct detection rate of 85%. It is likely that some high confusion rates are caused by the overrepresentation of certain classes.

Table 6. Confusion matrix using maximum probability for pairwise fusion. The column headings show the ground truth and the rows show inferences. Average accuracy is 72%. A random choice would result in 11% accuracy.

	absorbed	excited	interested	joyful	opposed	stressed	sure	thinking	unsure
absorbed	74	0	2	0	0	1	2	1	1
excited	0	75	2	6	0	2	6	0	1
interested	4	0	69	0	0	2	2	3	1
joyful	4	10	6	79	16	11	4	3	4
opposed	0	2	0	2	62	1	2	0	0
stressed	4	8	6	3	8	67	9	1	8
sure	0	0	2	2	5	2	63	0	0
thinking	7	0	8	3	0	4	11	86	17
unsure	7	4	6	4	8	8	2	6	68

Table 7. Confusion matrix using thresholding for pairwise fusion. The column headings show the ground truth and the rows show inferences. Average accuracy is 86%. A random choice would result in 11% accuracy.

	absorbed	excited	interested	joyful	opposed	stressed	sure	thinking	unsure
absorbed	93	4	15	0	0	4	12	23	24
excited	15	85	10	29	27	46	24	6	14
interested	22	2	83	14	3	10	11	17	14
joyful	15	35	21	91	41	39	22	23	22
opposed	0	14	6	22	73	11	17	7	8
stressed	15	60	31	56	51	92	31	24	29
sure	11	19	6	4	16	9	74	11	9
thinking	48	15	42	19	24	19	28	93	56
unsure	48	8	52	24	22	31	26	56	91

5 Conclusion

We have presented a framework for real-time speech emotion classification whose accuracy outperforms previous work using the same corpus [3]. We have also shown that the novel application of the system for assessing public speaking skills achieves high classification accuracies.

The framework consists of $n(n-1)/2$ pairwise SVMs for n labels, each with a differing set of features selected by a correlation-based feature selection algorithm. We demonstrated a considerable improvement in classification accuracy from optimising the misclassification and exponentiation coefficients (C, γ) in (1) and (4) using a grid search algorithm. Improvements between 10% and 25% were observed.

Overall, this paper presented a high-accuracy training and classification framework for emotion detection from speech, and shows that it can be successfully applied for real-time assessment of public speaking skills.

References

1. Scherer, K.R.: Vocal affect expression: A review and a model for future research. Psychological bulletin 99, 143–165 (1986)
2. Haynes, J.D., Rees, G.: Decoding mental states from brain activity in humans. Nature Reviews Neuroscience 7, 523–534 (2006)
3. Sobol Shikler, T.: Analysis of affective expression in speech. PhD thesis, Cambridge University (2007)

4. Baron-Cohen, S., Golan, O., Wheelwright, S., Hill, J.J.: Mind Reading: The Interactive Guide to Emotions. Jessica Kingsley Publishers, University of Cambridge (2004) ISBN 1 84310 214 5
5. Golan, O., Baron-Cohen, S., Wheelwright, S., Hill, J.J.: Systemizing empathy: Teaching adults with asperger syndrome and high functioning autism to recognize complex emotions using interactive multimedia. Development and Psychopathology 18, 589–615 (2006)
6. Sobol Shikler, T., Robinson, P.: Classification of complex information: Inference of co-occurring affective states from their expressions in speech. IEEE Transactions on Pattern Analysis and Machine Intelligence 99 (2009)
7. Hall, M.A., Frank, E., Holmes, G., Pfahringer, B., Reutemann, P., Witten, I.: The WEKA data mining software: An update. SIGKDD Explorations 11 (2009)
8. Vapnik, V.N.: The nature of statistical learning theory. Springer, Heidelberg (1998)
9. Eyben, F., Wöllmer, M., Schuller, B.: openEAR – Introducing the Munich opensource emotion and affect recognition toolkit. In: Proc. 4th International HUMAINE Association Conference on Affective Computing and Intelligent Interaction 2009 (ACII 2009). IEEE, Amsterdam (September 2009)
10. Altun, H., Polat, G.: New frameworks to boost feature selection algorithms in emotion detection for improved human-computer interaction. In: Mele, F., Ramella, G., Santillo, S., Ventriglia, F. (eds.) BVAI 2007. LNCS, vol. 4729, pp. 533–541. Springer, Heidelberg (2007)
11. Hall, M.A., Smith, L.A.: Feature selection for machine learning: comparing a correlation-based filter approach to the wrapper. In: Florida Artificial Intelligence Symposium, pp. 235–239 (1999)
12. Qing-kun, L., Pei-wen, Q.: Model selection for SVM using mutative scale chaos optimization algorithm. Journal of Shanghai University 10, 531–534 (2006)
13. Pöyhönen, S., Arkkio, A., Jover, P., Hyötyniemi, H.: Coupling pairwise support vector machines for fault classification. Control Engineering Practice 13, 759–769 (2005)
14. Schuller, B., Steidl, S., Batliner, A.: The Interspeech 2009 emotion challenge. In: Interspeech, Brighton, UK (2009)
15. Schuller, B., Reiter, S., Müller, R., Al-Hames, M., Lang, M., Rigoll, G.: Speaker independent speech emotion recognition by ensemble classification. In: IEEE International Conference on Multimedia and Expo. (2005)
16. Lee, C., Mower, E., Busso, C., Lee, S., Narayanan, S.: Emotion recognition using a hierarchical binary decision tree approach. In: Interspeech, Brighton, UK (2009)

Dominance Signals in Debates

Isabella Poggi and Francesca D'Errico

Dipartimento di Scienze dell'Educazione – Università Roma Tre
Via Manin 53 – 00185 Roma, Italy
{Poggi,fderrico}@uniroma3.it

Abstract. The paper analyzes the signals of dominance in different modalities displayed during TV talk shows and debates. Dominance is defined, according to a model in terms of goals and beliefs, as a person's having more power than others. A scheme is presented for the annotation of signals of dominance in political debates: based on the analysis of videotaped data, a typology is proposed of strategies to convey dominance, and the corresponding signals are overviewed. Strategies range from the aggressive ones of imperiousness, judgement, invasion, norm violation and defiance, to the more subtle touchiness and victimhood, ending up with haughtiness, irony and ridicule, easiness, carelessness and assertiveness.

Keywords: Dominance, Social signals, Debates.

1 Dominance

The notion of *dominance* reflects different research approaches and sometimes it is confused with notions like *status* or *power*.

In the sociological perspective the notion of *status* refers to a hierarchical position in a group or organization that is determined by native (e.g., gender or ethnic belonging) or gained characteristics (e.g., work position). In Social Psychology, according to the *expectation states theory* [1] the concept of status is replicated at the interpersonal level by *expectations of status*, evaluative beliefs about positive or negative competences associated to this nominal feature, and at the personal level by *expectations of performance*, which anticipate the contribution needed for a specific task. In the *social identity theory* [2], the awareness of belonging to a social group is a central part of the self concept, with associated emotional, motivational, behavioural responses; so people tend to evaluate the *stability* and *legitimacy* of status differences to decide what cognitive strategy is useful in their condition: re-categorization, social creativity, individual or collective mobility across the hierarchy [3].

Power is defined as "the ability to influence or to control other persons or groups" [4]. Status may well be a condition for power in that sense, but does not necessarily imply attitude change and control, and it is focused not on personal competence but on a nominal or structural position in a social group or institution.

Dominance might be seen as a combination of status and power since it is defined as "ability to influence or control others, but it also involves *groupness*. Specifically, dominance concerns power relationships within a relatively enduring social organization" [4].

A.A. Salah et al. (Eds.): HBU 2010, LNCS 6219, pp. 163–174, 2010.

As to its roots, some authors view dominance as a personality trait [4], stressing its being a steady feature of an individual, others propose a situational view: dominance as gained from time to time depending on the context [5; 6; 7].

In recent literature, for the *social dominance theory* [8] one possible explanation of discrimination phenomena is the psychological construct of *social dominance orientation* (SDO), i.e. the personal preference for hierarchical relationships between social groups. The degree of social dominance is determined by group membership because members of more powerful groups are more dominant then less powerful ones (e.g., men more dominant than women); further, SDO is a way to fulfil the social hierarchies, since people with high level of social dominance tend to legitimate racism, nationalism and conservatism.

In the *dyadic power theory* [9] dominance is seen from an interpersonal point of view: "interpersonal dominance is a relationally-based communication strategy dependent on the context and motives of the individuals involved" [6]. This definition of dominance is a dynamic combination of personal and contextual characteristics and it is based on a relational model, pointing out that the influence or control of powerful individuals depends on the submission or acquiescence of another one. Thus dominance is seen as a dynamic communicative act based on a relation, by means of which an individual exerts power or influence over another individual.

From this perspective much research has focused on the verbal and non verbal indicators of dominance (for ample reviews see 10; 11; 7; 9).

2 Signals of Dominance

Signals of dominance in various modalities have been explored. Within studies on gaze, Keating [12] demonstrated that in western cultures lowered eyebrows are perceived as a strong signal of dominance. Argyle [11] pointed out that the dominant person gazes less and during interaction reduces the amount of gaze and breaks mutual gaze first. Yet, in close relationships the dominant person has a more expressive face, he looks more than the less dominant and shows higher *visual dominance*, i.e. higher looking while speaking than while listening [4; 7]. As to hand movements, the dominant person uses more gestures, more illustrators than adaptors, but giving an impression of relaxation and confidence [7]. Posture and spatial behaviour are salient in the expression of pride [13], where expanded postures are typical especially in males [14]. In vocal behaviour, dominance passes through speech intensity, tempo and pitch [10; 15], but also through turn taking management [16]: perception of dominance is strictly connected to amount of speaking [17], topic introduction [18], frequency and maintenance of turns, and interruptions [19].

3 A Definition of Dominance in Terms of Goals and Beliefs

We propose a definition of dominance according to a model of cognitive and social action in terms of goals and beliefs [20; 21]. In this model, the life of natural and artificial, individual and collective systems consists of pursuing goals, regulatory states which, if not realized, trigger action. To achieve goals a system performs a hierarchically arranged plan of actions by using internal resources (action capacities and beliefs) and external resources (world conditions, material resources, others' help in goal pursuit). In this framework, *"power of"* is defined as the likeliness for a system to achieve its goals.

If system A has a goal G but does not have the *"power of"* achieving it for the lack of capacities or conditions, while B has them, A may "depend on" B to achieve G. The devices of *adoption* and *influence* stem from this *dependence*: if A depends on B, A can achieve G only if B adopts A's goal G, putting one's resources to the service of A's goal. So, both A and B may have the goal to influence each other, i.e., to have each other pursue or give up some goal. When A depends on B, B has the *"power to influence"* A; but if dependence is not reciprocal, B can both influence A and refuse to adopt A's goal, thus having *"power over"* A.

Besides *"power to influence"* and *"power over"* power may also stem from comparison: B has *"more power than"* A. Adoption enhances the power of systems of achieving goals thanks to resource exchange; but to decide whose and what goals to adopt, a system needs to evaluate other systems, to form an image of them. In humans, image is the set of evaluative and non-evaluative beliefs that others conceive of about a person. We strive to present a positive image of ourselves to have others adopt our goals. In rare cases we obtain adoption by presenting an image of lack of power (e.g., when C helps A out of compassion); but generally we must elicit positive evaluations, show an image of power (e.g., C adopts B's goals because she esteems him). To choose whether to adopt A's or B's goal, C compares their respective power as to specific goals. In an electoral debate, to decide which candidate to vote, elector C compares the respective powers of A and B as to the goal of fulfilling C's political expectations.

These "social" notions of power, *power to influence*, *power over* and *more power than*, are strongly intertwined. If I have *more power than* you I may have *power over* you, and this gives me the *power to influence* you. So, to state social hierarchies, assessing who has *more power than* others (e.g., who is the alpha male winning contests) is a basis to institutionalize his *power over others*, to credit him with a higher status than others, and this gives him the *power to influence*.

We can now state a correspondence between the classical notions of status, power and dominance and the three social notions of power defined above. *Power over others* corresponds to having a higher status than others, *power to influence* to the classical notion of power, and dominance, in our terms, is the fact that one has *more power than* another. Dominance thus entails power comparison; B is dominant compared with A if B has more power than A with respect to goal G. So B may be dominant in some fields but not in others, and his dominance may either be a personality trait or be gained in a specific situation thanks to A's behaviour.

Dominance is the basis for *power over* and hence for *power to influence*, but only if others know it. This is why signalling dominance is so important, in humans and other animals. We define as "signal of dominance" any signal, in whatever modality, that conveys the belief "I have more power than B" to either B himself or to C.

4 Dominance in Debates

This work presents a study on the signals of dominance displayed during TV debates. In a debate a person may want to appear dominant, i.e., to signal "I have more power than you", to do so he may use a number of different strategies – from more direct and aggressive to more subtle and indirect ones – and these strategies exploit specific signals in various modalities. The point of our work is to single out these strategies and their typical signals.

4.1 Method

To single out different dominance strategies, we performed a qualitative analysis of multimodal communication in 7 political debates in Italian TV talk shows and 1 judicial debate in a trial of high political import (the "Clean Hands Trial", see 4.2.2.). The analysis is based on a model [22] that views communication as a social action whereby a Sender S, in order to the (conscious, unconscious or biological) goal of having an Addressee A assume some belief B, produces a signal (a sentence, gesture, facial expression, gaze, posture, body movement) that conveys belief B as its meaning. Each signals has a literal meaning, and possibly indirect meanings that the Sender wants the Addressee to understand through inference.

We analyzed fragments for a total of 80 minutes using the annotation scheme in Table 1. Column 1 contains time in the video and name of the Sender of the analyzed behaviour, cols. 2 and 4 describe, respectively, the speaker's verbal and nonverbal behaviours, and cols.3 and 5 their meaning. Col.6 mentions the indirect meaning: what the Sender wants to be inferred from the meanings of col. 3 and/or 5. Col.7 classifies the behaviour as being a signal of dominance (D) or not, assigning it to a specific "dominance strategy".

Let us see a fragment from a political talk show in 2008.

(1)   Eugenio Scalfari, founder and president of "La Repubblica", an important leftist newspaper in Italy, argues against Roberto Castelli, a Minister of the government of the right, who has just maintained that Scalfari is not an expert in economic issues, since he hardly knows what a company is. Scalfari says: *"Voglio dire all'... onorevole, eh... che io conosco le aziende, sa. Io ne ho fatta una, che adesso ha cinquecento giornalisti"*. (I want to tell... Lord ... well... that I know companies, you know, I made one that now has 500 reporters).

The first part of the sentence, *"Voglio dire all'"* (I want to tell) (col. 2) is uttered in a *low voice* (col.4), meaning the Sender is quiet (col. 5), thus indirectly conveying (col. 6) that Scalfari does not worry about Castelli's argument. So Scalfari exhibits a dominance strategy of "calm strength" (col.7; see Sect.4.2.9). Before saying *"Onorevole"* (which is the name credited in Italy to members of Parliament, but literally means "Honourable"), he makes a *pause* (col. 4), conveying he is uncertain (col. 5) whether the literal meaning "honourable" can apply to Castelli: an insinuation implying (col. 6) contempt towards his opponent, exploiting a dominance strategy of "haughtiness" (col. 7). While finally saying *"onorevole"*, he *looks at Moderator* (col. 4), and ignores Castelli (col.5), conveying he is not worth taking into account (col. 6). A strategy of "careless attitude" (col.7). Then Scalfari says: *"Eh... che io conosco le aziende, sa?"* (well... that I know companies, you know) (col. 2), and he *looks at Castelli* (col. 4), meaning he is now addressing him (col. 5). By saying *"sa?"* (do you know it?) he literally asks Castelli (col. 3) if he ever knows that Scalfari is the founder

Table 1. An annotation scheme for dominant communicative acts

1. Time, Send.	2. Speech	3. Meaning	4. Signal	5. Meaning	6. Indirect meaning	7. Dominance Strategy
Scalfari 3.39	*Voglio dire... all'...* I want to tell....	I tell Moderator that I want to tell something to my opponent			I do not consider my opponent at all	D: Careless attitude
3.39			*Low voice intensity*	I am quiet	I am not worried or afraid	D: Calm strength
3.39			*Pause*	I am uncertain if he deserves being called "honourable"	I feel contempt toward my opponent	D: Haughtiness
3.39	*Onorevole* Lord...	My opponent is a member of Parliament (but he is not honourable)	*Looks at Moderator (not to the opponent)*	I ignore him	I do not consider my opponent at all	D: Careless attitude
3.46	*Eh... che io conosco le aziende* Ehm... that I know companies	I affirm I do know companies			It is not true that I cannot speak of economic issues	Counter argument
3.49	*Sa* You know	I ask you, my opponent, if you know this	*Looks at opponent*	I address you now	I am ironic about your not taking this into account	D: Irony
3.57	*Io ne ho fatta una* I made one	I remind you that I made a Company	*High voice intensity*	I remark this, this is important	You should take it into account	D: Assertive-ness
3.58	*che adesso ha cinquecento giornalisti* That now has 500 reporters		*Slow voice*	I need not hurry up in talking	I am quiet, I don't fear you	D: Calm strength

of "La Repubblica", but being this a well known thing, the question sounds ironic (cols. 6 and 7). Finally, he says: *"Io ne ho fatta una"* (I made one) (col.2) in a *loud voice* (col. 4) remarking his statement (col. 5), as if reminding this to Castelli, and inviting him to take it into account (col.6). He is now "assertive" (col. 7), i.e., maintaining his point without aggressing the other. Then he adds: *"che ora ha cinquecento giornalisti"* (that now has 500 reporters) (col.2), with a *slow voice*: he conveys he is not in a hurry (col.5), hence showing not worried nor afraid of the opponent (col. 6) and displaying "calm strength" again (col. 7).

4.2 Results. Dominance Strategies

Based on our qualitative analysis we concluded that people in debates adopt various strategies to show dominance, each exploiting peculiar signals in various modalities. We define a strategy as a set of behaviours directly or indirectly aimed at conveying a specific message, like those in column 6 of the annotation scheme. Conveying that particular message implies one has the particular attitude towards the other, or wants to project the particular image, that is written in column 7 of Table 1.

The dominance strategies we singled out are the following.

4.2.1 Aggressiveness

A first trivial way to show dominant in a debate is aggressiveness. The message conveyed is: I am stronger than you, and if you do not do what I want, I intend to, and I can, punish you. This strategy subsumes the following behaviours: imperiousness, judgement, invasion and norm violation.

a. *Imperiousness.* A straightforward way to exhibit dominance is imperiousness. The message conveyed in this strategy is: I give you commands, hence I can afford to do so, hence I have power over you. The types of signals used to this end are primarily requestive communicative acts and deontic words like *must*, *ought to*, *necessarily*.

Let us take a case of a requestive gesture.

(2) Luigi De Magistris, a former judge, now a leftist member of the European parliament, is talking. Roberto Castelli starts speaking during De Magistris' turn, trying to interrupt him. De Magistris does not stop speaking and, while continuing, simply *raises his right hand, spread fingers, palm to Castelli*, as if saying: "Stop (speaking)".

This gesture counts as an imperative sentence conveying a peremptory order, namely, that Castelli should not interrupt, and. Let us now see a use of a deontic verb.

(3) Ignazio La Russa, a Minister from the government of the right, has been invited in a talk show of a leftist channel to discuss about the wiretapping of the premier's phone-calls, its constitutional validity, and whether the actions mentioned in the wiretapped dialogues were illicit or not. La Russa is trying to manage the turn-taking himself, and instead of letting the Moderator do so, he says: *"Un minuto di fila io devo parlare"*. (A whole minute continued I **must** speak!).

Verbs of this kind imply one makes appeal to right, to law, which is supposed to win over individuals' goals.

b. *Judgement.* A typical aggressive dominance strategy is playing the judge, showing entitled to judge others. This conveys the message: I can judge you, so I have power over you. One way to do so is to use insulting words or strong negative evaluations. Let us see a case of this.

(4) La Russa shows indignation about the Premier's phone call wiretapping through a rhetorical question: *"È impossibile dire in questa televisione, che è il regno della libertà, che è una **fetenzia** quello che sta succedendo?"* (Is it impossible to say in this TV, which is the realm of freedom, that what is happening is really a **filthy thing**?).

The word *fetenzia* (filthy thing) is a case of dysphemism: an ostentatiously negative and insulting word, used with the aim of offending, i.e., aggressing the opponent's image. Moreover, if the Speaker affords using evaluative words, while not bothering to extenuate the strongly negative evaluation through politeness or euphemism, this implies he feels entitled to judge others.

Another device to imply one is acting as a judge is showing severity: this can be conveyed through communicative (verbal or nonverbal) acts of accusation, blame, reproach, but also by displaying anger. Since anger is generally due to norm violation, showing angry implies that some of one's rights (possibly the right to be obeyed) have been violated, or that one's will (deserving obeyence), has not been fulfilled. Anger is displayed by eyebrow frowning, wide open eyes, and complete absence of smile; but also by those parameters of gesture and voice that are a cue to high activation, like hectic gestures and high voice intensity. Besides revealing emotional arousal, these aspects of gesture and voice also convey emphasis, implying that what one is saying is more important and worth being heard than what said by others.

c. *Invasion.* A person adopting an aggressive dominance strategy typically takes more room than he is entitled to, to widen one's territory at the expense of the other's, in both time and space. Signals invading space are ample gestures, while a typical way to invade time is aggressive turn taking behaviour, characterized by frequent interruptions and overlapping, and by taking more time for one's turn, often ignoring the Moderator's requests.

(5) La Russa says to the Moderator, who is trying to put him a question: *"Non ho bisogno della domanda. Mi faccia rispondere. Lo lasci dire a me."*. (I don't need the question. Let me answer. Let me say this). His *voice* has a *high intensity*; he *tilts his head upward-forward*, then he makes *repeated jerky nods* and *batonic gestures.*

La Russa refuses the Moderator's question, he does not accept to submit to her turn taking management, and does so not only by his very explicit sentence ("I don't need the question"), but also by voice and gesture intensity, displaying high activation and strength. A case of multimodal aggressive floor management.

d. *Norm violation.* Invasion in turn taking behaviour is also a cue to another aggressive strategy: norm violation. Blatant violation of generally accepted rules implicitly conveys the idea that one is so strong as to be above rules.

(6) La Russa goes on talking far beyond the turn assigned to him by the Moderator, and continuously overlaps on her attempts to manage turn taking with the other invited politician. When she finally asks him: *"E mi fa fare la domanda?"* (And do you let me put the question?) he says: *"Beh, per questa volta gliela lascio fare"* (Well, for this time I will).

With this self-ironical concession to the Moderator, he is reversing the roles, hence indirectly communicating: "It is me who have the right to turn management in this debate".

4.2.2 Defiance

A way to express dominance, mainly from a down to an up position, is defiance. Interesting cases of this strategy come from the "Clean Hands trial": a trial of high political importance for Italy, viewed as a "degradation ritual" [23; 24; 25], i.e., a ceremony in which someone guilty of juridical or moral faults gets publicly devoid of his public identity and status, as an outcome of public moral indignation. In the "Clean Hands" trial many previously important politicians charged of corruption were put pilloried and lost their face from a political and ethical point of view, losing all their power. Yet many of them, during the trial, tried to make appeal to their previous power and to challenge the judicial power accusing them. Here is an example.

(7) The politician Paolo Cirino Pomicino is examined by the public accuser, Antonio Di Pietro, for having taken money on behalf of his party by Italian industry owners. Di Pietro is hunting him down by continuous sarcastic questions about how much money he has got while pretending it was legal, and the judge appears quite convinced that Di Pietro is right. So Di Pietro (the judicial power) is now winning over Cirino Pomicino (the political power). Notwithstanding this, during nearly the whole examination, Cirino Pomicino keeps displaying a *defying stare* and *raised chin*, as if telling Di Pietro: "I am not afraid of you, I still have more power than you".

4.2.3 Touchiness

The dominance strategies seen so far are straightforward ways to claim one has more power than the other. Now we move to more indirect and subtle ways to display dominance: strategies of decreasing (apparent) aggressiveness and increasing subtlety.

A such strategy is showing touchiness. Being touchy means to have a low threshold for feeling offended. You feel offended when you feel that some communicative or non-communicative action of another caused a blown to your image. Image is the set of evaluative and non-evaluative beliefs others have about you [26], and their evaluations are beliefs about how much power you have: in brief, image is how much power people think you have. So, the more power you claim you have, the worthier your image, and the more severe a blow to it: as if a direct correlation held between severity of an offence and power of the offended one. So, if you want to let people infer you have more power, you simply have to show offended also for things that would not be so serious for other people.

During the debate with La Russa, Di Pietro, a leftist member of the parliament, accuses La Russa and the Premier of being already exalted about their future victory at the elections, which they consider certain. To describe their exaltation he uses the word *gasati* (gassed: something like "enflated with gas"), which is not a very insulting word, but rather an expression of Di Pietro's creative popular language. La Russa makes a scandal about this word: in a provocative way he asks Di Pietro to explain what *gasati* means, and asks the Moderator how can she stand that in her talk show one says words like this, to make it clear that he considers it a severe offence.

4.2.4 Victimhood

A strategy only apparently opposite to dominance is playing the victim. If you are a victim, others unduly did wrong to you violating your rights, so you are entitled to retaliate, and this strengthens your claiming of your rights.

Here is an example from La Russa's multimodal behaviour.

> (8) The Moderator invites La Russa to let other people speak, and he says: *"Ma perché non mi lasciate finire di parlare? Un minuto di fila io devo parlare"*. (But why don't you let me finish? A whole minute continued I must speak!). While saying: *"Ma perché non mi lasciate finire di parlare?"* (But why don't you let me finish?), he *moves his joint hands*, like praying hands, *up and down repeatedly*, as if begging for something. Then he goes on: *Un minuto di fila io devo parlare"* (a whole minute continued I must speak!), and *opens arms*, showing helplessness.

The first sentence asks why don't they let him finish to speak, but being a rhetorical question, it pretends to be allowed to speak. Praying hands and open arms adopt a strategy of victimhood, as if he were denied the right to speak. Then with the second sentence ("A whole minute continued I *must* speak!") he definitely claims his right to speak, moving to the imperiousness strategy.

4.2.5 Haughtiness

Opposed to a strategy of victimhood is one of haughtiness: the Sender wants the audience to understand his superiority over the opponent, and does so not through boasting, but in a covert and indirect way, conveying "I am superior; but so much so that I neither bother to communicate it explicitly". The "haughty dominant" has a prig and didactic attitude towards opponents, bystanders, even audience. He behaves as if all others were children or stupid: he explains things clearly, using gestures (like the "ring", *thumb and index f. in a circle moved up and down*) that convey precision and seriousness. He sits down with *trunk backward*, as if withdrawing from others to avoid contact, to take distance and to communicate "I am not like he is, I am different (superior)". One more signal of haughtiness are *half-closed eyelids*, that conveying relaxation mean "I need not worry about you" and again imply the other's inferiority.

4.2.6 Ridicule and Irony

Two more ways to show superiority are ridiculization and irony. Let us see why.

Laughter is an emotional expression triggered by surprise and then relief, caused by an incongruous event that violates an expectation, but after leaving you in a suspense, does not finally result in a dangerous outcome, so the previous worry results in relief and in a sense of superiority about the event or its cause [26]. Thus, laughing at something or someone makes you feel superior to events or other people. We *laugh at* someone who reveals some fault or lack of power that is finally innocuous, not threatening – simply impotence. The one *laughing at* feels superior while the one *laughed at* feels abased, humiliated, ridiculed: someone people make fun of. His impotence is publicly sanctioned, yet not through punishment, that would credit him with some threatening power, but through laughter: he does not scare or worry anyone. So, laughing at someone is an aggression to his image and self-image, possibly more humiliating than plain scorn.

In the "Clean Hands Trial", Cirino Pomicino often makes fun of Di Pietro, to demonstrate that he is still a well-known politician, while Di Pietro is an unknown prosecutor [27].

Also irony can be used as a dominance strategy. In irony the Sender's literal goal is to communicate a meaning x, but through this he wants the addressee to infer another meaning y, contrasting with or opposite to x [22]. Both the literal and the indirect meaning of an ironic statement often convey some evaluation: if the literal meaning is positive, the ironic one is negative (e.g., ironic praise), and vice versa (ironic blame).

Irony about another is often used to tease, to make fun of him. As we saw in Table 1, irony is used as a dominance strategy by Scalfari. By saying *"Io conosco le aziende, sa?"* (I know companies, you know), with his *"sa?"* (do you know it?) he literally asks Castelli if he knows he is the founder of an important newspaper. But since everyone knows this, the question is ironic, and aimed at ridiculing him. The real meaning Scalfari may be conveying is: "If you don't know I am the founder of "La Repubblica" you are such a poor thing that you would neither be worth being in this talk-show". And possibly, his attitude in asking *"sa?"*, apparently innocent, is in fact one of severity: "You should definitely know this". An aggressive move masked by the elegance of the rhetorical figure of irony.

4.2.7 Easiness

A way to communicate one is superior to others is to show totally at ease. Here the meaning conveyed is: I am satisfied, so I do not depend on you, you have no power over me.

> (10) Matteo Salvini belongs to a party of the right which had an unexpected victory at the elections. On the evening of the election day, when results are clear, he appears in a TV talk show with a gloating posture and face. He sits down on his chair in a very *relaxed posture*, and with a *smile* between exulting and ironic.

4.2.8 Carelessness

A subtle but very cruel way to show dominance is carelessness: behaving as if the other did not exist or were not there. Its message is: you are nothing, I do not care you at all. Its typical signal is not gazing at the opponent, even if talking about him, while possibly looking at another participant. Like does Scalfari (see Table 1, at time 3.39).

4.2.9 Assertiveness and Calm Strength

The last dominance strategy is assertiveness. Assertiveness [28] is a communicative strategy opposed to aggressiveness and passivity, oriented to self-affirmation and defence of one's own right but also to respect for the other. The assertive person is self confident, certain he will succeed without needing to aggress others, which gives him a "calm strength". Scalfari in Table 1 provides three examples of this strategy. At time 3.57, as he speaks of his having founded a Company, his *high voice intensity* remarks his own accomplishment. But his *low voice intensity* at 3.39 and *slow tempo* at 3.58 express calmness.

5 Conclusion

The goal of this work was to provide a qualitative analysis of dominance displays in debates, and to single out dominance strategies; later works will conduct quantitative analysis about the frequency of these strategies and their relation to personality and cultural factors.

Looking for signals of dominance in TV debates, we found several strategies to show dominant: from the more aggressive ones of imperiousness, judgement, invasion, norm violation and defiance, to more subtle ones like touchiness and victimhood, ending up with the distancing ones of haughtiness and other ways of showing superior, like irony and ridicule, easiness, carelessness and assertiveness. In all of these ways people try to show better – stronger, more intelligent, noble or important – than others. But why do people want to appear dominant? Probably due to an important law of power: that exhibiting an image of power is the first step to actually gain power...

Acknowledgements

This research is supported by the Seventh Framework Program, European Network of Excellence SSPNet (Social Signal Processing Network), Grant Agreement N. 231287.

References

1. Ridgeway, C.L.: Gender, status and leadership. Journal of Social Issues 57, 637–655 (2001)
2. Tajfel, H.: Interindividual behaviour and intergroup behaviour. In: Tajfel, H. (ed.) Differentation between social groups: Studies in the social psychology of intergroup relations, pp. 27–60. Academic Press, London (1978)
3. Tajfel, H., Turner, J.C.: The social identity theory of intergroup behaviour. In: Worchel, S., Austin, W.G. (eds.) Psychology of intergroup behaviour. Erlbaum, Hillsdale (1986)
4. Ellyson, S.L., Dovidio, J.F.: Power, dominance, and nonverbal behavior: Basic concepts and nonverbal behavior. In: Ellyson, S.L., Dovidio, J.F. (eds.) Power, dominance, and nonverbal behavior, pp. 1–27. Springer, New York (1985)
5. Aries, E.J., Gold, C., Weigel, R.H.: Dispositional and situational influences on dominance behavior in small groups. Journal of Personality and Social Psychology 44, 779–786 (1983)
6. Burgoon, J.K., Dunbar, N.E.: An interactionist perspective on dominance submission: Interpersonal dominance as a dynamic, situationally contingent social skill. Communication Monographs 67, 96–121 (2000)

7. Dunbar, N.E., Burgoon, J.K.: Perceptions of power and interactional dominance in interpersonal relationships. Journal of Social and Personal Relationships 22, 231–257 (2005)
8. Prato, E., Sidanius, J., Stallworth, L.M., Malle, B.F.: Social dominance orientation: A personality variable predicting social and political attitudes. Journal of Personality and Social Psychology 67, 741–763 (1994)
9. Dunbar, N.E., Bippus, A.M., Young, S.L.: Interpersonal Dominance in Relational Conflict: a view from Dyadic Power Theory. Interpersona 2(1), 1–33 (2008)
10. Ridgeway, C.L.: Nonverbal Behavior, Dominance, and the Basis of Status in Task Groups. American Sociological Review 52, 683–694 (1987)
11. Argyle, M.: Bodily Communication, 2nd edn. Methuen, New York (1988)
12. Keating, C.F., Bai, D.L.: Children's attributes of social dominance from facial cues. Child Development 57, 1269–1276 (1986)
13. Tracy, J.L., Robins, R.W.: The prototypical pride expression: Development of a nonverbal behavioral coding system. Emotion 7, 789–801 (2007)
14. Cashdan, E.: Smiles, speech, and body posture: How women and men display sociometric status and power. Journal of Nonverbal Behavior 22, 209–228 (1998)
15. Gregory, S.W., Webster, S.: A nonverbal signal in voices of interview partners effectively predicts communication accommodation and social status perceptions. Journal of Personality & Social Psychology 70, 1231–1240 (1996)
16. Jayagopi, D.B., Hung, H., Yeo, C., Gatica-Perez, D.: Modeling dominance in group conversations using nonverbal activity cues. Trans. Audio, Speech and Lang. Proc. 17(3) (2009)
17. Stein, R.T., Heller, T.: An empirical analysis of the correlations between leadership status and participation rate reported in literature. Journal of Personality and Social Psychology 37, 1993–2003 (1979)
18. Brooke, M.E., Ng, S.H.: Language and social influence in small conversation groups. Journal of Language and Social Psychology 5, 201–210 (1986)
19. Ng, S.H., Bradac, J.J.: X Power in language. Sage Publication, N.P (1986)
20. Conte, R., Castelfranchi, C.: Cognitive and social action. University College of London Press, London (1995)
21. Castelfranchi, C.: Micro-Macro Constitution of Power, ProtoSociology. International Journal of Interdisciplinary Research, 18-19, 208-265 (2003)
22. Poggi, I.: Mind, hands, face and body. In: A goal and belief view of multimodal communication. Weidler, Berlin (2007)
23. Giglioli, P., Cavicchioli, S., Fele, G.: Rituali di degradazione. Anatomia del processo Cusani, Bologna, il Mulino (1997)
24. Garfinkel, H.: Studies in ethnometodology. Prentice-Hall, Englewood Cliffs (1967)
25. Goffman, E.: Modelli di interazione, Il Mulino, Bologna (1967)
26. Castelfranchi, C.: Che figura. Emozioni e immagine sociale, Bologna, Il Mulino (1988)
27. Poggi, I.: Irony, humour ad ridicule. Power, image and judicial rhetoric in an Italian political trial. In: Vion, R. (ed.) La corporalité du langage. Multimodalitè, discourse, écriture. Hommage à Claire Maury-Rouan. Publications de L'Université de Provence, Aix-en-Provence (2010)
28. Kelly, J.A., Kern, J.M., Kirkley, B.G., Patterson, J.N., Keane, T.M.: Reactions to assertive versus unassertive behavior: Differential effects of males and female and implications for assertiveness training. Behavior Therapy 11, 670–682 (1980)

Author Index

Printing: Mercedes-Druck, Berlin
Binding: Stein+Lehmann, Berlin